Multidimensional Grief Therapy

"*Multidimensional Grief Therapy* provides a remarkable integration of a theoretical model of grief with measures and intervention strategies that are tailored to identify and treat the unique needs of different bereaved children. The book provides an impressive review of the scientific foundations of their approach. The approach provides guidance for clinicians to support adaptive grieving processes and to identify and treat maladaptive processes. The manual in the book provides step-by-step exercises clinicians can use to guide their practice, with each exercise nicely tied to the underlying theory of distinct dimensions of children's grief. The authors are distinguished scholars who have made significant contributions to our scientific understanding of children's grief. In this book they have brought all of their scientific research together to provide clinicians with a uniquely comprehensive model they can use to support bereaved youth."

Irwin Sandler
Research Professor (FSC), ASU Psychology REACH
Emeritus Professor, Emeritus College
Arizona State University

"This is a remarkably cogent volume on an assessment and treatment (*Multidimensional Grief Therapy*) of childhood grief – developed after decades of clinical experience and empirical confirmation by a team of respected authors who recognize that "one-size-fits-all" grief treatments lack effectiveness."

Ted Rynearson, M.D.
Clinical Professor of Psychiatry
University of Washington

"*Multidimensional Grief Therapy* fills an important gap by providing everything a clinician needs to implement this easy to use and developmentally appropriate evidence-based therapy. The authors have incorporated years of research and work with grieving children into this text which provides helpful handouts, a range of suggested assessment tools for each session and direct practical advice for working with bereaved children and their caregivers who are often grieving themselves."

Julie Cerel, Ph.D.
Professor, Licensed Psychologist
University of Kentucky
College of Social Work
Director, Suicide Prevention & Exposure Lab (SPEL)
Wilson Professor in Mental Health

Multidimensional Grief Therapy

A Flexible Approach to Assessing and Supporting Bereaved Youth

Julie B. Kaplow
Tulane University School of Medicine

Christopher M. Layne
Nova Southeastern University

Robert S. Pynoos
University of California Los Angeles

William Saltzman
California State University–Long Beach

Shaftesbury Road, Cambridge CB2 8EA, United Kingdom

One Liberty Plaza, 20th Floor, New York, NY 10006, USA

477 Williamstown Road, Port Melbourne, VIC 3207, Australia

314–321, 3rd Floor, Plot 3, Splendor Forum, Jasola District Centre, New Delhi – 110025, India

103 Penang Road, #05–06/07, Visioncrest Commercial, Singapore 238467

Cambridge University Press is part of Cambridge University Press & Assessment, a department of the University of Cambridge.

We share the University's mission to contribute to society through the pursuit of education, learning and research at the highest international levels of excellence.

www.cambridge.org
Information on this title: www.cambridge.org/9781107566507
DOI: 10.1017/9781316422359

© Julie B. Kaplow, Christopher M. Layne, Robert S. Pynoos, and William Saltzman 2023

This publication is in copyright. Subject to statutory exception and to the provisions of relevant collective licensing agreements, no reproduction of any part may take place without the written permission of Cambridge University Press & Assessment.

First published 2023

A catalogue record for this publication is available from the British Library.

ISBN 978-1-107-56650-7 Paperback

Cambridge University Press & Assessment has no responsibility for the persistence or accuracy of URLs for external or third-party internet websites referred to in this publication and does not guarantee that any content on such websites is, or will remain, accurate or appropriate.

Every effort has been made in preparing this book to provide accurate and up-to-date information that is in accord with accepted standards and practice at the time of publication. Although case histories are drawn from actual cases, every effort has been made to disguise the identities of the individuals involved. Nevertheless, the authors, editors, and publishers can make no warranties that the information contained herein is totally free from error, not least because clinical standards are constantly changing through research and regulation. The authors, editors, and publishers therefore disclaim all liability for direct or consequential damages resulting from the use of material contained in this book. Readers are strongly advised to pay careful attention to information provided by the manufacturer of any drugs or equipment that they plan to use.

Contents

Acknowledgments   page vi

1 Overview of Multidimensional Grief Therapy   1

2 Multidimensional Grief Theory: The Foundation of Multidimensional Grief Therapy   5

3 MGT Pretreatment Assessment Interview: Using Evidence-Based Assessment and Goal Setting to Guide Individual Treatment Using MGT   18

4 Caregivers as "Cofacilitators" of Children's Grief   32

References   37

Multidimensional Grief Therapy Sessions

Session 1 Grief Psychoeducation: What Is Grief?   43
Session 2 Emotion Psychoeducation and Identification: What Am I Feeling and Why?   70
Session 3 Grief Psychoeducation Continued: How Has My Grief Changed over Time?   79
Session 4 Understanding Caregivers as Key Grief Facilitators: What Can My Caregiver Do to Support Me?   83
Session 5 Understanding Loss Reminders and Trauma Reminders: What Reminds Me That They're No Longer Here or about How They Died?   96
Session 6 Sizing Up a Situation: How Can Our Thoughts Change the Way We Feel or Act?   115
Sessions 7–9 Loss Narrative: Telling the Story of My Person   149
Session 10 Graduation and Launching into the Future: What Does It Mean to Have a "Good Goodbye"?   159

Index   163

Acknowledgments

We are grateful to the many individuals who contributed to the development of this book. The authors wish to thank Stephanie Yudovich for her clinical insights and critical editorial feedback, and Trauma and Grief Center clinicians Nikki Adeleke, Donna Dozier, Jackie Garza, Tamara Johns, and Marisa Nowitz, who were instrumental in refining and adapting the exercises in *Multidimensional Grief Therapy* with diverse populations. We greatly appreciate the artistic talent of David Pfendler, whose illustrations brought the exercises to life. We also thank Alan Steinberg for reviewing the historical origins of the three conceptual grief domains. We are grateful to David Schuldberg, Marit Netland, and Joseph Olsen for their generous support in working on challenging research questions that have informed our thinking, and Lauren Alvis, Ryan Hill, Ben Oosterhoff, and Evan Rooney for their help in rigorously evaluating the effectiveness of Multidimensional Grief Therapy. We thank Blake A. Yoder and Ayesha Ahmad (graduate research assistants in Nova Southeastern University's Trauma & Bereavement Research Lab), and Puneetha Goli and Becka Hoppe (research assistants at the Trauma and Grief Center) for assisting with proofreading and compiling references. We thank Micki Burns for her collegial review of our theory chapter. We are also indebted to our mentors and colleagues in the field who have taught us so much about children's grief and bereavement over the past few decades, including Albert Cain, Mardi Horowitz, Colin Murray Parkes, Irwin Sandler, Nadezda Savjak, and the late Dora Black. Finally, our deepest gratitude goes to the many children and families who have shown us firsthand what it means to "grow from grief" as well as to our own families for their unwavering love, support, and encouragement.

1 Overview of Multidimensional Grief Therapy

Multidimensional Grief Therapy (MGT) is a strength-based intervention designed to carry out a range of important therapeutic tasks with bereaved children and adolescents. These tasks include (1) reducing unhelpful grief reactions (grief that keeps kids "stuck" and unable to adjust); (2) promoting adaptive grief reactions (grief that helps kids to feel and cope better after a death); (3) reducing associated symptoms of psychological distress (e.g., posttraumatic stress and depressive symptoms), and (4) helping bereaved children and adolescents to lead healthy, happy, productive lives. Consistent with its assessment-driven, flexibly tailored design, MGT is divided into a *pretreatment assessment interview* and an *assessment feedback interview*, followed by a two-phased treatment approach.

Pretreatment Assessment Interview. The pretreatment assessment interview is preferably conducted by the same clinician who will be facilitating the MGT sessions. Its primary goals are to obtain sufficient information about the perceived needs of the child or youth, determine whether MGT is an appropriate intervention, and make initial decisions regarding which dimensions of grief require clinical attention. This work is based on the assumption that children and adolescents grieve in different ways, and that "one-size-fits-all" grief treatments (which treat them as if they have the same grief reactions) often lack effectiveness (see Kaplow, Layne, & Pynoos, 2019, for a review). To assist in case conceptualization and treatment planning, the clinician interviews both the youth and their caregiver(s) and administers selected measures (reviewed in Chapter 3) to gather information regarding the client's functioning across a range of symptom domains, especially grief reactions.

Assessment Feedback Interview. Following the pretreatment assessment interview, the clinician reviews the assessment results with the client and their caregiver(s). Using both the assessment results as well as clinical judgment, the clinician then makes recommendations for intervention using a three-tiered referral system. This system refers cases based on the seriousness and urgency of each client's difficulties and need for general versus more specialized bereavement care (Layne et al., 2008; Saltzman et al., 2003). Different tiers of intervention include the following:

Tier 1: Use MGT Phase 1 to provide general bereavement support focused on facilitating adaptive grieving (e.g., psychoeducation, strengthening coping skills, improving family communication). This general support (i.e., MGT Phase 1 alone) can also be provided by community-based bereavement support facilities, faith-based organizations, or other youth-serving organizations (often as implemented by trained paraprofessionals – e.g., school-based or community-based grief support groups).

Tier 2: Implement a full therapeutic dose of MGT consisting of both Phase 1 (general grief support focused on facilitating adaptive grief) followed by Phase 2 (therapeutic support focused on both reducing maladaptive grief reactions and facilitating adaptive grief reactions) in a therapeutic setting. Potential therapeutic settings include school-based clinics, community mental health centers, hospitals, and clinical private-practice offices.

Tier 3: If risk screening efforts detect severe symptoms requiring urgent care (e.g., significant suicide risk), refer for emergency care (e.g., emergency room evaluation). Depending on the client's condition, this may involve admission to inpatient treatment or enrollment in an intensive day treatment program.

We discuss how youths' individual assessment profiles can be used to guide professional decisions about which tiers of service to offer in Chapter 3.

Regarding Tier 2, our assessment-driven, two-phased approach for implementing MGT with bereaved youth and families is based on the basic premise that *not every client needs both phases of MGT* (Hill et al., 2019). This determination (whether to proceed from Phase 1 to Phase 2) is made typically by readministering the assessment battery at the completion of Phase 1 and evaluating whether the client has experienced clinically significant reductions in the symptoms/diagnoses that were targeted as intervention objectives in the treatment plan. Chapter 3 describes this decision-making process in detail.

Phase 1 of MGT (Sessions 1–6) focuses on teaching youth and families about the different dimensions of grief as explained by multidimensional grief theory, different grief-related challenges, ways in which grief reactions can change over time, how grief is different for each family member, how certain reminders of the deceased person or reminders of how the person died can evoke different grief reactions, and teaching coping skills to decrease unhelpful grief-related thoughts.

Phase 2 of MGT (Sessions 7–10), guides the client through his/her own story about the death by focusing on each dimension of grief (emphasizing those that are most problematic for the client), reducing maladaptive grief reactions, promoting adaptive grief reactions, making meaning of the death, and finding ways to move forward in life while still maintaining a healthy connection to the deceased person. MGT sessions also include a number of caregiver-child exercises that help to build positive communication and *caregiver grief facilitation* (caregiver behaviors or activities that help youth to grieve in adaptive ways).

Including the pretreatment assessment and assessment feedback session, the full version of MGT (both Phase 1 and Phase 2) typically takes 14 weeks to implement (given that certain sessions, such as the loss narrative, often require 2–3 weeks to complete), with each session lasting approximately 50 minutes. MGT is designed to be tailored flexibly to the specific needs and strengths of each individual client. For example, different youth may need more, or fewer, sessions depending on their individual assessment profiles. Although this manual is designed to be conducted as an *individual* grief-focused treatment (i.e., conducted one-on-one with a therapist), the exercises can be adapted and tailored for a *group-based* treatment modality. Similar grief-focused work has been implemented successfully in a group modality (i.e., see the Grief module of *Trauma and grief component therapy for adolescents* [Saltzman et al., 2017]), including with adolescents exposed to domestic violence, community violence, gang violence (Grassetti et al., 2014; Grassetti et al., 2018; Herres et al., 2017; Layne, Pynoos, & Cardenas, 2001; Saltzman et al., 2001), and war (Layne et al., 2001, 2008); and youth in the juvenile justice system (Clow et al., 2022; Olafson et al., 2018).

What Makes MGT Unique?

It is reasonable to ask what makes MGT unique and how this treatment supports best-practice bereavement care – especially given the recent inclusion of prolonged grief disorder (PGD) in both *Diagnostic and statistical manual of mental disorders* (5th ed.) (DSM-5-TR) and *International statistical classification of diseases and related health problems* (11th ed.) (ICD-11) and the growing need, across the world, for child-focused grief support (e.g., at the time of writing, over 300,000 US youth had lost a parent or caregiver to COVID-19). Drawing on features and lessons learned from a companion intervention, Trauma and Grief Component Therapy for Adolescents (TGCTA; Saltzman et al., 2017), MGT has six built-in strengths that set it apart as a cutting-edge intervention for bereaved children and adolescents:

1. *Developmentally tailored.* MGT contains exercises that are designed to specifically address the developmental needs, strengths, risks, challenges, tasks, and life circumstances of both children and adolescents. Specific language and practice elements for each age/developmental group are provided. For example, descriptions of the various grief domains are modified according to the child's age/developmental level (e.g., use of the grief characters versus a general description of each grief domain). In addition, the grief sketches found in Session 6 are designed to represent a wide range of bereavement-related challenges that can occur among younger children as well as adolescents.

2. *Interplay between trauma and bereavement.* A second strength of MGT is its integrative focus on bereavement, trauma, and the interplay between grief reactions and posttraumatic stress reactions. Several MGT authors served on the American Psychiatric Association's DSM-5 Posttraumatic Stress Disorder, Trauma, and Dissociative Disorders Sub-Work Group, in which capacity they provided age-specific recommendations for both posttraumatic stress disorder (PTSD) criteria and newly proposed PGD criteria (Layne et al., 2019; Layne, Oosterhoff, et al., 2020). MGT aligns with the latest diagnostic and treatment considerations for these particular bereavement- and trauma-related outcomes. Although many interventions that treat grief reactions in youth are primarily designed to address trauma (treating bereavement as simply another form of trauma), or conflate PTSD with grief reactions (as in the case of "traumatic grief"), MGT approaches bereavement and trauma as related yet meaningfully distinct causal risk factors (Layne, Beck et al., 2009; Layne, Steinberg, & Steinberg, 2014). The design of MGT reflects a clear conceptual understanding of the causal links between bereavement (a causal risk factor) and grief (an outcome); trauma (a causal risk factor) and posttraumatic stress reactions (an outcome) (Layne, 2021b). Its design also reflects an understanding of the crisscrossing interplay between grief and posttraumatic stress reactions over time and the importance of this dynamic process for case conceptualization and differential diagnosis (Layne et al., 2017; Layne, Kaplow, & Pynoos, 2022b; Pynoos, 1992), as well as individually tailored treatment (Kaplow, Layne, & Pynoos, 2019; Saltzman et al., 2017).

Bereavement and trauma may occur in different configurations in youth's lives. For example, they may co-occur simultaneously, as in the case of *traumatic bereavement* – in which their loved one dies under traumatic circumstances (Layne et al., 2017). Alternatively, bereaved youth may also be directly exposed to imminent life threat or serious injury themselves (e.g., being involved in a car accident in which a loved one is killed) (Saltzman et al., 2017). Regardless of their particular configuration, co-occurring bereavement and trauma each exert their own effects on distress and functioning. MGT reflects the understanding that both grief reactions and posttraumatic stress reactions can exert enormous demands on the inner resources of children and adolescents (Pynoos, 1992). Further, the demands of one set of reactions can intersect in complex ways with the social, physical, psychological, and spiritual resources available to cope with the other set of reactions (Layne, Beck et al., 2009; Saltzman et al., 2017).

3. *Two-phased, assessment-driven format.* A third strength of MGT is its two-phased format, which supports assessment-driven, flexibly tailored intervention. When paired with evidence-based assessment methods, MGT helps practitioners to carry out a central task of evidence-based practice: to gather and use the best available evidence to tailor the intervention in accordance with clients' specific needs, strengths, life circumstances, values, informed wishes, and the practitioners' clinical wisdom and expert judgment (Layne, Strand, et al., 2014). Based on assessment information gathered in the pretreatment assessment interview, this data can be used to develop an *individual assessment profile* that summarizes the client's degree of distress as measured along specific dimensions of grief (see Chapter 3). This information can be used to select specific practice elements (e.g., specific sketches reflecting those dimensions) that will be most relevant and beneficial for the youth. The individual assessment profile also helps to identify key benchmarks of functioning and developmental progression versus derailment that can be used to evaluate clinically significant impairment at baseline and at the completion of Phase 1, and monitor clinically significant improvement as treatment progresses (Layne et al., 2010).

Youth begin with Phase 1 and proceed through each of its sessions, after which they are reassessed to evaluate the effectiveness of treatment to that point. Youth who report few maladaptive grief reactions and/or for whom treatment goals have been met (e.g., significant reductions in PTSD and improved functioning) following completion of Phase 1 may not require additional treatment and may thus terminate therapy. In contrast, youth who manifest continued maladaptive grief reactions and/or PTSD symptoms are encouraged to continue on to Phase 2. Although the contents of Phases 1 and 2 are divided into specific sessions, MGT is designed to encourage "flexibility within fidelity" by tailoring treatment to meet each child's needs (Kendall & Frank, 2018). As dictated by a child's unique grief presentation, individual needs, family configuration, developmental level, and life circumstances, sessions may be expanded or condensed at the therapist's discretion (Hill et al., 2019).

4. *Multitiered intervention framework.* A fourth strength of MGT, also derived from its two-phased format, is its capacity to support *multitiered* mental health and wellness interventions. Multitiered interventions are especially valuable in high-risk, high-need, under-resourced settings because they help service providers to balance both program effectiveness and program efficiency. MGT is built on a three-tiered conceptual framework (Saltzman et al., 2003) that allows practitioners to flexibly provide services ranging from general wellness promotion to specialized mental health therapeutic services (Cox et al., 2007). This conceptual framework draws on public mental health principles to help practitioners flexibly implement interventions that reach many beneficiaries while conserving and concentrating specialized services for those in greatest need (Layne et al., 2008). These tiers consist of grief-focused psychoeducation and skill building (e.g., Phase 1 of MGT; Tier I), more specialized treatment for youth continuing to exhibit elevated maladaptive grief and/or posttraumatic stress reactions (Phase 2 of MGT; Tier 2), and referral to intensive specialized psychiatric/mental health treatment (only as needed, either as stand-alone treatment or a supplement to Tier-2 treatment) for youth at severe risk (Tier 3). A similar multitiered system has proven effective in high-risk and resource-poor settings (Cox et al 2007; Layne et al., 2008).

5. *Individual or group-based format.* A fifth strength of MGT is its flexibility with regard to treatment modality – specifically, MGT can be used individually or in groups. Although MGT has shown evidence of reducing psychological distress in youth when used in individual therapy (Hill et al., 2019), it is also ideally suited to treat groups of children or adolescents with loss histories in settings where a group-based modality is more efficient. These settings include bereavement centers, schools, juvenile justice settings, residential care, diversion programs, and community-based mental health centers (e.g., Grassetti et al., 2014). A sizable literature documents that groups are generally as effective as, and often more efficient than, individual treatment for many problems (Davies, Burlingame, & Layne, 2006). A group-based modality can also improve access to care, especially in underresourced areas where evidence-based interventions for childhood bereavement/grief may be especially difficult to find.

6. *Grounded in cutting-edge theoretical and empirical developments.* A sixth strength of MGT is that it draws on recent clinical and scientific advances in the field of child and adolescent bereavement. For example, Phase 1 components draw on advances in the study of *loss reminders and trauma reminders,* and ways in which they differentially evoke grief and posttraumatic stress reactions (Layne et al., 2006). Phase 2 components draw on advances in the study of children's loss narratives and the most effective strategies for helping youth to process a death (Kaplow, Wardecker et al., 2018). MGT also draws heavily from multidimensional grief

theory to guide assessment, case formulation, treatment planning and tailoring, monitoring treatment progress, and treatment outcome evaluation (Kaplow, Layne et al., 2013; Kaplow, Layne, & Pynoos, 2019; Layne & Kaplow, 2020; Layne, Kaplow, & Pynoos, 2022c).

A core assumption of multidimensional grief theory is that grief is an inherently *beneficial* yet often taxing process of responding to, and making ongoing efforts to adjust to, a world in which the deceased person is no longer physically present (Layne et al., 2019). These theoretical underpinnings carry major implications for both grief-informed assessment and treatment. First, measures and interventions that address grief must acknowledge *both* adaptive grief reactions and maladaptive grief reactions to avoid overpathologizing normative grief reactions and set the stage for strength-based components that promote positive adjustment (Layne, 2018; Layne, 2021a). Second, interventions designed to address maladjustment and positive adjustment in bereaved youth should view children's grief reactions within a broad theoretical context comprised of both child-intrinsic and child-extrinsic socioenvironmental factors theorized to either reduce or promote these outcomes, respectively (Kaplow et al., 2012; Pynoos et al., 1995). Multidimensional Grief Therapy contains practice elements that focus explicitly on a range of child-intrinsic (e.g., developmental stage, coping strategies) and child-extrinsic factors (parent-child communication, parenting practices) that are associated with children's grief reactions.

A third implication is the need for an assessment-driven format that therapeutically leverages the "adaptive versus maladaptive" continuum proposed by multidimensional grief theory (Kaplow & Layne, 2014; Layne, 2018, 2021b; Layne et al., 2020). Multidimensional Grief Therapy matches individual or group assessment profiles with those treatment components that are most effective in therapeutically reducing (for maladaptive grief) and promoting (for adaptive grief) specific grief reactions (see also Saltzman et al., 2017). Multidimensional Grief Therapy thus invites practitioners to flexibly prescribe and tailor specific practice exercises (e.g., selecting specific sketches) within each session that carry the best theoretical rationale and empirical evidence for clients' specific grief profiles, including the three primary dimensions proposed by multidimensional grief theory: separation distress, existential/identity distress, and circumstance-related distress. As discussed in Chapter 3, MGT also encourages practitioners to monitor each client's therapeutic progress along these conceptual dimensions in combination with PGD diagnostic status (Layne & Kaplow, 2020; Layne, Kaplow, & Pynoos, 2022c).

In closing, we know firsthand how challenging this work can be. We also recognize the immense power of an effective intervention that can ease the pain of loss and help children to lead healthy, happy, fulfilling lives in the face of tragedy. It is our hope that you will find MGT to be as user friendly, flexible, meaningful, and transformative as we have. In the next chapter, you will learn more about how MGT came to be, its theoretical underpinnings, and the ways in which multidimensional grief theory has served as the foundation for all of the practice elements found in each session.

2 Multidimensional Grief Theory
The Foundation of Multidimensional Grief Therapy

What Is Multidimensional Grief Theory?

Both multidimensional grief *theory* and multidimensional grief *therapy* (MGT) draw upon a rich history of the clinical and scientific study of child and adolescent (hereafter youth) bereavement. This history offers a diverse array of conceptual lenses and therapeutic tools that support a broad, integrative approach to understanding, assessing, and intervening with bereaved youth and families. As a theory derived from decades of field study and clinical practice, multidimensional grief theory is both practical and powerful in its ability to describe, explain, predict, and therapeutically address a broad range of grief reactions. As we will discuss, the theory is an outgrowth of three major streams of clinical research, theory, and practice: attachment theory, existential philosophy, and disaster mental health (Layne, 2021b). Multidimensional grief theory incorporates, but also extends beyond, these three major approaches by integrating their core principles into a coherent conceptual framework, adopting a developmental and ecological emphasis, and clarifying their many implications for assessment, case conceptualization, and treatment planning. Multidimensional grief theory not only describes how grief reactions can manifest in bereaved youth (as depicted in an individual grief assessment profile (Layne, Kaplow, & Pynoos, 2022c); see Layne, Kaplow, & Pynoos, 2022c). It also facilitates a balanced, strength-based, problem-focused intervention for bereaved youth and families that offers a broad array of engaging activities for clinicians and care providers (see also Saltzman et al., 2017).

Multidimensional grief theory's broad scope encompasses all primary features of Prolonged Grief Disorder as listed in both DSM 5-TR (American Psychiatric Association, 2022) and ICD-11 (World Health Organization, 2019) diagnostic criteria, and will help you to "see" many different facets of grief and guide you in deciding how to address them (Saltzman et al., 2017). The theory's dual emphasis on both helping adaptive (helpful) grieving to *proceed* and maladaptive (unhelpful) grieving to *recede* (Layne et al., 2017; Layne, 2018; Layne, Kaplow, & Pynoos, 2021a, 2021b) makes it a useful framework for integrating grief-focused *general support* interventions found in Phase 1 (e.g., focusing on grief psychoeducation, facilitating helpful caregiver-child communication, and facilitating adaptive grieving that brings comfort); with grief-focused *therapeutic* interventions found in Phase 2 (e.g., utilizing different practice elements to help both maladaptive grief reactions to *recede*, and adaptive grief reactions to *proceed*). Combined with developmentally-appropriate assessment methods that align with the theory (e.g., Layne, Kaplow, & Pynoos, 2022a, 2022b), multidimensional grief theory will help you to build a grief assessment profile (Layne et al., 2022c), case conceptualization, and intervention plan that you can tailor flexibly according to each youth's profile (Kaplow & Layne, 2019; Layne & Kaplow, 2020). This manual will help you to tailor your intervention based on such factors as each youth's developmental level (this manual is designed for bereaved youth aged 7–18), culture, relationship to the deceased, exposure to the death, current functioning, life circumstances, strengths, and informed wishes.

We use the following terminology throughout this manual (Layne, 2021b):

- *Bereavement*: a life event involving the loss of a loved one through death
- *Bereaved*: a person who has experienced bereavement
- *Grief*: voluntary and involuntary emotional, psychological, spiritual, and behavioral reactions to bereavement (and more generally, to other forms of loss that do not involve the death of a loved one – e.g., prolonged separation, estrangement, abandonment, former way of life)
- *Mourning*: ritualized, often culturally influenced ways – both public and private – of recognizing the meaning, significance, and value of the deceased person's life and death; and of acknowledging the ongoing impact of their loss in the lives of an individual, family, community, and/or nation

Overview of Multidimensional Grief Theory

A Model of Multidimensional Grief Theory's Primary Conceptual Domains

Figure 2.1 is a model of the three primary conceptual domains of multidimensional grief theory. It depicts a multidimensional approach to understanding, assessing, and intervening with grief in both directions (horizontally and vertically). This three-domain model of grief has guided our assessment, intervention, training, and public advocacy efforts for over two decades (Layne, 2020, 2021b). These efforts include the authors' early field trainings in the model (CL and RP, 2008), treatment outcome studies (Layne et al., 2008), scientific presentations (Layne, Kaplow, & Pynoos, 2012), and applications to military families (Kaplow et al., 2013) and traumatically bereaved youth (Layne et al., 2017). The model has three major distinguishing features (Layne, Kaplow, Oosterhoff, & Hill, 2019).

First, the model is multidimensional along the horizontal axis (the bottom) (Layne et al., 2019). Multidimensional grief theory proposes that grieving and mourning are generally normal, expectable processes that promote adaptive adjustment to the death of a loved one. The adaptive/helpful versus maladaptive/not helpful two-headed arrow at the base of the model is a guide to recognize – and distinguish between the helpfulness of – different grief reactions for specific individuals and their particular life context. This most basic distinction (between helpful and less helpful/unhelpful grief reactions) in multidimensional grief theory has been replicated in multiple settings (e.g., Layne et al., 2001; Layne et al., 2008; summarized in Layne et al., 2019). Nevertheless, this distinction is only conceptual and not a true "either-or" continuum. To the contrary, the theory proposes that adaptive and maladaptive grief reactions can and frequently do *co-occur*. For example, grieving people can shift from intense emotional pain to comforting reminiscing from one moment to the next. Further, measures of adaptive versus maladaptive grief reactions tend to correlate positively in the moderate range (Layne, Kaplow, & Pynoos, 2012; Layne et al., 2001; Layne et al., 2008; Layne et al., 2019; Layne et al., 2020). This potentially high degree of co-occurrence between adaptive versus maladaptive grief reactions can make it challenging to differentiate between these two sets of reactions in assessment (e.g., differential diagnosis), therapeutic work, and research studies (Layne, Kaplow, et al., 2014; Layne & Kaplow, 2020). We discuss this challenge and ways to address it in the next chapter on assessment.

Second, the model is multidimensional along the vertical axis (Layne et al., 2019). Multidimensional grief theory proposes that a broad range of grief reactions can arise after the death of a loved one (Kaplow, Layne et al., 2013; Layne et al., 2008; Layne et al., 2017; Pynoos, 1992), and that a given reaction can vary in its helpfulness in facilitating adaptive adjustment to a given death. The theory proposes that grief reactions generally fall within three primary conceptual domains or dimensions (which are vertically stacked in the model). These conceptual domains consist of the following:

- *Separation distress* (e.g., missing the person who died, longing for their return). Separation distress is positioned at the top of the model because it is the most easily recognized – and perhaps prototypical – grief reaction (Layne et al., 2019). It is common to all age groups (although it may be somewhat more intense in younger children; Kaplow et al., 2012) and all types of death, and commonly seen in clinical practice. Consistent with its high prevalence rate and key role as an early "gateway" grief reaction that can, if severe and persisting, lead to clinically significant distress, separation distress is a required "B" symptom in both DSM-5-TR and ICD-11 prolonged grief disorder (Layne et al., 2019; Layne, Oosterhoff, Pynoos, & Kaplow, 2020).
- *Existential/identity distress* (e.g., diminished sense of life meaning and purpose or of personal identity). Existential/identity distress is positioned in the middle of the model because it is a common reaction to many types of deaths – both "traumatic" and otherwise – but is often less understood and less well recognized than separation distress, sometimes appearing as apathy, aimlessness, resignation, nihilism, or despair (Layne et al., 2019; Layne et al., 2020). In our experience, existential/identity distress is more likely to (1) become clinically prominent in adolescence and young adulthood following the loss of identity-defining relationships and/or relationships that provide a sense of purpose, meaning, drive to one's life, and hope for the future; and (2) call for clinical attention due to its tendency to erode youths' sense of optimism, life ambitions, and preparations for the future (Layne, Pynoos, & Cardenas, 2001; Layne et al., 2008; see also Saltzman et al., 2017, Module 4).
- *Circumstance-related distress* (e.g., distress over *how* the person died). Circumstance-related distress is positioned at the bottom of the model because it is more likely to arise in the aftermath of traumatic or tragic deaths and thus may be less commonly recognized as a form of grief that is separate and distinct from posttraumatic stress reactions/PTSD (Layne et al., 2019). Circumstance-related distress can arise after

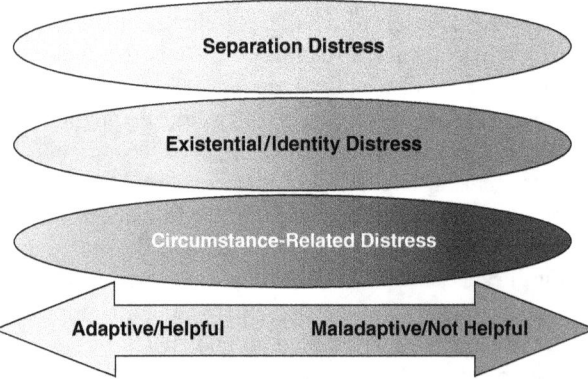

Figure 2.1 Multidimensional grief model (Layne, Kaplow, & Pynoos, 2012)

deaths due to either natural or unnatural causes, or following anticipated or unanticipated deaths. Indeed, deaths due to natural, foreseeable causes can contain highly distressing elements (e.g., witnessing a loved one's intense suffering and progressive deterioration) that evoke more posttraumatic stress reactions than deaths due to sudden natural causes (Kaplow, Howell, & Layne, 2014). Conceptually, this dimension of the multidimensional grief model is most closely akin to – but *not* functionally interchangeable with, nor should be confused with – what is sometimes termed "traumatic grief" (Layne et al., 2017; Pynoos, 1992).

Third, the model is built on the proposition of *differential relations* (Layne, Kaplow, & Pynoos, 2012, 2014). That is, the distinctions between adaptive versus maladaptive grief reactions (the horizontal dimension), and between different conceptual domains of grief (the vertical dimension), are meaningfully distinct and clinically useful because they convey different types of information (e.g., create different grief assessment profiles – see Layne et al., 2022c), can arise from different causes, lead to different causal consequences, and can call for different interventions. Later in this chapter, we explain how the twin propositions of multidimensionality and differential relations guide multidimensional grief theory and our unique approach to grief-informed assessment, case conceptualization, and intervention.

A Brief Review of the Scientific and Theoretical Roots of Multidimensional Grief Theory

The Scientific Roots of Multidimensional Grief Theory

Multidimensional grief theory is a direct outgrowth of decades of careful fieldwork in building assessment tools, manualized interventions, and training curricula for professionals working with youth, families, and communities bereaved under diverse conditions (Layne, 2020). Its core propositions have coevolved with the authors' efforts to advance the fields of traumatic stress and bereavement along seven fronts (Layne, Kaplow, & Pynoos, 2012). These fronts are (1) theory building, (2) test construction, (3) naturalistic research, (4) intervention development and evaluation, (5) education and training, (6) implementation and dissemination, and (7) public outreach and advocacy. A number of relevant advances have been developed, field-tested, and refined over more than three decades:

- *Clinical-descriptive and treatment-outcome studies of bereaved youth* whose loved ones died due to community violence (Layne, Pynoos, & Cardenas, 2001; Saltzman et al., 2001), civil war (Howell, Kaplow et al., 2015; Layne et al., 2001; Layne et al., 2008), terrorist attacks (Hoagwood, Layne, & CATS Consortium, 2007, 2010), homicide (Douglas et al., 2021; Layne et al., 2001; Nader et al., 1990; Pynoos, 1992), and natural causes (Kaplow, Howell, & Layne, 2014; Layne et al., 2008; Saltzman et al., 2001).
- *Developmental and ecological theory* that can explain trauma-induced developmental impacts, distinctions between adaptive versus maladaptive grief, and the roles of trauma reminders, loss reminders, and secondary adversities in prolonging distress (Kaplow, Layne et al., 2013; Kaplow et al., 2006; Kaplow & Layne, 2014; Layne, Kaplow, & Pynoos, 2012; Layne, Pynoos, & Cardenas, 2001; Layne et al., 2006; Pynoos, 1992; Pynoos, Steinberg, & Wraith, 1995; Saltzman et al., 2003).
- *Theories of resilience*, including the roles of such stress-buffering resources as social support, self-efficacy, optimism, courage, and altruism (Layne et al., 2007; Layne & Hobfoll, 2020), insights into how adaptive grieving can facilitate resilience (Layne et al., 2018, 2021a, 2021b), and the roles of both promotive and protective factors in enhancing positive growth, wellness, and positive youth development (Layne, Beck et al., 2009; Layne, Ruzek, & Dixon, 2021).
- *Naturalistic studies of posttraumatic/postbereavement* factors theorized to influence the course of grief. These include circumstances of the death (Kaplow, Howell, & Layne, 2014; Kaplow et al., 2020), parenting practices in facilitating youth adjustment (Al-Sabah et al., 2015; Alvis, Dodd et al., 2022; Houston, 2006; Howell et al., 2016; Shapiro, Howell, & Kaplow, 2014; Wardecker et al., 2017), caregiver-child communication regarding the death (Shapiro, Howell, & Kaplow, 2014; children's coping (Howell, Shapiro et al., 2015); children's use of language in describing the loss (Kaplow, Wardecker et al., 2013); and spirituality, and religiosity (Howell, Shapiro et al., 2015; Rooney et al., 2019).
- *Developmentally appropriate measures* of trauma exposure, trauma reminders, loss reminders, secondary adversities, parenting practices, posttraumatic stress reactions, and grief reactions (Alvis et al., 2020; Kaplow, Layne et al., 2018; Kaplow, Rolon-Arroyo et al., 2020; Layne, Kaplow, & Pynoos, 2014, 2022a, 2022b, 2022c; Layne, Pynoos, & Cardenas, 2001; Layne et al., 2008, 2010; Nader & Layne, 2009; Pynoos, 1992).
- *Theories of mechanisms of therapeutic change*, including the therapeutic alliance, parenting self-efficacy, and group cohesion (Davies, Burlingame, & Layne, 2006; Layne et al. 2008; Warren et al. 2011).
- *A manualized, assessment-driven, individually tailored treatment* containing four modules designed specifically for traumatized and bereaved youth (TGCTA). Early locally published versions of TGCTA were extensively field-tested and refined in war-torn Bosnia (CL, WS, RP, & Alan Steinberg, 1997), and in post-September 11th New York State (CL, WS, RP, & Alan Steinberg, 2002). Since its worldwide publication (Saltzman et al., 2017), TGCTA is now being implemented in many countries around the globe.
- *A stepped-care intervention model* that integrates schools with community-based mental health clinics. It consists of (Tier 1) broad public/classroom-based outreach, risk

screening, psychoeducation, and coping skills; (Tier 2) school-based therapeutic care (e.g., TGCTA) for seriously distressed students by trained school counselors; and (Tier 3) referral of high-risk (e.g., suicidal) students for emergency/highly specialized treatment services (Layne et al., 2008; Saltzman et al., 2003).

- *A TGCTA training curriculum* covering risk screening, clinical/diagnostic assessment, case conceptualization, treatment planning, and assessment-driven individual tailoring. This curriculum has been refined over decades of trainings in such field settings and institutions as school-based health clinics, community mental health centers, juvenile justice settings, bereavement support centers, government ministries, and university training clinics. The TGCTA training curriculum has been adapted by the authors over many years to address the needs of youth and families exposed to war (CL, WS, & RP, 1997); terrorism, as well as community and domestic violence (CL, WS, & RP, 2002); rural life (CL & RP, 2008); and community, gang, and domestic violence (WS, CL, & JK, 2017). A recent edition of the training curriculum focused on fostering post-hurricane resilience (JK, CL, WS, & instructional designer Dr. Hannah Grossman). This version integrates instructional tools and exercises from the National Child Traumatic Stress Network's Core Curriculum on Childhood Trauma (Layne, Strand et al., 2014) to strengthen core competencies relating to trauma- and bereavement-informed assessment, case conceptualization, treatment planning, and critical reasoning (see Layne, 2022; TGCTA.com for further information about TGCTA).

Multidimensional grief theory has also guided the development of a manualized intervention for traumatized, bereaved, traumatically bereaved, and developmentally disrupted adolescents (TGCTA [Saltzman et al., 2017]) and its predecessors (Layne et al., 1997; Layne et al., 2002). These manualized interventions have been shown to reduce symptoms of psychological distress including PTSD, depression, and grief reactions; and to improve functioning, including school performance, in diverse populations and settings. Populations included youth exposed to community, gang, and domestic violence (Layne, Pynoos, & Cardenas, 2001; Saltzman et al., 2001), war (e.g., Davies et al., 2006; Layne et al., 2001; Layne et al., 2008), terrorism (Hoagwood, Layne, & CATS Consortium, 2010), and incarcerated youth with extensive histories of trauma and bereavement (Clow et al., 2022; Olafson et al., 2018). Multidimensional grief theory has been used to guide training and practice with mental health professionals serving Native American and rural youth (CL & RP, 2008), military families (Kaplow, Layne et al., 2013), and traumatically bereaved adolescents (Layne et al., 2017). An open trial of MGT with bereaved inner-city youth found significant pre- to post-treatment improvement in multiple domains of maladaptive grief reactions, PTSD, and depressive symptoms (Hill et al., 2019).

Core Propositions of Multidimensional Grief Theory and Their Scientific Roots. The foundations of multidimensional grief theory and this manualized treatment are built upon the twin propositions of *multidimensionality* (of grief reactions) and *differential relations* (between different types of grief reactions and different external factors, such as causal risk factors and treatment components) (Layne, Kaplow et al., 2014). Using correlation matrices, statistical prediction, expert ratings, factor analysis, and other test construction tools, the authors identified – through extensive field research (e.g., Layne et al., 2001; Layne et al., 2008; Layne et al., 2010; Layne, Kaplow, & Pynoos, 2012) – an increasingly broad range of grief reactions characterized by both adaptive and maladaptive responses to the deaths of loved ones. Over time, a scientific method – the differential validity matrix (Layne, Kaplow et al., 2014) – evolved. This multidimensional framework guides our approach to carrying out many bereavement research- and treatment-related tasks (Layne, Kaplow et al., 2012; Layne, Kaplow, & Pynoos, 2022c):

- Building a multidimensional and clinically useful theory that can account for a broad range of grief reactions across a range of developmental periods, cultures, and ecological settings
- Constructing multidimensional measures for assessing grief reactions
- Differentiating between generally adaptive versus maladaptive grief reactions
- Differentiating between grief versus related conditions (e.g., PTSD, depression)
- Creating an individualized grief assessment profile for each client
- Using each client's assessment data to create an individually tailored case conceptualization
- Creating supportive/therapeutic grief exercises to address different grief dimensions and the central coping challenge for each grief domain
- Using each client's assessment data and case conceptualization to create a flexibly tailored treatment plan (Kaplow, Layne, & Pynoos, 2019; Layne, Kaplow, & Youngstrom, 2017; Layne & Kaplow, 2020; Saltzman et al., 2017)

The core propositions of multidimensional grief theory arose as direct implications of the differential validity matrix (Layne, Kaplow, & Pynoos, 2012; Layne et al., 2014, 2019; Layne, 2021a, 2021b). This scientific approach offers an ecologically grounded, contextualized, and clinically useful understanding of a broad range of grief reactions. Most relevant to MGT, this approach offers a clear rationale as to why the core propositions of multidimensional grief theory are clinically useful – that is, why these distinctions make a real-world and clinically actionable difference (Layne, Kaplow et al., 2014). As used in the theory, multidimensionality refers to basic distinctions between the horizontal axis (i.e., adaptive versus maladaptive) and vertical axis (i.e., primary conceptual domains of grief) of the multidimensional grief model (Layne et al., 2019). That is, each of these grief domains are theorized to be meaningfully distinct and clinically useful, in that they are not functionally interchangeable with one another in performing a range of important tasks, including coping with a central coping task or challenge associated with each domain (Layne et al., 2017). The basic distinctions between adaptive versus maladaptive grief reactions (the horizontal axis of the model), and grief conceptual domains (the vertical axis: Separation Distress, existential/identity distress, and circumstance-related distress), are clinically useful because they can lead to *different clinical decisions* about important aspects of bereavement-informed care (Layne, Kaplow, & Youngstrom, 2017; Layne et al., 2019; Layne, 2021a, 2021b), such as understanding

- which individuals, based on exposure to specific types of causal risk factors, vulnerability factors, and protective factors, are most likely to experience which types of grief reactions;
- the origin, locus, and essential nature of their grief-related distress and difficulties;
- the primary coping challenge associated with each type of grief reaction;
- intervention objectives (therapeutic goals) associated with each conceptual grief domain;
- how to help in effective, flexible ways (Kaplow, Layne, & Pynoos, 2019; Layne & Kaplow, 2020).

The differential validity matrix approach to unpacking and differentiating between grief reactions (Layne, Kaplow et al., 2014) demonstrates that different grief dimensions are meaningfully distinct *because they relate differently* to one or more of four different types of external factors: correlates, moderators, causal precursors, and causal consequences (see Layne, Beck et al., 2009, for examples). To illustrate how this guides bereavement-informed care and decision-making, Table 2.1 lists these different factors and briefly summarizes the growing scientific evidence base.

Table 2.1 Four different types of factors and their differential relations to grief domains

Primary correlates (things that co-occur and correlate significantly with grief reactions)

- *Primary correlates* (e.g., PTSD, depression, functional impairment, risky behavior)
  - Evidence: Compared to adaptive grief reactions, maladaptive grief reactions correlate significantly more strongly with distress (e.g., depression, PTSD symptoms, somatic distress), impairment (school grades), and risky behavior (suicide ideation) (reviewed in Layne et al., 2019; Layne et al., 2020).
  - Grief reactions correlate more strongly with other grief reactions than they correlate with either PTSD or depression, showing that grief reactions are internally coherent and distinguishable from other types of distress (Geronazzo-Alman et al., 2019).

Moderators (protective factors and vulnerability factors that interact with bereavement to mitigate/reduce, or intensify/exacerbate, its harmful effects on a given outcome)

- *Protective factors and vulnerability factors* can influence postdeath adjustment. These include relationship to the deceased, social support, the well-being of surviving caregivers, and parenting practices. Other potential moderating factors include age, culture/ethnicity, gender, race, socioeconomic status, and prior loss history (Coffino, 2009).
  - Evidence: Bereaved children whose surviving caregivers help them to feel connected to their deceased parent (e.g., help them to reminisce, identify positive traits they share in common) report fewer maladaptive grief reactions and more adaptive grief reactions (Alvis et al., 2022; Kaplow, Layne, & Pynoos, 2014a; Sandler et al. 2003; Shapiro, Howell, & Kaplow, 2014).

Causal precursors (factors that precede, and are theorized to cause, grief reactions)

- *Causal risk factors* (e.g., witnessing traumatic deaths or death scenes; exposure to traumatic details about deeply disturbing death circumstances such as eyewitness accounts, police or medical reports/photographs, legal testimony).
  - Evidence: Youth exposed to violent deaths report higher levels of circumstance-related grief distress than youth exposed to nonviolent deaths (Douglas et al., 2021; Layne et al., 2019).
  - Bereavement predicts grief regardless of the manner of death; many different trauma types (including nondeath-related events) predict PTSD symptoms (Layne et al., 2010).
- *Mediators* (e.g., trauma reminders, loss reminders, and/or secondary adversities)
  - Evidence: Grief reactions correlate significantly more strongly with loss reminders; conversely, PTSD correlates more strongly with trauma reminders (Layne et al., 2006).
  - Compared to severe financial hardships, interpersonal hardships (fights at home, living with a depressed or alcoholic caregiver) are a stronger mediator of the links between wartime trauma and postwar PTSD, depression, and grief five-plus years later (Layne et al., 2010).
- *Treatment components/mechanisms of therapeutic change*
  - Evidence: PTSD symptoms respond to trauma-focused treatment components; grief reactions respond better to loss-focused treatment components (Grassetti et al., 2014).

Causal consequences (theorized causal effects of grief reactions)

- *Causal consequences* (poor school grades, risky behavior, suicide ideation).
  - Evidence: Reductions in maladaptive grief reactions over treatment are linked to improvements in school behavior and performance (Layne et al., 2001; Layne et al., 2008; Saltzman et al., 2001).

Applying this method to drawing distinctions between different grief dimensions based on their differential relations with external factors (Layne, Kaplow et al., 2014), multidimensional grief theory proposes that different dimensions of grief may (Layne et al., 2012, 2017; Layne, 2021b)

- be more prominent at different developmental stages (e.g., age may *moderate* the effect of bereavement on different grief domains, such that children report more separation distress, whereas adolescents report more existential/identity distress [Layne et al., 2019, 2020]);
- be more prominent in some demographic groups (e.g., socioeconomic status [SES], gender, culture, prior history) than others – for example, SES may act as a vulnerability factor that *moderates* the effect of bereavement on different grief domains (e.g., adaptive vs. maladaptive grief), such that maladaptive grief is more prominent in low-SES groups;
- vary across different types of relationship with the deceased as a *moderator* – for example, youth bereaved by the loss of very close/highly dependent relationships (e.g., a parent) may experience more separation and/or existential/identity distress than by the loss of a friend;
- vary across different types of bereavement as a *causal risk factor* (e.g., youth bereaved by traumatic deaths may experience more circumstance-related distress);
- relate differently to different *causal consequences* – for example, compared to adaptive grief, maladaptive grief may cause greater functional impairment, developmental disruption (school problems) (Layne & Kaplow, 2020), and risky behavior (Hill et al., 2019);
- and most relevant to MGT, different dimensions of grief may
  ◦ call for different treatment components (*causal precursors*) – a key principle of our modularized approach to tailoring treatment flexibly using each client's individual grief assessment profile (similar to TGCTA's approach [Saltzman et al., 2017]);
  ◦ produce different grief profiles that can support individually tailored intervention.

Multidimensional Grief Therapy uses individual grief assessment profiles generated using appropriately designed measures (e.g., Kaplow, Layne et al., 2018; Layne, Kaplow, & Pynoos, 2022a, 2022b, 2022c) to tailor treatment for each client. Using multidimensional grief theory as a guide, MGT aligns four levels of intervention (Layne, Strand et al., 2014). This involves using an individual's grief assessment profile to select and align the following:

1. A given *dimension of grief* and its central coping task as a therapeutic focus
2. *Intervention objectives* (therapeutic goals) that focus on that conceptual domain/coping task
3. *Practice elements* (therapeutic strategies) intended to achieve those intervention objectives
4. *Skills* (ways of implementing practice elements to maximize their effectiveness for a client that take into account such factors as their age, culture, prior history, life circumstances, etc.)

Multidimensional Grief Therapy helps practitioners use individual assessment data to tailor their intervention plan for each client across each of these four levels (Layne & Kaplow, 2020; Layne et al., 2022c). This can be done in creative ways while adhering to the principle of *flexibility within fidelity* to multidimensional grief theory and to MGT (Kendall & Frank, 2018). This design feature of MGT offers practitioners great flexibility in selecting the best-fitting intervention strategies for a client's individual grief reactions assessment profile. MGT offers the flexibility needed to address as many of the three primary grief domains as require therapeutic attention. (As noted in Chapter 3, the PGD Checklist has an accompanying guide for calculating grief dimension-specific scores and evaluating general severity [Layne, Kaplow, & Pynoos, 2022a, 2022b, 2022c].) As a concrete example of how multidimensional grief theory can guide treatment planning, if a youth presents with (see Layne, Strand et al., 2014):

1. prominent separation distress (conceptual grief dimension) in their assessment profile, a practitioner can then
2. focus on creating comforting ways to connect with the deceased (intervention objective) and
3. use the Good Grief Jar to collect comforting mementos and memories (practice element), and
4. implement the Good Grief Jar activity in ways that are engaging and appropriate for the client's developmental level and cognitive ability, culture, history, and life circumstances (skills).

Multidimensional Grief Therapy can be tailored at each of the four levels, beginning with the use of client assessment data to select a grief dimension and its central coping challenge (described later), and to align it with appropriate intervention objectives, practice elements, and skills. Other brief examples can be given of ways in which MGT aligns grief domains with intervention objectives and practice elements:

- Address circumstance-related distress (intervention objective: reduce distress over the way the person died) by using the MGT loss narrative (a practice element) and empathic skills.
- Address both separation distress (intervention objective: find comforting ways to connect by working through ambivalent feelings about the deceased) and existential/identity distress (objective: identify positive attributes to integrate into one's own maturing personal identity) by using the Sticks and Stones exercise (a practice element) and engagement/empathic skills.

The Theoretical Roots of Multidimensional Grief Theory

A recent advance in the development of multidimensional grief theory involves efforts to clarify the theoretical roots of its three conceptual dimensions (Layne, 2021a, 2021b). This recent work helps to ground and integrate the theory into the decades-deep child and adult grief literatures while increasing its generalizability, explanatory power, and clinical utility.

Historical Roots of Separation Distress. The conceptual domain of separation distress mainly traces back to attachment theory (e.g., Bowlby, 1980), which proposes that loss leads to disruptions in primary attachment relationships and manifests as distress over the persisting separation and the loved one's failure to physically return. Child bereavement studies contain rich examples of separation distress across different developmental stages. These manifestations of separation distress can vary, reflecting ongoing revisions in children's internal representations of the attachment relationship and their current developmental needs. Early studies of infants and preschoolers found that the loss of caregivers can evoke strong fears of abandonment – including clinging to surviving caregivers – that can appear as simple separation anxiety to the untrained eye, as well as disorganize body rhythms and disrupt child-caregiver interactions during daily care routines (see Lieberman et al., 2003). Early studies also revealed age-related differences in the ways in which separation distress can manifest. Young children may experience fantasies of concrete physical reunion with the deceased (e.g., climbing a ladder to join Mommy in heaven) (Cerny & Buskirk, 1991; Pynoos, 1992), whereas adolescents may experience suicidal ideation or reunification fantasies (e.g., dying to join the deceased in an afterlife) (Balk, 1983). Separation distress can also reemerge later in life as youth mature, take on new developmental tasks, and undergo new life changes. For example, an early adolescent girl experienced renewed grief reactions when her mother was not present to guide her through her first menstruation (Goenjian et al., 1994). Other studies described adolescents' ambivalence in approaching developmental tasks and the risks associated with each option, such as feeling pulled either to never leave home or to prematurely embark on independent living. For example, following sibling loss, youths' reduced reliance on adult caregivers through precocious independence seeking can lead to deprivations in meeting developmental needs for parental guidance and support (Balk, 1983).

Building on these contributions, early childhood bereavement studies reframed Horowitz's adult model of grief (1990). Horowitz originally proposed that, over time and in response to repeated encounters with "empty situations," bereaved adults gradually reschematize their inner working models to successfully transition to new attachment figures; namely, bereaved adults are able to revise their attachment relationships with the deceased in ways that allow them to form new close bonds, potentially including new romantic partners. Over time, children and adolescents may also accept substitute attachment figures that allow them to gain the social support needed to cope with life challenges and opportunities (e.g., a youth whose father died allows herself to form a close bond with a new stepfather) (Layne, Warren et al., 2009). However, beyond revising their internal working models of the deceased to accommodate the formation of new attachments, bereaved children and adolescents face an additional developmentally linked challenge: Early bereavement researchers (Pynoos, 1992; Silverman et al., 1992) proposed that youth retain an inner working model of a deceased parent that requires them to renegotiate key features of their parent-child relationship as they mature into adulthood and encounter new life experiences. That is, bereaved youth relate to their internal working model of a deceased parent in different ways at different developmental stages and life circumstances, such as relating to a deceased mother first as a teenager, then as a young college student, and then as a young mother (Layne, 2021b). Grieving may thus include both updating one's internal working model of the deceased over time (e.g., let Mom age along with me). In addition, given that needs for different types of support can change over time with ongoing maturation and new life events (Layne, Warren et al., 2009), bereaved people may seek different types of support from their working model in relation to new life roles (e.g., high school student), at different life stages (late adolescence), in relation to new developmental tasks (preparing for college and serious dating). This naturally ongoing work of relationship renegotiation can be complicated by a preexisting history of injuries to one's relationship with the deceased (e.g., abuse, neglect) that requires the bereaved child to contend with ambivalent feelings arising from memories of both positive and negative experiences – something addressed by the Sticks and Stones exercise (a practice element offered in MGT as well as TGCTA).

Historical Roots of Existential/Identity-Related Distress. The conceptual domain of existential/identity distress traces back to both early and modern existential philosophers (Layne, 2021a, 2021b). This school of philosophy explores positive approaches to death and dying through meaning construction (e.g., Alborn, 1997; Frankl, 2006; Neimeyer & Currier, 2009; Pausch & Zaslow, 2008). This work also includes early clinical-descriptive studies of personal existential crises among bereaved youth who experienced a loss of life purpose and ambition ("I've lost what I cared about the most, so nothing matters anymore") or identity-related crises ("A big part of me died with him"; "I'm nobody without her") (Kaplow, Layne et al., 2013; Layne et al., 2008; Layne et al., 2017). These personal crises were often marked by a sense of historical discontinuity in identity (e.g., "Part of me died with them"; "I'm not the same person I was before") and developmental disruption (e.g., one's future is blighted by the loss of a loved one as prospects for a successful life disappeared with them) (Layne, Pynoos, & Cardenas, 2001).

Early prototypes for identity and existential bereavement-related crises are found throughout the child literature. For example, early studies described negative self-concept among bereaved youth (Balk, 1983). Others documented children's reluctance to identify with a deceased loved one given fears that wanting to be like them would lead to the same tragic fate (Cain & Fast, 1972; Furman, 1974; Wolfenstein, 1969). Early studies also identified existential themes among bereaved youth, especially pessimistic expectations about the future (Worden & Silverman, 1996) and fears that one is doomed to share the same fate as a deceased loved one. These findings of negative self-concept, pessimism, and risk of underachieving developmental tasks were largely replicated in later longitudinal studies of bereaved youth (see Layne & Kaplow, 2020, for a review).

Historical Roots of Circumstance-Related Distress. The conceptual domain of circumstance-related distress traces back to studies of traumatic bereavement and disaster mental health (Layne, 2021a, 2021b). These include studies of youth exposed to war (e.g., Layne et al., 2001; Layne et al., 2008; Nader et al., 1993), terrorist attacks (Hoagwood, Layne, & CATS Consortium, 2010; Nader et al., 1990; Pynoos, 1992; Pynoos et al., 1987), and community violence including homicide (e.g., Layne, 1996; Layne, Pynoos, & Cardenas, 2001). This conceptual domain is also enriched by the disaster literature (e.g., Lindemann, 1944), including constructive responses to mass disasters and family tragedies (e.g., Layne, 2018; Rosenfeld, 2018). Early studies of bereaved children documented distress reactions to the circumstances of the death and highlighted diverse ways in which tragic and traumatic deaths can influence children's grief reactions and therapeutic needs. In the pioneering study *A child's parent dies*, Furman (1974) reported that privately held distressing concerns over the circumstances of a death often lay behind children's difficulties following bereavement. These concerns commonly arose during the course of the parent's terminal illness and death by natural causes. This key finding – that even deaths due to natural causes (typically excluded from PTSD criteria) can evoke intense distress over the manner of death – presages more recent findings (Kaplow, Howell, & Layne, 2014) about the many troubling reactions that youth bereaved by traumatic and tragic deaths can experience.

Notably, the prominent attachment theorist Bowlby (1980) described how stigma and issues of human accountability surrounding the manner of death can cause adults to misdirect children in ways that contradict and invalidate a child's own understanding and feelings. These distortions in the narratives that families weave about the circumstances of the death can lead to chronic disruptions in children's attachment relationships, emotional regulation, and development. Eth and Pynoos (1985) described special challenges that can arise when deaths occur under traumatic circumstances – including homicide and suicide – when witnessed by children. The encounter with physically mutilating death required *therapeutically reconstituting an intact image of the parent* that the child could then use to grieve in comforting ways (Pynoos, 1992). A longitudinal study of youth bereaved by a school sniper attack (Nader et al., 1990) shed light on the interplay that arose between traumatic stress reactions (to the circumstances of the death) and grief reactions (to the ongoing loss). The dual challenges of coping with posttraumatic stress reactions *and* grief reactions depleted youths' coping resources and led to a more prolonged and severe clinical course of both sets of reactions. These early studies set the stage for later work that focused on ways in which trauma, bereavement, and developmental factors can intersect following traumatic bereavement to intensify and prolong posttraumatic stress and grief reactions (Layne et al., 2017). This makes case conceptualization and treatment planning more complex and calls for specialized intervention that addresses trauma, bereavement, their interplay, and potential developmental disruption (see also TGCTA [Saltzman et al., 2017]).

Core Assumptions and Central Challenges of Multidimensional Grief Theory Domains

This early clinical-descriptive and theory-building work (e.g., Kaplow et al., 2012; Kaplow et al., 2013; Layne, Kaplow, & Pynoos, 2012, 2014; Layne, Pynoos, & Cardenas, 2001; Layne et al., 2008; Layne et al., 2017; Saltzman et al., 2017) set the stage for a developmentally informed, multidimensional, strength-based conception of grief. There are four core assumptions of MGT (Layne et al., 2021b; Layne et al., 2017, 2019):

1. Grief reactions are largely encompassed and explained by three primary conceptual domains: separation distress, existential/identity distress, and circumstance-related distress.
2. Each grief domain is linked to a central coping challenge specific to that domain.
3. Both adaptive and maladaptive adjustment (grief reactions and associated coping responses) can arise within each of the three conceptual domains.
4. The particular ways in which bereaved individuals react to and cope with the specific challenges of each grief domain make up their individual grief assessment profile.

Next, we describe each conceptual domain reaction in detail, including its central coping challenge, key functions, and examples of adaptive versus maladaptive grief reactions.

Separation Distress. The central coping challenge for separation distress centers on the question "How can I continue to feel connected to the person who died so that they remain an important part of my life?" (Layne et al., 2017). Separation distress-related reactions can be viewed as "classic" or prototypical grief responses and are positioned at the top of the multidimensional grief model because they are often most readily recognized (Layne et al., 2019). These reactions include missing the deceased person, heartache over their failure to return, yearning and longing to be physically reunited, and protest over the ongoing physical separation. Separation distress can be evoked by *loss reminders*, such as hearing the loved one's name or encountering their belongings, picture, empty situations they formerly inhabited, and former activities such as work, chores, hobbies, and favorite songs (Layne et al., 2006). Separation distress reactions typically recede over time in their frequency, intensity, and capacity to interfere with important developmental tasks as bereaved youth find meaningful ways to feel connected to the deceased (Clark, Pynoos, & Goebel, 1996). The specific ways in which separation distress manifests in bereaved children and adolescents can reflect both their increasing capacity across development to comprehend the meaning (e.g., permanence) of physical death, as well as their age-specific reactions to the ongoing loss (Kaplow, Layne et al., 2013; Layne et al., 2017; Lieberman et al., 2003; Nader & Layne, 2009). For example, a young child may protest a parent's failure to return by sitting next to the front door and crying inconsolably, whereas a school-age child may feel deprived of the caregiver's constant physical support (e.g., "I miss Mom's cooking"). Manifestations of separation distress in teenagers may take the form of seeking guidance or support from the deceased (e.g., "I wish Dad was here to give me advice" or "I wonder what Mom would say").

Multidimensional grief theory proposes that *adaptive reactions* to the central coping challenge of separation distress function by helping the bereaved to form a sense of ongoing emotional, psychological, and spiritual connectedness to the deceased that brings a sense of comfort and reassurance (Layne, 2021a, 2021b; Rando, 1993). Core tasks of adaptive coping with the central challenge of separation distress include the following (Kaplow, Layne, & Pynoos, 2019; Kaplow, Layne et al., 2013; Layne et al., 2009; Layne et al., 2017; Saltzman et al., 2017; Wolfelt, 1996):

- Recognizing and accepting the reality and permanence of the death
- Experiencing and learning to regulate the pain and discomfort of the permanent separation
- Successfully working through ambivalent thoughts and feelings about the deceased
- Renegotiating the relationship with the deceased to one based in memories and ongoing psychological and spiritual connection
- Revising attachment relationships with the deceased over time to reflect maturation, life stage, circumstances, experiences, and differing needs (e.g., relating to their deceased mother first as a teen, then as a young parent, then as a mother of teenagers)
- Working through unresolved injuries and strains to the attachment relationship with the deceased (e.g., working through guilt over how one treated the deceased before or during their death, including assumptions about how one may have contributed to the death)
- Recognizing the deprivations (e.g., love, companionship, guidance, security, physical help) formerly provided by the relationship with the deceased
- Finding constructive ways to address those deprivations and meet one's ongoing needs for support, such as by grafting on other relationships and activities (e.g., learning social support recruitment skills, joining afterschool clubs, volunteering in community activities)

In contrast, theorized *maladaptive reactions* to the central coping challenge of separation distress can be conceptualized as unhealthy, self-defeating, and/or socially destructive efforts to maintain a sense of connection to the deceased (Layne et al., 2017, 2022c). These maladaptive reactions carry a common theme of inability to renegotiate one's personal relationship with the deceased from one based in physical presence to one based in memory, or otherwise retaining an unhealthy connection to the deceased. In contrast to adaptive reactions to separation distress, maladaptive manifestations of separation distress carry significantly greater risk for severe persisting distress, functional impairment, risky behavior, and developmental disruption, and, conversely, a reduced likelihood to engage in positive growth-enhancing activities (Layne, Kaplow et al., 2014). Acting as causal risk factors or vulnerability factors, these maladaptive reactions are theorized to promote or prolong problems with adjustment (Layne et al., 2019; Layne, 2021b). Theorized manifestations of maladaptive reactions to the central coping challenge of separation distress include the following (Kaplow, Layne et al., 2013; Layne et al., 2017, 2019, 2022c; Rando, 1993; Saltzman et al., 2017):

- Retaining an unhealthy connection with the deceased by assuming their same unhealthy or destructive habits; feeling doomed to share their same tragic fate, etc.
- Inability or refusal to accept the physical reality and irreversibility of the death
- Avoiding opportunities to form healthy new attachments appropriate to one's life circumstances
- Developmental freezing, slowdowns, or regressions (e.g., trying to stay connected with the deceased by remaining stuck in the same developmental stage; persisting in immature/self-defeating behavior patterns one was in while the deceased was still alive; fears that moving on with life will involve abandoning, negating, or disrespecting the person who died)
- Identifying with unhealthy or dysfunctional elements of the deceased's life, values, behaviors, or roles as a way of feeling an ongoing sense of connection to them (e.g., taking on destructive habits, roles, or values the deceased person used to do or embrace)
- Persisting suicidal ideation motivated by a wish to be quickly reunited in an afterlife
- Distress over strains and injuries to one's relationship with the deceased while they were alive ("I feel guilty about what I said the last time I saw him"; "I never got to say goodbye")
- Excessive behavioral or cognitive avoidance of loss reminders that interfere with accepting the reality of the death or remembering and reminiscing about the deceased ("I can't stand to talk about Mom"; "Every time someone brings up my dad in a conversation, I have to leave the room")

Viewed from a broader psychosocial context, the wellbeing and parenting strategies of surviving caregivers can influence separation distress. For example, youths' separation distress can intensify if the relationship with the surviving caregiver is strained, or if the caregiver has difficulty talking about the deceased or is also experiencing intense separation distress. Conversely, caregivers can facilitate adaptive reactions to separation distress by helping to remember, reminisce, and form positive psychological and spiritual connections (Alvis et al., 2022; Kaplow, Layne, & Pynoos, 2014a; Sandler et al., 2003; Shapiro, Howell, & Kaplow, 2014).

In summary, multidimensional grief theory's domain of separation distress provides you with a conceptual lens and space to recognize how maladaptive grief reactions can arise through an inability to accept the reality of the death (permanent physical separation) or through unhealthy identification with the deceased (Layne et al., 2022c). This lens will also guide you in facilitating adaptive grief reactions by helping clients to form more comforting, constructive, and portable psychological, emotional, and spiritual attachments to their deceased loved ones that clients can carry forward in their lives. Multidimensional Grief Therapy provides a flexible set of practice elements to help promote adaptive coping with separation distress (by creating a comforting sense of ongoing connection) and reduce maladaptive coping (by revising and letting go of unhealthy, risky, and developmentally restricting connections) (see also Saltzman et al., 2017).

Existential/Identity Distress. The central coping challenge for existential/identity distress centers on addressing the question "Who am I as a person, and what is the purpose of my existence, now that my loved one is physically absent from my life?" (Layne et al., 2017). Multidimensional grief theory proposes that *adaptive reactions* to the coping challenge of existential/identity distress function by helping the bereaved to revise and renegotiate one's sense of self, personal identity, and the purpose of one's life and existence in a world in which the deceased is physically absent. This includes accommodating to a new way of life, including new rituals, roles, assumptions, and expectations about one's future prospects, place in the world, and reason for being (Clark, Pynoos, & Goebel, 1996; Pearlman et al., 2014; Rando, 1988; Saltzman et al., 2017). Core tasks of adaptive responding to the coping challenge of existential/identity distress include the following (Layne et al., 2017, 2022c; Layne, 2021b):

- Successfully managing and coping with challenges to one's self-concept
- Successfully managing and coping with disruptions in future life plans
- Finding a sense of purpose and fulfillment in life (e.g., career aspirations, life ambitions)
- Developing new daily routines and ways of living
- Adjusting to the physical absence (e.g., making room in my life for Mom's new boyfriend)
- Finding alternative sources of healthy gratification to help compensate for those previously furnished by the relationship (e.g., forming new friendships and hobbies)
- Growth (taking over roles formerly carried out by the deceased, developing new skills)
- Making meaning of the deceased person's life and ongoing loss (e.g., revising personal values and life priorities; reflecting on the impact of the deceased's life; carrying on their legacy, doing healthy and constructive things that would make them pleased or proud)
- Prosocial behavior and civic engagement (volunteerism, altruism, advocacy; making the world a better place for new generations) (see Saltzman et al., 2017, Module 4)

In contrast, theorized *maladaptive reactions* to the central coping challenge of existential/identity distress involve a severe, persisting personal existential crisis and/or personal identity crisis precipitated by the loss (Layne et al., 2017, 2022c). In contrast to adaptive reactions to existential/identity distress, maladaptive reactions are characterized by a significantly greater risk of severe persisting distress, functional impairment, risky behavior, and developmental disruption (Layne, 2021b; Layne et al., 2014). Theorized clinical manifestations include the following (Kaplow et al., 2012; Kaplow et al., 2013; Layne, Kaplow, & Pynoos, 2022a, 2022b; Layne et al., 2017, 2019, 2022c; Saltzman et al., 2017):

- Diminished personal identity (e.g., feeling like part of you died with them)
- A sense of being "different" from peers ("I'm the only one without a mom")
- Historical discontinuity in one's sense of self ("I'm a different person since they died")
- Loss of a sense of life purpose and meaning; existential nihilism ("I've lost my reason for living"; "I've lost what was most precious to me, so nothing else matters anymore")
- Risk taking, recklessness, or indifference to one's safety or well-being (e.g., not wearing seat belts; not looking before crossing the street); self-neglect ("I don't care if I live or die")
- Lack of realistic yet positive life aspirations ("I don't care about my future")
- Survivor guilt or the sense that one's "true" fate was thwarted by remaining alive ("I should have died with them"; "I shouldn't still be here")
- Hopelessness, despair, or resignation in anticipation of a grim future that has been irreparably blighted by the death (e.g., "I'll never find anyone like him"; "My life is over")
- The sense that all of life has lost its savor (e.g., beliefs that current relationships or activities are no longer gratifying and worth investing in)

In contrast to PTSD (and its sense of *foreshortened* future – "I feel like I won't live long"), existential/identity distress can reflect a sense of *blighted* future: One expects to still exist, but in a world that lacks personal meaning, fulfillment, and is not worth hoping for, investing in, or preparing for (e.g., abandoning future aspirations) (Layne, Pynoos, & Cardenas, 2001; Layne et al., 2017).

In summary, existential/identity distress provides you with a clinical lens and conceptual space in which to understand how deaths – even "peaceful" deaths due to natural causes – can evoke devastating personal existential crises and/or identity crises. These crises can erode survivors' sense of hope and optimism, derail their life aspirations and future ambitions, and disrupt their personal identity or sense of life purpose. These personal crises can appear as a loss of meaning, purpose, and hope for the future; demoralization over the belief that one's future prospects are irreparably blighted, loss of a sense of continuity in personal identity, or a marked sense of being diminished and depleted (Layne et al., 2017). Indeed, this distress can appear as other conditions including depression, pessimism, identity or role confusion, aimlessness, apathy, passivity, resignation, indifference towards one's life or the future, and losing the will to live (Layne et al., 2019, 2022c). Multidimensional Grief Therapy's flexible array of practice elements can assist you in facilitating adaptive grief reactions by helping clients to re-form their daily lives and personal identity, make meaning of the deceased person's life and death, and find a sense of life purpose that motivates them to hope for and invest in a meaningful future (see also Saltzman et al., 2017).

Circumstance-Related Distress. The central coping challenge for circumstance-related distress centers on addressing the question "How do I manage my distressing thoughts, beliefs, wishes, fantasies, emotions, and impulses evoked by how this person died?" (Layne et al., 2017). This challenge can be conceptualized as emanating from *how* the person died, whereas the challenges of separation distress and existential/identity distress emanate from the fact *that* the person died, regardless of the circumstances (Layne, 2021a, 2021b; Layne et al., 2017). This conceptual domain is very broad, encompassing both "traumatic" deaths as well as "tragic" deaths that evoke intense distress. Multidimensional grief theory proposes that a range of expectable distress reactions can arise in the short-term aftermath of such deaths, including anger, disgust, horror, troubling thoughts and mental images ("No one should have to die like that"), and indignation ("He deserved better") (Pearlman et al., 2014). Although often intensely painful, these distress reactions tend to recede over time, diminishing in their frequency, intensity, and distractibility as survivors learn to cope with their distress and move forward with their lives (Clark, Pynoos, & Goebel, 1996; Kaplow, Layne et al., 2013; Layne et al., 2017; Pynoos, 1992).

This conceptual lens will help you to recognize distress over "traumatic" deaths (e.g., accidents, homicides, suicide) that *do* meet PTSD diagnostic criteria as a traumatic stressor (Layne et al., 2019). This includes understanding processes through which both posttraumatic stress and grief reactions can intersect and exacerbate one another in the aftermath of traumatic deaths, creating an interplay that can intensify and prolong distress (Layne, Kaplow, & Youngstrom, 2017; Layne et al., 2017; Nader, 1997; Nader et al., 1993). For example, PTSD symptoms (intrusions, avoidance, numbing) can interfere with and inhibit adaptive grief reactions in a classic "traumatic grief" presentation (Pynoos, 1992). Conversely, grief reactions (e.g., existential crises, demoralization, denial of the reality of the death, fixation on avenging the death before allowing oneself to grieve) can undermine efforts to participate in trauma treatment that involves confronting the reality and distressing nature of the death and its circumstances (Kaplow, Layne, & Pynoos, 2019; Layne et al., 2017; Layne & Kaplow, 2020). Multidimensional grief theory thus proposes that circumstance-related distress evoked by the manner of death is most likely to be clinically prominent after deaths (causal risk factors) that contain potentially traumatic, tragic, or otherwise deeply troubling elements. There is growing evidence supporting this proposition (summarized in Layne et al., 2019; Layne et al., 2020; Layne & Kaplow, 2020).

This conceptual domain will also help you to recognize and understand how many other types of deeply distressing deaths (e.g., deaths due to natural causes) that although *not* meeting formal PTSD Criterion A diagnostic criteria as "traumatic," can nevertheless evoke intense persisting distress over the tragic way in which the loved one died (Layne et al., 2019). Examples of intense distress over the death circumstances include deep sadness that they died young, died alone, felt excruciating pain; feeling like they deserved a better death; bitterness over senseless or meaningless deaths; shame or guilt over stigmatized deaths; intense anger over deaths caused by negligence or medical error; bewilderment over deaths of undetermined cause; or feeling frustrated and angry at the deceased for not taking better care of themselves (Layne et al., 2017; Saltzman et al., 2017). Indeed, Kaplow, Howell, and Layne (2014) found that, for children and adolescents, deaths due to natural causes (e.g., slow, painful deaths due to wasting illness) may contain more traumatogenic elements than sudden deaths. This conceptual lens will also help you to understand how factors surrounding the death (e.g., bitter last words, not being able to or not saying goodbye, not being present at the time of death, unresolved hard feelings, believing one contributed to their death, feeling angry at them for contributing to their own death) can create severe persisting distress without being necessarily or overtly "traumatic."

Multidimensional Grief Therapy proposes that *adaptive reactions* to the central coping challenge of circumstance-related distress share a common theme of representing a constructive answer to the way in which the person died (Layne et al., 2017; Layne, Pynoos, & Cardenas, 2001; Pynoos, 1992; Saltzman et al., 2017). Traumatic deaths can evoke powerful responses that motivate individuals, communities, and society to take action to prevent similar deaths in the future, compassionately support those afflicted by loss, and to hold the responsible parties accountable to uphold the social contract and restore moral order (Layne, 2018; Pynoos, Sorenson, & Steinberg, 1993). In contrast to general altruism, constructive responses to circumstance-related distress by definition thematically relate to the *manner* of death. These responses can often be conceptualized as vicarious wish fulfillment in preventing, protecting against, repairing, or seeking appropriate retribution for similar deaths; or in reducing the suffering that follows (Layne et al., 2017). This vicarious wish fulfillment can be illuminated by reframing constructive responses as counterfactual "if-then" contingencies: "If only this had been in place before they died, then it might have prevented their death"; or "If this were available to us at the time our loved one died, then it would have made it easier to bear." The following are examples of adaptive coping with the central challenge of circumstance-related distress:

- Prosocial behavior (e.g., volunteering to ease the burden for other victims, public advocacy for victims, referring those at risk to specialized help) (Saltzman et al., 2017)
- Aspiring to be a detective, attorney, or judge (who remove dangerous people from society); counselor (who helps people in crisis); paramedic or doctor (who saves injured people); dietician (who helps prevent heart attacks); scientist (who discovers cures for fatal diseases); engineer or architect (who designs safer planes and buildings); and lawmaker (who passes safety and victim assistance legislation) (Kaplow, Layne et al., 2013; Layne, 2018; Layne et al., 2017)
- Learning to protect and assist oneself and others in safe and responsible ways (e.g., martial arts, learning first aid skills, being trained in psychological first aid to help others in need)

On a societal level, many safety-related innovations arose in direct response to traumatic deaths, including emergency exit signs, air bags, fire escapes, suicide hotlines, lifeboats, Mothers against Drunk Driving, Amber Alert, and America's Most Wanted (Layne, 2018; Layne et al., 2017).

In contrast, theorized *maladaptive reactions* to the central coping challenge of circumstance-related distress involve the encroachment of severe persisting mental preoccupation and distress to the *way* the person died on adaptive grieving and mourning (Kaplow, Howell, & Layne, 2014; Layne et al., 2017, 2019, 2022c; Pynoos, 1992). The following examples may arise in response to the specific circumstances of the death:

- Efforts at positive reminiscing involuntarily segue into intrusive distressing mental images, thoughts, and emotional reactions to the manner of death ("Whenever I think about them, I start to feel angry over what their last moments must have been like")
- Feeling bewildered or deeply confused about the cause or manner of death in ways that interfere with acceptance of its reality or making necessary changes in life roles and plans
- Persistent psychic numbing that inhibits grieving and mourning ("I'm too numb to cry")
- Intense guilt or shame linked to how the person died (e.g., stigmatized deaths such as murder, suicide, or overdose; survivor guilt)
- Intense preoccupation with retaliatory or vindictive fantasies and rageful desires for revenge (Layne, Pynoos, & Cardenas, 2001; Saltzman et al., 2017)
- Refusal to accept the reality of the death due to the deeply objectionable or socially stigmatized circumstances under which it occurred (homicide, negligence, overdose, suicide, murder-suicide, drunk driving, cause undetermined or suspiciously not divulged [Pynoos, 1992; Pynoos et al., 1993; Rynearson, 2001])

Multidimensional grief theory proposes that risk for clinically significant circumstance-related distress increases when the manner of death (as a causal risk factor) contains highly distressing and traumatic features to which victims have been directly or indirectly exposed (Layne et al., 2017; Pynoos, 1992). Channels of exposure include witnessing, hearing about, or viewing accounts and photographs about the death. These traumatic features can include violence (e.g., gruesome or mutilating deaths), volition (malicious intent), the violation of the social contract (homicide, negligence, indifference, malpractice, abusing the dead body) (Rynearson 2001), or extreme tragedy (e.g., excruciating pain). A variety of causes of death (e.g., witnessing the progressive deterioration of a parent dying of cancer, intense physical suffering, or others' emotional agony) may contain traumatic elements capable of evoking circumstance-related grief reactions, PTSD, or both in youth (Kaplow, Howell, & Layne, 2014).

Circumstance-related distress may be especially prominent among individuals who are both exposed to direct life threat and witnesses to the traumatic death (Nader et al., 1990; Nader et al., 1993; Pynoos, 1992). This is because they can be contending with a complex array of: (1) PTSD reactions to the manner of death, (2) PTSD reactions to direct life threat, (3) grief reactions to the loss, as well as an aftermath of (4) trauma reminders of life threat, (5) trauma reminders related to witnessing the traumatic death, and (6) loss reminders (Layne et al., 2006; Pynoos, 1992).

In summary, circumstance-related distress provides a clinical lens and conceptual space in which to understand how distress over the tragic and often traumatic manner of death can interfere with survivors' efforts to grieve. This includes the ability to recognize how classic PTSD symptoms (traumatic stress reactions to the manner of death) and grief reactions (to the death and ongoing loss) can intersect with one another to prolong and exacerbate distress (Layne et al., 2017). This conceptual lens will also help you to see how tragic and disturbing deaths (e.g., deaths due to natural or undetermined causes) that do *not* meet PTSD Criterion A (and therefore cannot "cause" PTSD by definition) can nevertheless evoke deep distress over the manner of death and its aftermath (Layne et al., 2019). This lens also helps with differential diagnosis, given that circumstance-related distress can be mistaken for other conditions, including PTSD, rejection of the social contract following wrongful deaths, and aggressive fantasies (Layne & Kaplow, 2020). Recognizing that many different types of deaths (e.g., extended illness) can contain traumatogenic elements can also provide a useful check against a biased tendency to search for "traumatic grief" only among "traumatically bereaved" youth, while overlooking bereaved youth who are distressed over the circumstances of less dramatic yet nevertheless deeply troubling deaths (e.g., due to "natural" causes [Layne et al., 2022c]).

Conclusion

Multidimensional grief theory provides a diverse set of conceptual lenses to understand how the death of a loved one, its circumstances, secondary adversities, trauma and loss reminders, and the meaning survivors attach to the death and ongoing loss can each influence ongoing adjustment (Layne et al., 2006). Multidimensional grief theory is a broad and flexible theory. It offers space in which to conceptualize maladaptive grief as arising from disruptions in primary attachment relationships, disruptions in meaning-making systems, and distress over the manner of death (Layne, 2021b). Further, the proposition that *each conceptual domain contains a central coping challenge*, and that individuals' coping responses vary in their utility (Layne et al., 2017), allows it to crosspollinate with a large literature on coping strategies (e.g., Benson et al., 2011; Howell, Kaplow et al., 2014; Kaplow et al., 2014). Multidimensional grief theory's strong developmental emphasis also underscores the importance of carefully considering bereaved youths' social and physical ecologies and the key role that caregivers play in shaping youths' life experiences and facilitating their grief reactions (Alvis et al., 2022; Howell et al., 2016; Shapiro, Howell, & Kaplow, 2014). Last, the theory's strong ecological emphasis underscores the importance of considering the effects of bereavement and its aftermath on youths' and families' daily lives, including the roles played by loss reminders, trauma reminders, change reminders, and secondary adversities, and ways in which these can impede adaptive developmental progression for years and even decades into the future (Layne & Kaplow, 2020; Layne et al., 2006).

3 MGT Pretreatment Assessment Interview
Using Evidence-Based Assessment and Goal Setting to Guide Individual Treatment Using MGT

Note: The pretreatment assessment interview is usually conducted on an individual basis between a MGT clinician who will be facilitating the individual sessions and a prospective client. Primary aims of this interview include (1) gathering information needed to determine whether MGT is an appropriate treatment for this particular youth, or whether a referral for other services is appropriate; if MGT is indicated, (2) gathering information regarding losses and (in cases of multiple deaths) ranking them according to their severity/current impact to decide which should be a primary focus of treatment; (3) beginning to build a shared vocabulary for describing losses, grief reactions, and their consequences; and (4) building trust and therapeutic rapport, which you will draw on in subsequent sessions.

Selecting Appropriate Participants for MGT

Participants Should Meet the Following Criteria:

Age:	Eight or older
Inclusion Criteria:	1. A *history of bereavement* accompanied by
	2. severe persisting *distress* (especially maladaptive grief reactions and/or posttraumatic stress reactions), and evidence of
	3. *functional impairment*. This can include impaired performance in developmentally important life domains (e.g., school behavior, academic performance, interpersonal difficulties with friends or family). It can also manifest as developmental disruptions or risky behavior in the form of
	• *developmental slowdowns* (setbacks, regression, freezing, delays – e.g., failing a grade, loss of previously acquired competencies, reluctance to take on age-appropriate developmental tasks),
	• *precocious developmental accelerations* (e.g., becoming sexually active at an early age, taking on adult roles and responsibilities prematurely),
	• *developmental derailment* (drastic changes in life course, such as dropping out of school or incarceration),
	• *risky behavior* (especially in adolescents) (e.g., fighting, drug use, drunk driving, reckless driving, criminal activity).
Exclusion Criteria:	In general, youth who show signs of psychosis, severe psychopathology, or substance abuse should be referred for more in-depth diagnostic assessment and intensive targeted services that go beyond MGT.
Structure:	Multidimensional Grief Therapy is primarily designed to be implemented in an individual treatment modality. It can also be implemented in groups or combined school classroom/group-based settings:
	• Groups ranging from 5 to 9 members tend to benefit most from group cohesion (Burlingame, McClendon, & Alonso, 2011). If potential attrition is a significant risk in your setting, consider starting with up to 10–11 members.

- Groups formed of youth who share *similar* bereavement experiences (e.g., traumatic deaths) tend to form cohesion faster. Nevertheless, groups formed of youth with *dissimilar* loss-related experiences can also develop therapeutic cohesion, produce therapeutic change, and facilitate learning as members share their diverse life experiences and perspectives (Davies, Burlingame, & Layne, 2006). For example, Layne et al. (2008) combined war-exposed Bosnian youth whose loss-related experiences involved traumatic deaths, natural deaths, and/or internal displacement (loss of home and community) with significant beneficial effects.
- Cox et al. (2007) and Layne et al. (2008) describe a school-based trauma- and grief-focused program implemented by school counselors. The program integrated public outreach and advocacy (e.g., presentations to school staff, to parents at parent-teacher meetings), classroom-based risk screening, in-depth assessment, triage to different services, classroom-based psychoeducation and skills training for many students, and school-based small group treatment for severely distressed students.

Prepare for the Assessment

Various measures may be useful for such assessment tasks as risk screening, case conceptualization, formulating a working diagnosis, treatment planning, monitoring response to treatment over time, and assessing posttreatment outcomes. Published resources (Kaplow, Layne et al., 2018; Layne & Kaplow, 2020; Layne, Kaplow, & Youngstrom, 2017; Layne, Youngstrom, & Kaplow, 2020) can help you to apply principles of evidence-based assessment to your practice. Later in the chapter we present a list of *suggested* measures that have proven useful in different settings where MGT has been implemented (the final choice is left to your judgment); each measure is paired with a brief description of the test and information on how to obtain it. We divide the list into Primary measures (Table 3.1) (strongly recommended because they are very useful in identifying youth who are eligible for MGT and for tailoring the treatment) versus Secondary (optional) measures (Table 3.2). Some measures are in the public domain and can be used without cost; others are proprietary and may be obtained for a modest fee. The tables provide links for obtaining each measure. Please do not feel obligated to use all the measures, especially from the Secondary measures list. Use only those measures that you judge to be reasonable for your particular clients, assessment questions, and setting.

In general, we do *not* recommend that you fully hand score the measures during the assessment itself because doing so can lengthen the session, create awkward moments of silence, make the youth feel more self-conscious, and detract from rapport building. Instead, use this pretreatment assessment interview to help you efficiently gather basic information about key factors. These factors include bereavement (the death of a loved one), exposure to the circumstances of the death, current grief reactions, potential posttraumatic stress reactions, and other potential difficulties (see Chapter 1). Your goal is to integrate this information into your assessment feedback session (which follows the pretreatment assessment session).

Set aside time to score your measures completely *after* the pretreatment assessment session (or carefully review test scores if the tests are scored electronically). Capturing pretreatment baseline scores on key measures (particularly those that focus on grief reactions and posttraumatic stress symptoms) allows you to carry out *key assessment-related goals*:

- Evaluate the severity level of your client's total grief and posttraumatic stress scores. For example, is either score in the clinical range? Do they meet diagnostic criteria for either disorder (i.e., PGD, PTSD)?
  - Given its newness at the time of writing (March 2022), following is a brief summary of diagnostic criteria for PGD (American Psychiatric Association, 2022):
    - *Criterion A:* Death of a close person at least 12 months ago (for adults) and at least 6 or more months ago (for children and adolescents)
    - *Criterion B:* Development of persisting grief reactions since the death characterized by (1) intense yearning or longing for the deceased person, and/or (2) preoccupation with thoughts or memories of the deceased (and in children and adolescents, preoccupation with the circumstances of the death)
    - *Criterion C:* At least three of the following eight symptoms have been present most days and to a clinically significant degree:
      1. Identity disruption
      2. Marked disbelief about the death
      3. Avoidance of loss reminders (in youth, can also include efforts or strong desires to avoid loss reminders)
      4. Intense emotional pain relating to the death
      5. Difficulty with reintegrating into one's relationships and life activities
      6. Emotional numbing
      7. Feeling that life is meaningless
      8. Intense loneliness

- *Criterion D:* The disturbance causes clinically significant distress or impairment in important areas of functioning.
- *Criterion E:* Duration and severity exceeds social, cultural, or religious norms for the client's culture and context.
- *Criterion F:* Rule out major depressive disorder, PTSD, other mental disorders, and physiological effects of a substance (e.g., medication, alcohol, other drugs) or another medical condition.

• Use *multidimensional grief theory* as a set of conceptual lenses to assess which grief domains may be clinically prominent in your client's assessment profile. The PGD Checklist contains two separate test scoring procedures:
  ○ The first procedure, found in the PGD Checklist itself, allows you to make a PGD diagnosis according to DSM-5-TR criteria as outlined above. For individual clients, this can be useful for such applications as assessing diagnostic status at pre-/mid-/post-treatment and providing individual feedback. On a broader organizational level, this diagnostic scoring method can help you to implement principles of evidence-based assessment (EBA) (Layne & Kaplow, 2020; Layne, Kaplow, & Youngstrom, 2017; Layne, Youngstrom, & Kaplow, 2020). The principles of EBA will help you to gather and use assessment data to guide professional decisions regarding client care. Specific EBA procedures include the following:
    ▪ Tracking the prevalence rates of different diagnoses seen in your setting
    ▪ Assembling an assessment test battery that covers commonly seen diagnoses
    ▪ Evaluating whether you are implementing evidence-based interventions that effectively address the disorders commonly seen in your setting, and/or are linked to specialized service providers who do
    ▪ Creating procedures for risk screening, in-depth clinical assessment, and referral to appropriate mental health services that help to establish continuity of clinical care
  ○ The second, supplemental procedure is found in the appendix of the PGD Checklist. This supplemental procedure allows you to create *domain-specific grief scores* that align with multidimensional grief theory's conceptual domains (producing separation distress, existential/identity distress, and circumstance-related distress subscale scores). These domain-specific subscale scores will help you to evaluate two things: (1) The average frequency with which the client has experienced each type of grief reaction during the past month; and (2) the overall assessment profile of grief reactions, including relative elevations among grief domain scores. This information will help you to identify specific types of grief reactions that, based on their overall frequency and relative elevation, may be given greater priority as intervention objectives and emphasized in treatment.

• Decide how to tailor MGT's many grief-related exercises to best fit the client's specific needs, as reflected in their grief assessment profile. After consulting with the client, you may choose to prioritize – as therapeutic objectives – specific types of grief reactions (assessed using the PGD Checklist supplemental scoring system) that they report experiencing most frequently, intensely, or that are otherwise most troubling to them.

• Identify areas of functional impairment, developmental disruption, or risky behavior that may require special attention.

• Evaluate whether traumatic stress reactions – especially those linked to the circumstances of traumatic or deeply tragic deaths – may interfere with the client's ability to engage in grief processing, particularly in relation to constructing the loss narrative.

Results of the assessment will also help you to prepare for future sessions by gathering details about different loss experiences and life adversities. This individualized information will help you to personalize your psychoeducational discussions, set the stage for in-depth processing of loss experiences, and highlight areas of developmental disruption that may require attention. The assessment will also allow you to monitor changes in your therapeutic targets (grief reactions, posttraumatic stress symptoms, etc.) over time.

We strongly encourage you to conduct an additional follow-up assessment after completing Phase 1 of MGT. Some youth may only require Phase 1 of MGT, especially if their distress symptoms have receded. This post-Phase 1 assessment will help you to evaluate whether to terminate intervention or to proceed on to Phase 2 (including the construction of a loss narrative). If you choose to implement Phase 2, we strongly encourage you to conduct a postintervention follow-up assessment after completing Phase 2 to evaluate the extent to which you achieved your intervention objectives and to assess for potential need for additional services. Tables 3.1 and 3.2 can help you to select appropriate measures and create an assessment plan (see Layne & Kaplow, 2020).

Overview of the Assessment Interview Procedure

1. Introduce yourself and begin to build rapport.
2. Describe the purpose of MGT and build motivation to participate.
3. Complete the assessments that you select.
4. Clarify possible connections between the youth's past loss experiences and current difficulties.
5. Explain that you will be reviewing their responses after the initial session and extend an invitation to

Table 3.1 Primary measures

Focus/Target	Reporter	Recommended Use	Title of Measure, Brief Description
• Bereavement • Maladaptive grief reactions (prolonged grief disorder [PGD], etc.)	Youth (optional caregiver report of functional impairment)	• Baseline (pretreatment) clinical assessment, diagnosis, case conceptualization, treatment planning • Post-Phase 1 (readiness to terminate vs. proceed to Phase 2) • Post-Phase 2 outcome assessment (to evaluate readiness to terminate Multidimensional Grief Therapy [MGT]) • Follow-up assessment (e.g., at follow-up booster sessions held weeks or months after formally terminating MGT)	Prolonged Grief Disorder Checklist (PGD Checklist) (Layne, Kaplow, & Pynoos, 2022a). Assesses PGD, a new diagnosis listed in *Diagnostic and statistical manual of mental disorders* (5th ed.) (DSM-5-TR; American Psychiatric Association, 2022). *Criterion A* (screening) items ask whether the youth has experienced the death of someone close, relationship to deceased, circumstances of death. *Criterion B* items (gateway symptoms including distress over circumstances of the death) and *Criterion C* items (full PGD symptom constellation) assess frequency of grief reactions during the last four weeks. *Criterion D* items include youth self-report and (optional) caregiver observational reports assessing functional impairment at home, school, with peers, and in developmental progression. The PGD Checklist contains procedures for generating a DSM-5-TR PGD diagnosis. Its appendix contains a supplemental scoring system. This supplemental system will generate multidimensional grief theory *conceptual domain subscale scores* (separation distress, existential/identity distress, circumstance-related distress) that creates an individual assessment profile to support case conceptualization and intervention planning/tailored intervention. Domain scores of two or above suggest moderate or higher distress levels and a need for therapeutic follow up. Proprietary, license available at www.reactionindex.com.
• Trauma exposure • Posttraumatic stress symptoms • Screen for/rule out PTSD diagnosis	Youth	• Baseline *risk screening* and case conceptualization (recommend using the UCLA PTSD Reaction Index for DSM-5, Brief Form [RI-5-BF; Rolon et al., 2020]) • Baseline *in-depth clinical assessment*, PTSD diagnosis, case conceptualization, treatment planning (recommend using the UCLA PTSD Reaction Index for DSM-5 [RI-5; Kaplow, Rolon-Arroyo et al., 2020; Pynoos & Steinberg, 2002]) • Post-Phase 1 (readiness to terminate vs. proceed to Phase 2) • Post-Phase 2 outcome assessment	*Two assessment tools are available:* • *For initial trauma/PTSD risk screening:* RI-5-BF. Includes brief trauma screen; 13 PTSD items provide a cutoff score with high hit rate (sensitivity & specificity) for predicting/ruling out PTSD diagnosis. Can be used at baseline, post-Phase 1, post-Phase 2 to predict/rule out PTSD. Available free of charge at www.reactionindex.com. If the youth tests positive on the RI-5-BF, then the full RI-5 (described next) is recommended as a follow-up second step to gather in-depth clinical information about the full PTSD symptom profile. • *For in-depth trauma-informed clinical assessment, diagnosis, case conceptualization, treatment planning for youth who test positive on the RI-5-BF:* RI-5. The RI-5 assesses all DSM-5 PTSD symptoms. Recommended when PTSD symptoms appear prominent and are a potential focus of treatment.

Table 3.1 Primary measures (cont.)

Focus/Target	Reporter	Recommended Use	Title of Measure, Brief Description
			The RI-5 consists of (1) a brief trauma screen; (2) a detailed Trauma History Profile assessing 20 types of trauma exposure across ages 0–18, to be administered at baseline given its length; (3) frequency of each PTSD symptom experienced during the past month; (4) functional impairment in major life domains (home, school, peers, developmental progression). Proprietary, license available at www.reactionindex.com.
• Depression	Youth, parent, parent self-report	• Baseline risk screening • Post-Phase 1 (readiness to terminate vs. proceed to Phase 2) • Post-Phase 2 outcome assessment	Mood and Feelings Questionnaire (MFQ) (Angold et al., 1995). Frequency of depressive symptoms experienced during the last two weeks is rated on a three-point scale consisting of *most of the time, sometimes, not at all*. Useful screening tool for identifying youth at risk for depression; not appropriate for clinical diagnosis of depression. • Total score of ≥8 on the Short Form MFQ is a marker of heightened risk for depression. • Available in many languages. (Short and long versions of each measure available without cost: https://devepi.duhs.duke.edu/measures/the-mood-and-feelings-questionnaire-mfq/.)

• Screen for suicide risk (ideation and plans)
• Assess for suicide risk (ideation and plans)
	Youth	• In settings with *low prevalence rates* of suicide ideation, use the Columbia-Suicide Severity Rating Scale (C-SSRS) Short Screening Form for baseline risk screening. Then use the C-SSRS for follow-up assessment for those who screen positive on the Screen Version.
		• In settings with *significant prevalence rates* of suicide ideation, use the C-SSRS for baseline/intake in-depth assessment, followed by the C-SSRS Short Screening Form for ongoing monitoring (post-Phase 1 or as needed; post-Phase 2). If youth test positive on the Short Form during ongoing monitoring, then readminister the full C-SSRS.
		• Be prepared for acute suicide preventive intervention (see King, Ewell-Foster, & Rogalski, 2013).
			Two assessment options are available:
			• *For risk screening*: C-SSRS Screen Version; assesses baseline risk level or as a follow-up monitoring instrument over the course of treatment.
			• *For in-depth assessment of suicide ideation/intent*: C-SSRS – a widely used clinician-administered instrument that covers risk and protective factors; suicidal ideation (active/passive), intensity, frequency, duration; suicidal behaviors, past attempts, preparatory acts, and lethality of methods. Instructions must be followed exactly. Available without cost in multiple languages.
			  ◦ C-SSRS (Full Length Form): https://cssrs.columbia.edu/wp-content/uploads/C-SSRS_Pediatric-SLC_11.14.16.pdf.
			  ◦ C-SSRS (Short Screening Form): www.cms.gov/files/document/cssrs-screen-version-instrument.pdf.
			Training in their use is strongly recommended; available at: http://c-ssrs.trainingcampus.net/.

Table 3.2 Secondary measures

Construct	Reporter	Recommended Use	Title of Measure, Brief Description
Avoidant coping	Youth	• Baseline risk screening • Post-Phase 1 monitoring • Post-Phase 2 outcome assessment	Active Inhibition Scale (AIS; Dodd et al., 2020). The AIS is an 11-item questionnaire that measures avoidance with regard to the child's thoughts and feelings. The child indicates the degree to which each statement is true by responding to a question about the frequency of each item on a scale ranging from 0 (never) to 4 (a lot). Scores 29 and over may indicate high avoidant coping. The AIS can be obtained without cost from the above article or from Dr. Irwin Sandler at Irwin.sandler@asu.edu.
Overall adjustment across multiple domains; critical items screen for risky conditions	Youth	• Baseline assessment • Session-by-session monitoring • Post-Phase 1 (readiness to terminate vs. proceed to Phase 2) • Post-Phase 2 outcome assessment	Youth Outcome Questionnaire (Y-OQ; Burlingame, Wells, & Lambert, 1995). A normed test consisting of seven subscales (intrapersonal distress, somatic distress, interpersonal relations, social problems, behavioral dysregulation, critical items). Test items were selected from the treatment outcome literature based on their sensitivity to clinical change (i.e., ability to show significant treatment effects). Provides early feedback regarding whether clients are on track to make significant improvement, creating opportunities for timely course corrections. Proprietary, license available at www.oqmeasures.com/.
Functional impairment/ positive adjustment	Youth, Teacher	• Baseline risk screening • Post-Phase 1 (readiness to terminate vs. proceed to Phase 2) • Post-Phase 2 outcome assessment	Strengths and Difficulties Questionnaire (SDQ; Goodman, 1997). Assesses functional impairment/positive adjustment across multiple developmental domains. The SDQ is available free of charge: www.sdqinfo.org/a0.html.

participate in the assessment feedback session following the pretreatment assessment session, where you will determine together the best course of treatment.

6. If you determine that the youth is not appropriate for MGT, have other treatment options available (e.g. substance abuse treatment referral).
7. If appropriate, evaluate the youth's willingness/readiness to participate in treatment.

Preparation before Meeting with the Client

- Review the introductory information about MGT and the content of this session so that you can explain it briefly and clearly.
- Have selected assessment tools available.
- Have pens, pencils or slim markers ready, or, if using online versions of the measures, have a computer or iPad available.

Meeting with the Client

1 Engagement

Greet the youth and, if the youth was not self-referred, ask what he/she knows about the treatment and how and why they were referred. Be as transparent and open as possible regarding the referral and what you already know about the youth. Present the interview as an opportunity to learn about the youth, describe the assessment process, answer any questions, and explain ways in which the assessment will help you to determine how you can best help them.

Explain the limits of confidentiality with the youth, as you would with any client in your setting. (Consider all content confidential unless you identify a threat to self or other.)

2 Explain the Purpose of the Assessment and the Process

Using the information below, describe the assessment process in your own words while emphasizing how children and adolescents grieve in different ways.

- It is important to remember that there is no "right" or "wrong" way to grieve. We all grieve in different ways after a loved one dies, and there is no set timeline for grief. In fact, because grief is a reflection of the love we had for the person, we don't really "stop" grieving. Our grief just changes over time, and usually it gets easier to cope with our loss as time passes.
- It is also possible to feel really "stuck" in our grief, and that can cause problems in our daily lives. For example, it may be harder to pay attention in school or get along with our friends or family. We may even feel hopeless or helpless about our future.
- It is my job to learn more about how you have been feeling, including ways that you may be feeling stuck. I do that by using what we call an "assessment." An assessment is made up of questions about how you've been thinking and feeling since the death that can help me figure out the best way to help you.
- An assessment is not like a test you take in school, because there are no right or wrong answers. The most important thing is to give me your honest answers, so I can really understand what your experiences have been like and how I can help.
- If a question is confusing or doesn't make sense, please ask me to explain it until you understand.
- Because some questions ask about the death and how you have been feeling, they may bring up different feelings, like sadness. Just remember that it's perfectly okay to feel that way, and we can take a break any time you want. Just let me know. I'll check in with you every now and then to see how you are doing.

You can ask the client if they have any questions before getting started with the assessment. We recommend having snacks on hand and/or fidget toys that the client can hold while answering the questions.

3 Conduct the Assessment

Begin the Formal Assessment

Step 1: Assess for Bereavement and Grief (PGD Checklist recommended)

- Fill out Part A of the PGD Checklist (if available) with the youth by sensitively exploring whether the youth has experienced the death of someone close, and if so, who died. (If the youth has not experienced the death of a significant life figure, discontinue and move to the next measure.)
- If the youth reports experiencing at least one significant death, then ask them to fill out the remaining questions regarding the frequency of specific grief reactions and functional impairment.
- Quickly scan the grief reaction items to see whether any are endorsed at "3" (*a lot of the time*) or "4" (*all of the time*). Note the number of grief reactions that fall within this range.
- As noted earlier, the PGD Checklist contains different tools for scoring the measure later, after the assessment session with the client has ended. These include:
  ○ A scoring system that provides a PGD diagnosis (using DSM-5-TR PGD criteria), which is found in the PGD Checklist.
  ○ A supplemental scoring system found in the appendix of the PGD Checklist, which provides a multidimensional grief assessment (including separation distress, existential/identity distress, circumstances-related distress subscale scores). These dimension-specific subscale scores can be used to create an individual grief assessment profile that can be used to tailor MGT according to each client's specific needs.
  ○ An accompanying Multidimensional Grief Assessment Feedback Form for summarizing assessment findings in client-friendly ways.

Step 2: Assess for Trauma and PTSD (UCLA RI-5-BF or the UCLA RI-5 recommended)

- To conduct a *brief trauma screen only*, complete the RI-5-BF (brief exposure and PTSD symptom questions). This will help you to determine whether the youth is at high risk for PTSD and should be considered for in-depth clinical assessment for trauma exposure and PTSD.
  ○ If the youth screens positive for trauma/PTSD, clarify whether the PTSD symptoms are *linked to the circumstances of the death*.
    - If yes (PTSD is linked to the death circumstances), consider administering the UCLA RI-5 to assess the full set of PTSD symptoms. This can guide you in integrating PTSD symptoms into your MGT assessment summary, case conceptualization, and treatment plan.
    - If no (PTSD is linked to other traumatic experiences – e.g., sexual abuse), confer with the client in your assessment feedback session. Acknowledge and validate their trauma history and PTSD as separate concerns apart from bereavement and grief. Work with them to prioritize treatment goals (e.g., first offer trauma treatment focused on traumatic experiences other than the death? *or* first offer MGT, and then reassess for PTSD and need for other trauma

treatment?). Trauma and Grief Component Therapy for Adolescents (Saltzman et al., 2017) can treat PTSD linked to both traumatic deaths and other traumatic experiences.
- For *in-depth trauma and loss assessment*, complete the RI-5 (including the Trauma History Profile, PTSD symptom questions, and functional impairment items).
  - Quickly scan the completed pages, looking for endorsed trauma and loss items and which trauma was identified as the greatest source of distress (p. 10 of the RI-5).
  - Note the number of PTSD symptom items endorsed at "3" (*much of the time*) and "4" (*most of the time*). These are PTSD symptoms that the youth is experiencing regularly.

STEP 3: Assess for Depression and Suicide Risk

- Assess/screen for depression and suicide risk by administering appropriate assessment tools (including those recommended in Table 3.1). Quickly review the items for each measure, paying close attention to the suicide assessment results in particular. If the youth appears to be at elevated risk for suicide, be prepared to either (1) complete a Suicide Prevention Plan as you normally would in circumstances of low risk, including alerting the caregiver/parent and providing safety guidance; or (2) refer the youth to their local emergency room if they appear to be at high risk. Have a prepared list of local emergency referral sources available to be able to respond in an effective and timely manner should the need arise. Although a detailed guide for assessing suicidality and managing risk is beyond the scope of this manual, excellent resources are available (see King, Ewell-Foster, & Rogalski, 2013).

STEP 4: Administer Supplementary Measures (as needed and as time permits)

- Based on your available time and your clients' needs, administer other measures (including those listed in Table 3.2) that, in your clinical judgment, are relevant for evaluating each youth.
- Take special note of measures that not only identify distress but also other markers of high risk, including functional impairment in developmentally important domains (e.g., school, interpersonal relationships), risky behavior, and developmental setbacks.

Note: Although in our experience it happens infrequently, it is possible that some clients may become upset by certain assessment questions. If a youth becomes distressed, the clinician should use clinical judgment to determine whether (1) a brief break is needed, accompanied by practicing self-calming skills (e.g., deep breathing, grounding), or (2) it is in the client's best interests to terminate the assessment, accompanied by offering praise and encouragement for the client's courage and effort. This may include some self-regulation work (e.g., breathing relaxation) to help them emotionally recover.

STEP 5: Conclude the Assessment Session

Thank the youth for working with you to discuss things that can be hard to talk about and for providing honest answers. Explain that you will be providing detailed feedback on what you learned from your work together in your next meeting (the assessment feedback session).

STEP 6: Assessment Feedback Session (after the initial assessment session)

Prior to beginning the assessment feedback session, score the client's assessment measures and evaluate goodness-of-fit for MGT as a primary treatment. Specifically, a child or adolescent is a good candidate for MGT if any of the following are true:

- Client either (1) meets criteria for PGD (if scoring the PGD Checklist according to DSM-5-TR diagnostic criteria) or (2) receives an average score of "2" or higher on any grief domain subscale score (if scoring the PGD Checklist according to multidimensional grief theory)

OR

- Client meets the clinical cutoff on the RI-5-BF (score ≥ 24) and you have clarified that the PTSD is linked to the circumstances of (started or worsened after) the death

OR

- Client meets the clinical cutoff on the RI-5 (score ≥ 35) and you have clarified that the PTSD is linked to the circumstances of (started or worsened after) the death

Appendix D of the PGD Checklist (Layne, Kaplow, & Pynoos, 2022a) contains the Multidimensional Grief Distress Assessment Feedback Form. This form graphically depicts the theory's three conceptual grief domains, provides a place for you to record and interpret each client's score on each domain, and offers clinical guidelines for interpreting scores for each grief domain as viewed through the lenses of multidimensional grief theory.

Form P.2 (found at the end of this chapter) contains the Child Assessment Feedback Form. This form will help you to summarize and review all measures included in our recommended assessment battery listed above. This form will help you to review scores from each measure, summarize your overall clinical impressions, and evaluate with your client whether MGT is the best treatment option available. We recommend covering the following assessment results:

- Summarize the clinical picture that has emerged of the youth's loss-related experiences, as well as current strengths and positive experiences. Interpret the results by beginning to "connect the dots" by showing possible connections between their loss experiences and their current life difficulties (e.g., it's too painful to do some of the things they used to enjoy doing because their person is no longer there).
- When present, note current grief reactions and posttraumatic stress reactions, and how they may be interfering with the youth's ability to enjoy life and do the things they want to do. Scores on supplementary

measures may shed additional light on affected life domains (e.g., home, school, peers).
- Whenever possible, highlight the youth's strengths and resilience, including times when they showed courage or accomplished something notable despite their challenges. For example, note a few of the youth's stressful experiences and express admiration at how well the youth is doing given what he or she has been through (e.g., "I'm impressed at how you've been able to … ").
- Validate and normalize their current difficulties, such as by recognizing how challenging life is at times for them and/or their loved ones right now.
- Express realistic hope and confidence that, especially if provided with the right kinds of support (like the support provided in MGT), they can successfully deal with their loss and still have a good/great life.
- Provide similar feedback to the client's caregiver, being sure to explain that (if MGT is indicated) treatment will involve the caregiver to some degree (e.g., attending some sessions, providing support, etc.).

In Cases Where MGT Is Not Appropriate:

- If you decide that the youth may benefit from some form of mental health treatment but is *not* appropriate for MGT, consider providing a referral for other services. When possible, keep a prepared list of possible referrals available going into the interview.
- If there are indications that the youth is clinically depressed and/or at risk for self-harm, suicide, or harm to others, follow your professional mandates and guidelines for assessing risk and taking appropriate steps to ensure safety.

Step 7: Explain the Benefits of MGT

If, in your judgment, the youth is appropriate for MGT, extend an invitation to participate. You may wish to cover the following points:

- Provide details regarding how the treatment will be conducted, including the frequency and length of the sessions, when and where meetings will take place, etc.
- Address questions they may have, including confidentiality or concerns that if they talk about their loss each week, it will only make them more sad. Reassure them that although talking about a loss can be sad, especially at first, you'll be working together to find ways to grieve that feel comforting, to deal with challenges they face, and to have a good life.
- Using your own words, convey the following information about the treatment itself:
  ○ MGT is a support program for kids and teens who have lived through some very difficult losses that can still be causing some problems. During our time together, we'll learn new things about grief, share ideas, and find new and helpful ways of coping.
  ○ Of course, MGT won't solve *all* of your difficulties. But we focus on creating *new choices*, finding new ways to deal with problems, and creating a positive future. We cover knowledge and skills that have helped other kids who have lost loved ones. These skills help kids in practical ways, like being able to sleep better, not being bothered so much by memories of what has happened, feeling calmer and not so angry or sad or scared, getting along better with people, doing better in school, and having more hope for the future.

Step 8: Develop One or Two Goals for Participating in MGT

A primary aim of MGT is for the youth to select, work on, and achieve one or two personally meaningful goals relating to their loss and its present consequences. These are to be noted on the Personal Goals Worksheet (Handout P.1). Earlier, you elicited and summarized how their loss experiences are linked to current grief and/or posttraumatic stress reactions and began to explore potential links between these reactions and things the youth is unhappy about in their life. Mapping out cause-effect connections between *past* losses and *current* symptoms and problems is a motivational interviewing strategy that increases youth insight, gives MGT greater traction, and helps to identify key benchmarks (things the youth really cares about) for measuring clinically significant change over time. Connections between prior loss and current difficulties that the youth feels motivated to change should be pointed out in clear and concrete ways – a recurrent process that begins in this interview and continues throughout the program.

Encourage youths to select goals that are: (1) related to their loss experience, (2) current problems that the youth is motivated to address, (3) concrete and specific, and (4) realistically achievable within the allotted time span. It also helps to choose goals that can be worked on both *within* and *outside* the individual sessions (Mendelsohn et al., 2011). Prompts for guiding the selection of appropriate treatment goals include the following:

1. Do you see a connection between this problem and the death of your _____? (loss related)
2. In what ways is your life still affected by your loss? What would you want to change in this area of your life? (focus on current problem)
3. How would you know if you accomplished that goal? How would your life look different? (concrete and specific)
4. Is there a particular area of your life in which you experience this problem the most? How is it affecting you in this area? (concrete and specific)
5. That sounds like an important but very large goal. Can we break it down into smaller goals that you could start achieving in the next few weeks? (realistically achievable)

6. What part of your goal can you practice *during* our sessions together? What part of your goal can you practice *outside* of our sessions together?

To identify a personally meaningful goal, start with a clear description of a real problem in daily living that the youth cares about. Work to assemble a good *problem statement* by using good active listening skills (e.g., listen closely, paraphrase, reflect feelings, use clients' words, review and refine the problem statement with the client) to distill a clear statement of what the youth finds most distressing at this time. Use any of the prompts above to refine the problem statement. Once you arrive at a problem statement that resonates with the youth, work to create a positively framed goal statement that addresses the problem. At each step, check in with the youth to make sure the problem and goal statements reflect their concerns and motivations.

Example of a Problem Statement:

"So it sounds like you really hate it when people at school ask you about your brother's death. This makes you feel angry and sad, and you end up pulling away from your friends and feeling all alone for hours or even days on end. Does that sound right?"

Example of a Possible Goal Statement:

"Tell me if this makes sense for one of your goals: Learning how to respond to peoples' questions and comments about your brother without shutting down or distancing yourself from your friends."

Examples of Making This Goal Concrete, Specific and Realistic, with a Part to Be Achieved within the Individual Sessions and a Part Outside of the Sessions:

- *Within the individual sessions:* "By the end of the program I want to be able to talk about my brother's death during the session without shutting down or feeling like I need to run away."
- *Outside of the individual sessions:* "By the end of the program I want to be able to talk about my brother's death when asked about it at school or other social settings in ways that don't leave me feeling bad or even more alone."

Be sure to write down the problem and goal statements as accepted by the youth, and refer to them throughout the treatment. Reassure the youth that they will have multiple opportunities to revisit and change the problem and goal statements as they progress through therapy. As youth continue to learn about links between their loss and current difficulties, they often get better at selecting appropriate experiences to focus on. The problem and goal statements should keep pace with this evolution.

4 Conclude the Session

Conclude the session, check in with the youth as well as the caregiver regarding any remaining questions, share the date for the first meeting, and express your enthusiasm for seeing the youth again at the next session.

Handout P.1

Personal Goal Worksheet

Name: _____

Date: _____

Problem Statement: _____
_____
_____
_____
_____

Goal Statement: _____
_____
_____
_____
_____
_____

Date: _____

Problem Statement: _____
_____
_____
_____
_____

Goal Statement: _____
_____
_____
_____
_____
_____

A PDF version of this handout is available for download on Cambridge Core and via www.cambridge.org/MGT

Handout P.2

Client: _____   Assessment Date: _____

MGT Assessment Feedback Form

1. Summary of Grief Conceptual Domain Scores (from the PGD Checklist)

How Much of the Time?	Grief Domain Distress Score
Experiencing Separation Distress 0 Not at All, 1 A Little, 2 Sometimes, 3 A Lot, 4 All the Time (average score range = 0 to 4)	Separation Distress Separation Distress Score: _____
Experiencing Existential/Identity Distress 0 Not at All, 1 A Little, 2 Sometimes, 3 A Lot, 4 All the Time (average score range = 0 to 4)	Existential/Identity Distress Existential/Identity Distress Score: _____
Experiencing Circumstance-Related Distress 0 Not at All, 1 A Little, 2 Sometimes, 3 A Lot, 4 All the Time (average score range = 0 to 4)	Circumstance-Related Distress Circumstance-Related Distress Score: _____

2. Screening/Diagnostic Test Summary

	RI-5-BF (Screening Test) Score/Notes	RI-5 (Assessment Test) Score/Notes	
PTSD (Reaction Index)			PTSD Risk (Y/N)
MFQ (Depressive Symptoms)	Score/Notes		Depression Risk (Y/N)
AIS (Avoidance)	Score/Notes		
C-SSRS (Suicide Ideation)	Score/Notes		Suicide Risk (Y/N)

A PDF version of this handout is available for download on Cambridge Core and via www.cambridge.org/MGT

Understanding Assessment Feedback

PGD Checklist

The PGD Checklist can be used not only to provide a PGD diagnosis, but also to assess grief reactions across three different domains: separation distress, existential/identity distress, and circumstance-related distress. Higher domain scores reflect higher levels of distress and suggest that grief-focused intervention may be beneficial.

- *Separation distress:*
  - Youth experiencing *separation distress* yearn to be reunited with the deceased and are very preoccupied with the deceased person's continuing physical absence. These youth may also experience intense loneliness (really missing the person who died), anger, or protest about the loss. They may also experience difficulty trusting or feeling close to others, and have fantasies about reuniting with the person who died.

- *Existential/identity distress:*
  - Youth experiencing *existential distress* tend to feel lost without their loved one. They may feel that they have lost a sense of purpose and direction to their lives, and that it is hard to find something to live for or look forward to. They may have a pessimistic outlook on life or on their future because of the hardships the loss has brought. They may also be reluctant to think about the future and may withdraw from meaningful or pleasurable life activities.
  - Youth experiencing *identity distress* tend to struggle with their sense of self (who they are) after the loss. They may feel like a big part of them died with the person, or that they are not the same person as before. They may feel different from others with whom they felt a sense of belonging/fitting in before the death.

- *Circumstance-related distress:*
  - Youth experiencing *circumstance-related distress* are preoccupied with the way their loved one died, or with the cause of their death. This distress can make it difficult to talk about or think about the deceased. Reminders of the person who died (e.g., their name) can bring up upsetting thoughts and feelings about their death. Examples include upsetting memories of how the person died, guilt/regret that the youth didn't do more to prevent it, anger towards others for not preventing the death, shame/distress over stigmatized death, or reluctance to grieve and mourn because the death seems so wrong and unacceptable.

UCLA PTSD Reaction Index

The UCLA PTSD Reaction Index assesses posttraumatic stress reactions. These may be reactions to the way the person died, reactions to other stressful life events, or both. Higher scores reflect higher levels of distress and suggest that intervention that includes a trauma focus may be helpful.

Mood and Feelings Questionnaire

The Mood and Feelings Questionnaire assesses symptoms of depression that the child may have experienced over the last two weeks. Higher scores suggest that interventions that include a focus on depressive symptoms may be helpful.

Active Inhibition Scale

The AIS measures avoidance with regard to the child's thoughts and feelings. Higher scores suggest that interventions that focus on greater emotional expression may be helpful.

Columbia-Suicide Severity Rating Scale

The C-SSRS assesses suicide risk. It helps practitioners decide how to respond, with options including (1) education and information, (2) safety planning, or (3) referral for more in-depth assessment and potential acute intervention.

4 Caregivers as "Cofacilitators" of Children's Grief

It is not surprising that parents and caregivers play a critical role in helping their child adjust to a "new normal" following the death of a loved one. One of the most challenging aspects of assisting a child after a death is that the caregivers themselves are usually grappling with their own personal grief reactions at the same time. The reality is that observing one's own child in emotional distress is extremely painful under most circumstances, but bearing witness to this emotional pain within the context of a death can greatly add to the sorrow and devastation that a bereaved caregiver is likely already experiencing. In addition, it is often hard for caregivers to separate their own intense emotions from those of their child. This tendency can predispose caregivers to believe that their child's experiences are similar to their own. However, members of the same family can grieve in very different ways as a result of many contributing factors. These include each family member's personal life experiences, developmental stage, cognitive ability, relationship to the person who died, family roles, coping strategies, temperament, and experiences surrounding the death (Kaplow, Layne, & Pynoos, 2019). Consequently, it can be difficult for caregivers to accurately recognize their child's own personal grief reactions and intuitively understand how to help their child grieve in adaptive ways (Furman, 1974). These differences in how family members grieve can create communication difficulties, misunderstandings, and greater distress over the long term (Kaplow, Layne, & Pynoos, 2014a).

The good news is that research in the area of bereavement and parenting is providing insights into what we refer to as "caregiver grief facilitation" (Alvis et al., 2022) – that is, how parents can facilitate healthy grieving in their own children. Below, we briefly review this growing body of literature, which provides the foundation for a number of the practice elements and exercises found in MGT.

Positive Parenting/Caregiving

Basic Types of Positive Caregiving Behaviors. A number of research studies have identified associations between "positive" caregiving behaviors and improved child outcomes following the death of a loved one (e.g., Haine et al., 2008; Kwok et al., 2005; Sandler et al., 2013; Shapiro, Howell, & Kaplow, 2014; West et al., 1991). These positive caregiver behaviors include (1) engaging in enjoyable family activities (e.g., games, cooking together, watching a family movie) that serve the functions of strengthening positive bonds and building family cohesion (Haine et al., 2008; Sandler et al., 2003); (2) helping children to "take a break" from grieving through healthy distraction; (3) enhancing family identity by redefining the relationship to the deceased person; (4) increasing warmth and communication (Alvis et al., in press; Haine et al., 2008; Sandler et al., 2003); and (5) maintaining continuity in family routines and activities. This helps to establish a sense of stability and order (Walsh, 2008), especially during a time when most children feel that the world around them is "out of control."

How can caregivers talk to their grieving child in a helpful way? We often hear from caregivers that they are concerned about what to say to their grieving child. They want to be able to talk about the death but worry about saying the "wrong thing" or fear that their own intense feelings of sadness may overwhelm the child or themselves. These worries may be heightened in the short-term aftermath of a death, when intense feelings and emotional reactivity are more pronounced or when the caregiver is experiencing significant distress. These concerns may be especially prominent in the charged atmosphere that can arise when the death occurs under "traumatic" or socially stigmatized circumstances.

Caregivers may be more confused or avoidant of opening conversations with children if: (1) the person's death was sudden, unexpected, violent, violated basic laws and civil protections, or involved human agency such as malice or negligence, in the case of potentially traumatic deaths; or (2) is linked to intense negative experiences including shame, social alienation, marginalization, and cultural or religious judgments, in the case of potentially stigmatized deaths such as suicides, drug overdoses, or deaths related to illegal acts (Layne et al., 2017; Pynoos, 1992).

Caregivers can benefit from the reassurance that, although increased caregiver-child communication is generally helpful in the face of bereavement (e.g., Horsley & Patterson, 2006), current research suggests that it is not so much what caregivers *say* to the child, but what they *do* that matters most. For example, physical affection, smiling, and consistent eye contact with bereaved children are associated with lower levels of child maladaptive grief and depressive symptoms (Shapiro, Howell, & Kaplow, 2014). Caregiver warmth (e.g., displaying general positive regard, conveying acceptance, and expressing affection), is also consistently associated with decreased mental health problems in bereaved children (Kaplow, Layne, & Pynoos, 2014a; Saler & Skolnick, 1992; West et al., 1991). In contrast, other caregiver behaviors are linked to negative outcomes in bereaved youth. For instance, avoidant coping (which involves not thinking about or talking about the deceased person and/or the way that he/she died) among both caregivers and children is associated with reduced levels of adaptive grief (Alvis et al., 2020; Kaplow, Layne, & Pynoos, 2019) and with increased levels of maladaptive grief in bereaved youth (e.g., Alvis et al., 2020; Dodd et al., 2020; Stroebe, Schut, & Finkenauer, 2013). Next, we draw on these findings and our own professional experience to offer guiding principles for facilitating adaptive grief reactions and resilience in bereaved children.

Guiding Principles for Caregiver Grief Facilitation

Interventions that strengthen caregiver-child relationships and foster emotional expression appear to promote resilience among bereaved youth (see Ayers et al., 2013; Hill et al., 2019; Sandler et al., 2013). To encourage and harness these beneficial processes, we offer five principles (referred to as the Five S's) that caregivers can draw upon to promote children's adaptive grief. These principles are embedded throughout MGT. They are also summarized in a handout that caregivers can use to remember these principles and put them into practice at home (see Session 4).

Principle 1: *Show* That You Are Listening and That You Care

Certain positive caregiving behaviors are linked to lower levels of distress in bereaved youth. These behaviors include: (1) caregiver expressions of warmth; (2) expressions of physical affection (e.g., hugging); (3) smiling; and (4) being fully "present" when the child is sharing his/her feelings (e.g., maintaining good eye contact, leaning towards the child, nodding in response to the child's comments, etc.) (Shapiro, Howell, & Kaplow, 2014). Notably, these forms of body language are more strongly associated with reductions in the child's distress than the verbal content of the parents' conversations. This finding suggests that it may be more helpful for parents to focus on being present and engaged rather than focusing on finding the "exact right words."

Bereaved children are often vigilant and very "tuned in" to the expressions and emotions of their surviving caregiver, and thus may worry that discussions about the deceased person will upset their parent. Consequently, children may avoid mentioning the deceased person out of a caring desire to protect their caregiver from further distress. The caregiver's ability to demonstrate (especially through nonverbal cues) a capacity to listen and a genuine interest in the child's thoughts or feelings about the deceased person (including difficult questions and emotions) can help to alleviate children's concerns. This can open the door to honest and supportive caregiver-child communication in ways that reduce the child's distress and foster a sense of positive connection to the deceased (Kaplow, Layne, & Pynoos, 2014a).

Principle 2: Be *Sensitive* to the Child's Reactions and Needs

Children grieve in personal and often private ways. It is normal for there to be fluctuations in what children need at any given point in time. For example, a child may enjoy reminiscing and joking about the deceased person on one occasion, have lots of questions about the deceased's life or death on another, and may need moments of alone time for reflection or distraction on a third occasion. Thus, caregivers can look for opportunities to "sync" how they talk about the deceased with how the child is grieving and mourning at a given moment, in ways that feel sensitive and supportive. This also involves appreciating individual differences in how bereaved children grieve, including among siblings. For example, some children may want to talk frequently about the deceased person and his/her death, whereas others may not want to discuss the topic at all (Kaplow, Layne, & Pynoos, 2014a; Saltzman et al., 2017).

Further, some youth may become extremely emotional (e.g., sad, tearful, angry, or bittersweet joyful) during these discussions, and others may show little emotion. Caregivers can remind themselves, and their children, that people within the same family grieve in many different ways and that there is no "right" or "wrong" way to grieve. One of the most important things that a caregiver can do is to meet their children where they are at in terms of their own readiness to discuss the death or engage in memorializing activities. This can involve asking children directly if they want to talk about it or providing an "open door policy" that allows children to approach the topic if and when they are ready (e.g., "I'm here to listen whenever you want to talk about Dad, and you can always feel comfortable asking me questions whenever they come up for you.") (Kaplow, Layne, & Pynoos, 2014a).

Principle 3: *Separate* and Distinguish Caregiver Grief from Child Grief

Although this principle may seem similar to Principle 2 above, its importance cannot be overstated. Using our multidimensional approach to assessing grief reactions (Kaplow, Layne, & Pynoos, 2019; Kaplow, Layne et al. 2013; Layne & Kaplow, 2020; Layne, Kaplow, & Youngstrom, 2017), we have found that caregivers' self-reported grief reactions do not correlate significantly with their children's self-reported grief reactions (Wardecker et al., 2017). Despite empirical evidence that caregivers' own grief reactions are quite different (and essentially independent) from their children's grief reactions, caregivers often assume that bereaved children experience the same grief reactions as they do and thus have the same grief-related needs and wishes. However, grieving and mourning are often intensely private experiences that even close attachment figures find very difficult to accurately identify and assess in children (Pynoos, 1992). In fact, as with other forms of internalizing symptoms such as anxiety and depression (e.g., De Los Reyes & Kazdin, 2005), caregivers tend to be poor reporters of their children's internal grief experiences (Wardecker et al., 2017). Indeed, caregivers' observational reports of their children's grief reactions tend to correlate more strongly with their own self-reported grief reactions than with their children's self-reported reactions (Wardecker et al., 2017).

If unchecked, caregivers' misperceptions regarding children's private grief experiences can lead to inaccurate conclusions, misunderstandings, and potential conflict. For example, based on their own desire to avoid holiday-specific loss reminders, a surviving caregiver may choose to discontinue former holiday traditions (e.g., playing the deceased person's favorite Christmas songs), whereas the child may instead wish to hold on to these longstanding traditions that he/she perceives as comforting and helpful in fostering a sense of positive connection to the deceased (Kaplow, Layne, & Pynoos, 2014a). This potential for dyssynchronies and misunderstandings in how children and caregivers grieve and mourn requires that caregivers remain aware of ways in which their own grief reactions may differ from their children's. Calmly and respectfully recognizing these differences can help to create a safe and supportive place for honest communication about individual differences in family members' grief-related needs and wishes. This openness towards – as well as acceptance and support of – individual differences between family members can help families to function in more flexible, adaptable, and resilient ways (Saltzman et al., 2013).

Before engaging in discussions about the deceased, caregivers often find it helpful to monitor their own grief reactions and levels of distress. This self-awareness can help them choose whether to initiate a conversation during times when they can be most emotionally available to their child. This self-monitoring can be challenging because grief reactions and associated distress can vary by the day and even by the hour. Nevertheless, this basic self-awareness skill can be key: A critical factor in effective grief facilitation is the caregiver's ability to be present with their child and (at least for the moment) put aside their own sorrow, fears, and other preoccupations in order to enter into their child's world, bear witness to the child's own experience, and provide sensitive support when and where they can. At the same time, caregivers should be cognizant of when they need to seek support for themselves, whether from family members, friends, clergy, or a therapist.

Principle 4: Keep It *Simple* and *Straightforward*

Children often have many questions regarding the circumstances surrounding a death, especially when those circumstances are ambiguous in some way. One of the major grief-related tasks for bereaved children is to make sense of the events leading up to the death. This understanding can help to alleviate circumstance-related distress, which can manifest as an intense preoccupation with the way the person died (e.g., "Did they suffer?"; "Is there something I could have done to save them?"; "What was going through their mind at the time?"). Circumstance-related distress may also manifest as a need to mentally revisit the death over and over again, including asking the caregiver questions about how the person died, even if the death was due to "natural" causes (Kaplow, Howell, & Layne, 2014; Layne et al., 2017; see also Chapter 2).

In an attempt to be open and honest about the death, caregivers may err on the side of providing too much detailed information about the death, which can sometimes overwhelm children. On the other hand, in an attempt to protect their children's feelings, caregivers may err on the side of not talking about the death at all, especially when the circumstances of the death are ambiguous, traumatic, or more difficult to discuss. We know that caregivers generally have the best of intentions by withholding certain facts about the circumstances of the death in order to "protect" their children. However, this can create problems by making children feel invalidated, confused, or distrusting towards their caregivers. In fact, our work suggests that children are almost always aware on some level of parents' attempts to hide information about a death (Kaplow, Howell, & Layne, 2014). As Bowlby (1980) so accurately stated, "children know what they are not supposed to know" about the death itself and typically react to the death in a way that is consistent with the "true" cause of death, even if this information is not openly shared by caregivers. For example, children who are told that "Dad died of a heart attack" when he actually died by suicide may ask questions like "Why would someone try to kill themselves?" (Kaplow, Howell, & Layne, 2014; Layne et al., 2017; Saltzman et al., 2017).

Keeping language about the death "simple and straightforward," involves meeting children where they are in their understanding and allowing them to guide the conversation whenever possible. For example, a caregiver may say: "I know you may have some questions for me about how Mom died. What would be helpful to know right now?" Providing age-appropriate information about the circumstances surrounding the death of a loved one by "titrating" facts based on children's developmental capacity to comprehend and accept the information appears to be an important part of facilitating adaptive grief in bereaved children (Kaplow, Layne, & Pynoos, 2014a).

Discussions about the death can be especially challenging or anxiety provoking for caregivers when the circumstances of the death were particularly tragic or violent, such as in cases of suicide, homicide, or fatal accidents (Furman, 1974). In these situations, it can be helpful to have an additional trusted and caring adult or grief therapist available to help facilitate the discussion and serve as a support to both the caregiver and the children. This can also involve coordinating grief facilitation efforts and the message that is conveyed with their spouse or partner, if applicable, to allow them to support one other and to keep the message clear, consistent, and developmentally appropriate. For example, it is important that both adults come to a shared understanding of how and what to talk about, as well as how to respond to the child's questions and concerns that are likely to arise. It may also be useful to enlist the help of a physician if children have specific questions about the physiological or biological aspects of the death. The more that caregivers and adults in children's lives are able to provide clear and honest answers, the more adaptive grief reactions that children tend to exhibit (Kaplow, Layne, & Pynoos, 2014a; Pynoos, 1992; Saltzman et al., 2017).

Principle 5: *Stay* Connected to the Deceased

One of the most important, yet challenging, tasks of childhood bereavement is to find healthy ways of remaining connected to the deceased person while "reinventing" the relationship, given that the person is no longer physically present (Rando, 1993). For children, this task often requires help and guidance from their caregiver by providing opportunities to feel more connected to the deceased. This can include sharing stories about the deceased person, looking at photos together, allowing children to hold onto a personal item of the deceased (e.g., necklace, T-shirt, etc.), or even reading condolence cards or sharing things heard at the memorial service that help to honor the deceased. Caregivers can also provide opportunities to memorialize the deceased person, such as planting a garden in his/her memory, lighting a candle, donating to a certain charity in his/her memory, etc. We have also found that caregivers' sharing of honestly held, comforting spiritual beliefs (e.g., Dad is your guardian angel and will protect you, or we will all be together again someday) can be particularly helpful in promoting children's adaptive grief reactions and reducing separation distress (Howell, Shapiro et al., 2015).

Assessment of Caregiver Grief Facilitation

Caregivers are often unaware of the behaviors that they are engaging in at home that may help to facilitate adaptive grieving in their children or, conversely, that may contribute to greater distress. Although a number of measures of parenting behaviors currently exist, none of these assessment tools directly examine grief-related parenting behaviors (e.g., how often the caregiver talks about the deceased person with children; how often the caregiver shares positive memories, etc.). We developed the Grief Facilitation Inventory (GFI; Kaplow & Layne, 2012; Alvis et al., 2020), a 36-item measure, as a clinical tool to help identify specific caregiving behaviors that are most helpful to children in the aftermath of a death and those that may actually hinder adaptive grieving in youth. Although we developed both a child-report and caregiver-report version of the GFI, our experience suggests that children tend to be better (more accurate) reporters of specific caregiving behaviors occurring in the home.

Items for the GFI were generated based on the extant childhood bereavement literature, clinical experience, and feedback from providers in a trauma- and grief-focused outpatient psychology clinic. Caregiving behaviors theorized to reduce post-bereavement distress include: verbal and nonverbal communication with the child about the deceased (e.g., "My caregiver talks with me about ___"), memorializing the deceased (e.g., "My caregiver does things with me to help me remember ___"), and activities aimed at establishing stability and family cohesion (e.g., "My caregiver does most things the same way we used to before my ___ died"). Behaviors theorized to exacerbate maladaptive grief reactions include avoidance (e.g., "My caregiver tries not to mention my ___'s name or his/her death") and emotional suppression (e.g., "My caregiver tries hard not to show how upset he/she is about my ___'s death") (Alvis et al., 2020). Session 4 describes ways in which therapists can utilize the GFI in session to help caregivers better understand the ways in which their behaviors at home may facilitate adaptive grieving in their children.

Conclusion

In summary, a number of the practice elements in MGT are designed to help caregivers with the essential elements of caregiver grief facilitation: (1) meeting their children where they are; (2) being present and open to continued discussions about the deceased; (3) recognizing and respecting individual differences in how family members grieve; (4) using developmentally appropriate language when talking about the deceased and/or the circumstances of the death, and (5) finding healthy ways of feeling connected to the deceased over time.

It is important for caregivers to have realistic expectations about grief facilitation, in that this is not meant to be one brilliant, sensitive, and perfect conversation. Instead, facilitating good grieving is an ongoing, lifelong process that will involve many different conversations and encounters. Caregivers should not assume that they only have one chance to "get it right." In fact, initial conversations with their child might just involve getting their mutual "toes wet" and feeling more comfortable with the idea of talking about the deceased. Caregivers should be patient with themselves, and even if a conversation does not go as well as they had hoped, they do not need to panic or come to the conclusion that they have somehow harmed their child. In fact, it can be helpful for caregivers to be transparent with their child about how it is often difficult to talk about these issues, that they are trying and will keep trying, and that they may need to help each other become more comfortable. Finally, caregivers should remember that grief facilitation does not necessarily have to involve "planned conversations" but can also involve more spontaneous shared moments in which they laugh together about a funny memory or engage in an activity together that they had previously done with their loved one. Creating new, happy memories, while also remembering and cherishing their memories of the deceased, is an essential step in the grief facilitation process.

References

Al-Sabah, R., Legerski, J. P., Layne, C. M. et al. (2015). Adolescent adjustment, caregiver-adolescent relationships, and outlook towards the future in the long-term aftermath of the Bosnian war. *Journal of Child and Adolescent Trauma, 8,* 45–60.

Alborn, M. (1997). *Tuesdays with Morrie.* Bantom Doubleday Dell.

Alvis, L., Zhang, N., Sandler, I., & Kaplow, J. (2022). Developmental manifestations of grief in children and adolescents: Caregivers as key grief facilitators. *Journal of Child and Adolescent Trauma.* https://doi.org/10.1007/s40653-021-00435-0.

Alvis, L. M., Dodd, C. G., Oosterhoff, B. et al. (2020). Caregiver behaviors and childhood maladaptive grief: Initial validation of the Grief Facilitation Inventory. *Death Studies, 46*(6), 1307–1315. http://doi.org/10.1080/07481187.2020.1841849.

American Psychiatric Association. (2022). *Diagnostic and statistical manual of mental disorders,* 5th ed. (DSM-5-TR). American Psychiatric Association.

Angold, A., Costello, E. J., Messer, S. C., & Pickles, A. (1995). Development of a short questionnaire for use in epidemiological studies of depression in children and adolescents. *International Journal of Methods in Psychiatric Research, 5*(4), 237–249.

Ayers, T. S., Wolchik, S. A., Sandler, I. N. et al. (2014). The Family Bereavement Program: Description of a theory-based prevention program for parentally-bereaved children and adolescents. *Omega, 68*(4), 293–314. https://doi.org/10.2190/om.68.4.a.

Balk, D. (1983). Effects of sibling death on teenagers. *Journal of School Health, 53,* 14–18.

Benson, M. A., Compas, B. E., Layne, C. M. et al. (2011). Measurement of post-war coping and stress responses: A study of Bosnian adolescents. *Journal of Applied Developmental Psychology, 32*(6), 323–335.

Bowlby, J. (1980). Attachment and loss. Vol. 3, *Loss: Sadness and depression.* Basic Books.

Burlingame, G. M., McClendon, D. T., & Alonso, J. (2011). Cohesion in group therapy. *Psychotherapy, 48*(1), 34–42. https://doi.org/10.1037/a0022063.

Burlingame, G. M., Wells, M. G., & Lambert, M. J. (1995). Youth outcome questionnaire (YOQ). OQ Measures, Salt Lake City, Utah.

Cain, A., & Fast, I. (1972). Children's disturbed reactions to parent suicide: Distortions of guilt, communication, and identification. In A. Cain (Ed.), *Survivors of suicide* (pp. 93–111). Charles C. Thomas.

Cerney, M. S., & Buskirk, J. R. (1991). Anger: The hidden part of grief. *Bulletin of the Menninger Clinic, 55,* 228–237.

Clark, D. C., Pynoos, R. S., & Goebel, A. E. (1996). Mechanisms and processes of adolescent bereavement. In R. J. Haggerty, I. R. Sherrod, N. Garmenzy, & M. Rutter (Eds.), *Stress, risk, and resilience in children and adolescents: Processes, mechanisms, and interventions* (pp. 100–146). Cambridge University Press.

Clow, S., Olafson, E., Ford, J. et al. (2022). Addressing grief reactions among incarcerated adolescents and young adults using Trauma and Grief Component Therapy. *Psychological Trauma: Theory, Research, Practice and Policy.* https://doi.org/10.1037/tra0001364.

Coffino, B. (2009). The role of childhood parent figure loss in the etiology of adult depression: Findings from a prospective longitudinal study. *Attachment & Human Development, 11,* 445–470.

Cox, J., Davies, D. R., Burlingame, G. M. et al. (2007). Effectiveness of a trauma/grief-focused group intervention: A qualitative study with war-exposed Bosnian adolescents. *International Journal of Group Psychotherapy, 57,* 319–345. http://dx.doi.org/10.1521/ijgp.2007.57.3.319.

Davies, D. R., Burlingame, G. M., & Layne, C. M. (2006). Integrating small group process principles into trauma-focused group psychotherapy: What should a group trauma therapist know? In L. A. Schein, H. I. Spitz, G. M. Burlingame, & P. R. Muskin (Eds.), *Group approaches for the psychological effects of terrorist disasters* (pp. 385–424). Haworth.

De Los Reyes, A., & Kazdin, A. E. (2005). Informant discrepancies in the assessment of childhood psychopathology: A critical review, theoretical framework, and recommendations for further study. *Psychological Bulletin, 131*(4), 483–509. https://doi.org/10.1037/0033-2909.131.4.483.

Dodd, C. G., Hill, R. M., Alvis, L. M. et al. (2020). Initial validation and measurement invariance of the Active Inhibition Scale among traumatized and grieving youth. *Journal of Traumatic Stress, 33*, 843–849. https://doi.org/10.1002/jts.22529.

Douglas, R., Alvis, L., Rooney, E., Busby, D., & Kaplow, J. (2021). Racial, ethnic, and neighborhood income disparities in childhood trauma and grief reactions: Exploring potential indirect effects through trauma and bereavement exposure. *Journal of Traumatic Stress, 34*, 929–942.

Eth, S., & Pynoos, R. (1985). Interaction of trauma and grief in childhood. In S. Eth & R. Pynoos (Eds.), *Post-traumatic stress disorder in children* (pp. 169–186). American Psychiatry Press.

Frankl, V. (2006). *Man's search for meaning: An introduction to logotherapy*. Beacon Press. First published 1946.

Furman, E. (1974). *A child's parent dies*. Yale University Press.

Geronazzo-Alman, L., Fan, B., Duarte, C. S. et al. (2019). The distinctiveness of grief, depression, and posttraumatic stress: Lessons from children after 9/11. *Journal of the American Academy of Child & Adolescent Psychiatry, 58*, 971–982.

Goenjian, A. K., Najarian, L. M., Pynoos, R. S. (1994). Posttraumatic stress disorder in elderly and younger adults after the 1988 earthquake in Armenia. *American Journal of Psychiatry, 151*(6), 895–901. https://doi.org/10.1176/ajp.151.6.895.

Goodman, R. (1997). Strengths and difficulties questionnaire: A research note. *Journal of Child Psychology and Psychiatry, 38*(5), 581–586.

Grassetti, S. N., Herres, J., Williamson, A. et al. (2014). Narrative focus moderates symptom change trajectories in group treatment for traumatized and bereaved adolescents. *Journal of Clinical Child & Adolescent Psychology, 44*, 933–941.

Grassetti, S., Williamson, A., Herres, J. et al. (2018). Evaluating referral, screening, and assessment procedures for middle school trauma/grief-focused treatment groups. *School Psychology Quarterly, 33*, 10–20.

Haine, R. A., Ayers, T. S., Sandler, I. N., & Wolchik, S. A. (2008). Evidence-based practices for parentally bereaved children and their families. *Professional Psychology: Research and Practice, 39*(2), 113–121. https://doi.org/10.1037/0735-7028.39.2.113.

Herres, J., Williamson, A. A., Kobak, R. et al. (2017). Internalizing and externalizing symptoms moderate treatment response to school-based trauma and grief component therapy for adolescents. *School Mental Health, 9*(2), 184–193.

Hill, R., Oosterhoff, B., Layne, C. M. et al. (2019). Multidimensional grief therapy: Pilot open trial of a novel intervention for bereaved children and adolescents. *Journal of Child and Family Studies, 28*, 3062–3074. https://doi.org/10.1007/s10826-019-01481-x.

Hoagwood, K. E., Layne, C. M., & CATS (Child and Adolescent Trauma Treatment and Services) Consortium. (2007). Implementing CBT for children and adolescents after September 11th: Lessons from the Child and Adolescent Trauma Treatments and Services (CATS) Project. *Journal of Clinical Child and Adolescent Psychology, 36*, 581–592.

Hoagwood, K. E., Layne, C. M., & CATS (Child and Adolescent Trauma Treatment and Services) Consortium. (2010). Implementation of CBT for children and adolescents affected by the World Trade Center disaster: Outcomes in reducing trauma symptoms. *Journal of Traumatic Stress, 23*, 699–707.

Horowitz, M. J. (1990). A model of mourning: Change in schemas of self and other. *Journal of the American Psychoanalytic Association, 38*, 297–324.

Horsley, H., & Patterson, T. (2006). The effects of a parent guidance intervention on communication among adolescents who have experienced the sudden death of a sibling. *American Journal of Family Therapy, 34*(2), 119–137. https://doi.org/10.1080/01926180500301519.

Houston, R. (2006). Associations among post-war adversities, parent well-being, parent-adolescent relationships, and adolescent outcomes in Bosnian youth and their caregivers. PhD diss., Brigham Young University.

Howell, K. H., Barrett-Becker, E. P., Burnside, A. N. et al. (2016). Children facing parental cancer versus parental death: The buffering effects of positive parenting and emotional expression. *Journal of Child and Family Studies, 25*(1), 152–164.

Howell, K. H., Kaplow, J. B., Layne, C. M. et al. (2015). Predicting adolescent posttraumatic stress in the aftermath of war: Differential effects of coping strategies across trauma reminder, loss reminder, and family conflict domains. *Anxiety, Stress, & Coping, 28*, 88–104.

Howell, K. H., Shapiro, D. N., Layne, C. M., & Kaplow, J. B. (2015). Individual and psychosocial mechanisms of adaptive functioning in parentally bereaved children. *Death Studies, 39*, 296–306.

Kaplow, J. B., Gipson, P., Horwitz, A., Burch, B., & King, C. (2014). Emotional suppression mediates the relation between adverse life events and adolescent suicide: Implications for prevention. *Prevention Science, 15*, 177–185.

Kaplow, J. B., Howell, K. H., & Layne, C. M. (2014). Do circumstances of the death matter? Identifying socioenvironmental risks for grief-related psychopathology in bereaved youth. *Journal of Traumatic Stress, 27*, 42–49.

Kaplow, J. B., Layne, C. M., Oosterhoff, B. et al. (2018). Validation of the persistent complex bereavement disorder (PCBD) checklist: A developmentally informed assessment tool for bereaved youth. *Journal of Traumatic Stress, 31*, 244–254.

Kaplow, J. B., & Layne, C. M. (2012). Grief Facilitation Inventory (GFI). University of Michigan.

Kaplow, J. B., & Layne, C. M. (2014). Sudden loss and psychiatric disorders across the life course: Toward a developmental lifespan theory of bereavement-related risk and resilience. *American Journal of Psychiatry, 171*(8), 807–810.

Kaplow, J. B., Layne, C. M., & Pynoos, R. (2014a). Parental grief facilitation: How parents can help their bereaved children during the holidays. *Traumatic Stress Points*. https://istss.org/public-resources/trauma-blog/2014-december/parental-grief-facilitation-how-parents-can-help-t.

Kaplow, J. B., Layne, C. M., & Pynoos, R. (2014b). Persistent complex bereavement disorder as a call to action: Using a proposed DSM-5 diagnosis to advance the field of childhood grief. *Traumatic Stress Points*. https://istss.org/public-resources/trauma-blog/2014-january/persistent-complex-bereavement-disorder-as-a-call.

Kaplow, J. B., Layne, C. M., & Pynoos, R. S. (2019). Treatment of Persistent Complex Bereavement Disorder in children and adolescents. In M. Prinstein, E. Youngstrom, E. Mash, & R. Barkley (Eds.), *Treatment of disorders in childhood and adolescence*, 4th ed. (pp. 560–590). Guilford Publications, Inc.

Kaplow, J. B., & Pincus, D. (2007). *Samantha Jane's missing smile: A story about coping with the loss of a parent*. Magination Press.

Kaplow, J. B., Layne, C. M., Pynoos, R. S., Cohen, J. A., & Lieberman, A. (2012). DSM-V diagnostic criteria for bereavement-related disorders in children and adolescents: Developmental considerations. *Psychiatry: Interpersonal & Biological Processes, 75*(3), 243–266.

Kaplow, J. B., Layne, C. M., Saltzman, W. R., Cozza, S. J., & Pynoos, R. S. (2013). Using multidimensional grief theory to explore effects of deployment, reintegration, and death on military youth and families. *Clinical Child and Family Psychology Review, 16*, 322–340.

Kaplow, J. B., Shapiro, D. N., Wardecker, B. M. et al. (2013). Psychological and environmental correlates of HPA axis functioning in parentally bereaved children: Preliminary findings. *Journal of Traumatic Stress, 26*(2), 233–240. https://doi.org/10.1002/jts.21788.

Kaplow, J. B., Rolon-Arroyo, B., Layne, C. M. et al. (2020). Validation of the UCLA PTSD Reaction Index for DSM-5 (RI-5): A developmentally-informed assessment tool for trauma-exposed youth. *Journal of the American Academy of Child and Adolescent Psychiatry, 59*(1), 186–194.

Kaplow, J. B., Wamser-Nanney, R., Layne, C. M. et al. (2020). Identifying bereavement-related markers of mental and behavioral health problems among clinic-referred adolescents. *Psychiatric Research and Clinical Practice, 3*(2), 88–96. https://doi.org/10.1176/appi.prcp.20190021.

Kaplow, J. B., Wardecker, B., Layne, C. et al. (2018). Out of the mouths of babes: Links between linguistic structure of loss narratives and psychosocial functioning in parentally bereaved children. *Journal of Traumatic Stress, 31*(3), 342–351.

Kaplow, J. B., Saxe, G., Putnam, F., Pynoos, R., & Lieberman, A. (2006). The long-term consequences of early childhood trauma: A case study and discussion. *Psychiatry, 69*, 362–375.

Kendall, P. C., & Frank, H. E. (2018). Implementing evidence-based treatment protocols: Flexibility within fidelity. *Clinical Psychology: Science and Practice, 25*(4), e12271. https://doi.org/10.1111/cpsp.12271.

King, C. A., Ewell-Foster, C., & Rogalski, K. M. (2013). *Teen suicide risk: A practitioner guide to screening, assessment, and management*. Guilford Press.

Kwok, O., Haine, R. A., Sandler, I. N. et al. (2005). Positive parenting as a mediator of the relations between parental psychological distress and mental health problems of parentally bereaved children. *Journal of Clinical Child & Adolescent Psychology, 34*(2), 260–271. https://doi.org/10.1207/s15374424jccp3402_5.

Layne, C. M. 1996. Effects of Community Violence on Minority Adolescents. Unpublished doctoral dissertation, University of California, Los Angeles.

Layne, C. M. (2018). *Fostering "good grief" in the aftermath of traumatic death*. Keynote address at the Restorative Support for Families after Traumatic Death: Building a Bereavement-Informed Community Conference. Baylor College of Medicine, Houston, TX, September 21. https://psychology.nova.edu/common-pdf/chris_layne_trauma/layne,-c.-m.-2018-fostering-adaptive-grieving-following-traumatic-death-keynote.pdf.

Layne, C.M. 2020. *Developmental recommendations and implications for a prolonged grief disorder (PGD) in DSM-5-TR: Become an informed consumer and advocate* [Webinar].[Online]. National Center for Child Traumatic Stress. [March 25, 2020]. Available from: https://learn.nctsn.org/enrol/index.php?id=533

Layne, C. M. (2021a). Preparing for the COVID-19 second wave: An overview of the new prolonged grief disorder through the lenses of multidimensional grief theory [Webinar]. Hathaway-Sycamores Research and Training Institute. January 29. https://psychology.nova.edu/faculty/profile/layne-christopher.html.

Layne, C. M. (2021b). Clinical perspectives on bereavement & grief: Past, present, and future [Webinar]. Keynote address at the Eating Recovery and Pathlight Foundation Annual Conference. August 25. https://psychology.nova.edu/faculty/profile/layne-christopher.html.

Layne, C. M., Beck, C. J., Rimmasch, H. et al. (2009). Promoting "resilient" posttraumatic adjustment in childhood and beyond: "Unpacking" life events, adjustment trajectories, resources, and interventions. In D. Brom, R. Pat-Horenczyk, & J. Ford (Eds.), *Treating traumatized children: Risk, resilience, and recovery* (pp. 13–47). Routledge.

Layne, C. M., & Hobfoll, S. E. (2020). Understanding posttraumatic adjustment trajectories in school-age youth: Supporting stress resistance, resilient recovery, and growth. In E. Rossen (Ed.), *Supporting and educating traumatized students: A guide for school-based professionals*, 2nd ed. (pp. 75–97). Oxford University Press.

Layne, C. M., & Kaplow, J. B. (2020). Assessing bereavement and grief disorders. In E. A. Youngstrom, M. J. Prinstein,

References

E. J. Mash, & R. A. Barkley (Eds.), *Assessment of disorders in childhood and adolescence*, 5th ed. (pp. 471–508). Guilford Press.

Layne, C. M., Kaplow, J. B., Netland, M., Steinberg, A., & Pynoos, R. (2014). The differential validity matrix: An innovative tool for "contextualized" test construction and theory building. In C. M. Layne (Chair), Improving methods for unpacking the ecologies of trauma and loss: Implications for two new DSM-5 disorders [Symposium]. The Annual Meeting of the International Society for Traumatic Stress Studies, Miami, FL.

Layne, C. M., Kaplow, J. B., Oosterhoff, B., Hill, R., & Pynoos, R. S. (2017). The interplay between posttraumatic stress and grief reactions in traumatically bereaved adolescents: When trauma, bereavement, and adolescence converge. *Adolescent Psychiatry, 7*, 220–239.

Layne, C. M., Kaplow, J. B., Oosterhoff, B., & Hill, R. (2019). Developmental perspectives on DSM-5-TR prolonged grief disorder criteria: Proposals for improvement. Presentation at the Workshop on Developing Criteria for a Disorder of Pathological Grieving for DSM-5-TR. Hosted by the American Psychiatric Association, New York City. www.researchgate.net/profile/Christopher-Layne-4.

Layne, C. M., Kaplow, J. B., & Pynoos, R. S. (2012). Using developmentally informed theory and evidence-based assessment to guide intervention with bereaved youth and families. In C. M. Layne (Chair), Integrating developmentally-informed theory, evidence-based assessment, and evidence-based treatment of childhood maladaptive grief [Symposium]. Annual Meeting of the International Society for Traumatic Stress Studies, Los Angeles, CA.

Layne, C. M., Kaplow, J. B., & Pynoos, R. S. (2014). Persistent Complex Bereavement Disorder (PCBD) Checklist – Youth version 1.0: Test and administration manual. The University of California, Los Angeles, Office of Intellectual Property (and later, Behavioral Health Innovations).

Layne, C. M., Kaplow, J. B., & Pynoos, R. S. (2022a). Prolonged Grief Disorder (PGD) Checklist for Bereaved Children and Adolescents DSM-5-TR Version (PGD-5TR-CA)©. Behavioral Health Innovations. www.reactionindex.com/.

Layne, C. M., Kaplow, J. B., & Pynoos, R. S. (2022b). Prolonged Grief Disorder (PGD) Checklist for Bereaved Children and Adolescents DSM-5-TR Version (PGD-5TR-CA)©. Supplementary Scoring Guide. Behavioral Health Innovations. www.reactionindex.com/.

Layne, C. M.; Kaplow, J. B.; & Pynoos, R. S. (2022c). Supplementary Scoring & Interpretation Guide for the Prolonged Grief Disorder (PGD) Checklist. Behavioral Health Innovations. (www.reactionindex.com/).

Layne, C. M., Kaplow, J. B., & Youngstrom, E. A. (2017). Applying evidence-based assessment to childhood trauma and bereavement: Concepts, principles, and practices. In M. A. Landholt, M. Cloitre, & U. Schnyder (Eds.), *Evidence-based treatments for trauma-related disorders in children and adolescents* (pp. 67–96). Springer International Publishing AG.

Layne, C. M., Oosterhoff, B., Pynoos, R. S., & Kaplow, J. B. (2020). *Developmental analysis of draft DSM-5-TR criteria for prolonged grief disorder: Report from the Child and Adolescent Bereavement Subgroup*. American Psychiatric Association. www.researchgate.net/profile/Christopher-Layne-4.

Layne, C. M., Olsen, J. A., Baker, A. et al. (2010). Unpacking trauma exposure risk factors and differential pathways of influence: Predicting post-war mental distress in Bosnian adolescents. *Child Development, 81*, 1053–1076.

Layne, C. M., Pynoos, R. S., & Cardenas, J. (2001). Wounded adolescence: School-based group psychotherapy for adolescents who have sustained or witnessed violent interpersonal injury. In M. Shafii & S. Shafii (Eds.), *School violence: Contributing factors, management, and prevention* (pp. 163–186). American Psychiatric Press.

Layne, C. M., Pynoos, R. S., Saltzman, W. R. et al. (2001). Trauma/grief-focused group psychotherapy: School-based post-war intervention with traumatized Bosnian adolescents. *Group Dynamics: Theory, Research, and Practice, 5*, 277–290.

Layne, C. M., Ruzek, J. I., & Dixon, K. (2021). From resilience and restoration to resistance and resource caravans: A developmental framework for advancing the disaster field. *Psychiatry, 84*(4), 393–409.

Layne, C. M., Saltzman, W. R., Poppleton, L. (2008). Effectiveness of a school-based group psychotherapy program for war-exposed adolescents: A randomized controlled trial. *Journal of the American Academy of Child and Adolescent Psychiatry, 47*, 1048–1062.

Layne, C. M., Saltzman, W. R., Pynoos, R. S., & Steinberg, A. M. (1997). *Trauma and grief therapy for adolescents*. Unpublished treatment manual. UNICEF Bosnia & Hercegovina.

Layne, C. M., Steinberg, J. R., Steinberg, A. M. (2014). Causal reasoning skills training for mental health practitioners: Promoting sound clinical judgement in evidence-based practice. *Training and Education in Professional Psychology, 8*(4), 292–302.

Layne, C. M., Saltzman, W. R., Pynoos, R. S., & Steinberg, A. M. (2002). *Trauma and grief component therapy for adolescents*. Unpublished treatment manual. New York State Office of Mental Health.

Layne, C. M., Warren, J. S., Hilton, S. (2009). Measuring adolescent perceived support amidst war and disaster: The Multi-Sector Social Support Inventory. In B. K. Barber (Eds.), *Adolescents and war: How youth deal with political violence* (pp. 145–176). Oxford University Press.

Layne, C. M., Warren, J. S., Saltzman, W. R. et al. (2006). Contextual influences on post-traumatic adjustment: Retraumatization and the roles of distressing reminders, secondary adversities, and revictimization. In L. A. Schein, H. I. Spitz, G. M. Burlingame, & P. R. Muskin (Eds.), *Group approaches for the psychological effects of terrorist disasters* (pp. 235–286). Haworth.

Layne, C. M., Warren, J., Watson, P., & Shalev, A. (2007). Risk, vulnerability, resistance, and resilience: Towards an integrative model of posttraumatic adaptation. In M. J. Friedman, T. M. Kean, & P. A. Resick (Eds.), *PTSD: Science & practice – A comprehensive handbook* (pp. 497–520). Guilford.

Layne, C. M., Strand, V., Popescu, M. et al. (2014). Using the Core Curriculum on Childhood Trauma to strengthen clinical knowledge in evidence. *Journal of Clinical Child & Adolescent Psychology, 43*(2), 286–300.

Lieberman, A. F., Compton, N. C., Van Horn, P., & Ippen, C. G. (2003). *Losing a parent to death in the early years: Guidelines for the treatment of traumatic bereavement in infancy and early childhood.* ZERO TO THREE/National Center for Infants, Toddlers and Families.

Lindemann, E. (1944). Symptomatology and management of acute grief. *American Journal of Psychiatry, 101*(2), 141–148.

Mendelsohn, M., Herman, J. L., Schatzow, E. et al. (2011). *The trauma recovery group: A guide for practitioners.* Guilford Press.

Nader, K. O. (1997). Childhood traumatic loss: The interaction of trauma and grief. In C. R. Figley, B. E. Bride, & N. Mazza (Eds.), *Death and trauma: The traumatology of grieving* (pp. 17–41). Taylor & Francis.

Nader, K. O., & Layne, C. M. (2009). Maladaptive grieving in children and adolescents: Discovering developmentally-linked differences in the manifestation of grief. *Traumatic Stress Points, 23*(5), 12–16.

Nader, K. O., Pynoos, R., Fairbanks, L., Al-Ajeel, M., & Al-Asfour, A. (1993). A preliminary study of PTSD and grief among the children of Kuwait following the Gulf crisis. *British Journal of Clinical Psychology, 32*(4), 407–416. https://doi.org/10.1111/j.2044-8260.1993.tb01075.x.

Nader, K., Pynoos, R., Fairbanks, L., & Frederick, C. (1990). Children's PTSD reactions one year after a sniper attack at their school. *American Journal of Psychiatry, 147*, 1526–1530. https://dx.doi.org/10.1176/ajp.147.11.1526.

Neimeyer, R. A., & Currier, J. M. (2009). Grief therapy: Evidence of efficacy and emerging directions. *Current Directions in Psychological Science, 18*, 352–356.

Olafson, E., Boat, B. W., Putnam, K. T. et al. (2018). Implementing trauma and grief component therapy for adolescents and think trauma for traumatized youth in secure juvenile justices settings. *Journal of Interpersonal Violence, 33*, 2537–2557.

Pausch, R., & Zaslow, J. (2008). *The last lecture.* Hyperion.

Pearlman, L. A., Wortman, C. B., Feuer, C. A., Farber, C. H., & Rando, T. A. (2014). *Treating traumatic bereavement: A practitioner's guide.* Guilford.

Pynoos, R. S. (1992). Grief and trauma in children and adolescents. *Bereavement Care, 11*, 2–10.

Pynoos, R. S., Nader, K., Frederick, C., Gonda, L., & Stuber, M. (1987). Grief reactions in school age children following a sniper attack at school. *Israel Journal of Psychiatry and Related Sciences, 24*, 53–63.

Pynoos, R. S., Sorenson, S. B., & Steinberg, A. M. (1993). Interpersonal violence and traumatic stress reactions. In S. Breznitz & L. Goldberg (Eds.), *Handbook of stress: Theoretical and clinical aspects*, 2nd ed. (pp. 573–586). Maxwell Macmillan.

Pynoos, R. S., & Steinberg, A. M. (2002). *UCLA trauma history profile.* Unpublished manuscript. National Child Traumatic Stress Network, Los Angeles, CA.

Pynoos, R. S., Steinberg, A. M., & Wraith, R. (1995). A developmental model of childhood traumatic stress. In D. Cicchetti & D. J. Cohen (Eds.), Developmental Psychopathology. Vol. 3, *Risk, Disorder and Adaptation* (pp. 72–95). Wiley.

Rando, T. A. (1988). *How to go on living when someone you love dies.* Lexington Books.

Rando, T. A. (1993). *Treatment of complicated mourning.* University of Michigan.

Rolon-Arroyo, B., Kaplow, J. B., Oosterhoff, B., Layne, C. M., Steinberg, A., & Pynoos, R. (2020). The UCLA PTSD Reaction Index for DSM-5 Brief Form: A screening tool for trauma-exposed youth. *Journal of the American Academy of Child and Adolescent Psychiatry, 59*(3), 434–443.

Rooney, E. E., Hill, R. M., Oosterhoff, B., & Kaplow, J. B. (2019). Violent victimization and perpetration as distinct risk factors for adolescent suicide attempts. *Children's Health Care, 48*(4), 410–427.

Rosenfeld, E. K. (2018). The fire that changed the way we think about grief. November 29. *Harvard Crimson.*

Rynearson, E. K. (2001). *Retelling violent death.* Brunner-Routledge.

Saler, L., & Skolnick, N. (1992). Childhood parental death and depression in adulthood: Roles of surviving parent and family environment. *American Journal of Orthopsychiatry, 62*(4), 504–516. https://doi.org/10.1037/h0079372.

Saltzman, W. R., Layne, C. M., Steinberg, A. M., Arslanagic, B., & Pynoos, R. S. (2003). Developing a culturally-ecologically sound intervention program for youth exposed to war and terrorism. *Child and Adolescent Psychiatric Clinics of North America, 12*, 319–342.

Saltzman, W. R., Layne, C. M., Pynoos, R. S. et al. (2017). *Trauma and grief component therapy for adolescents: A modular approach to treating traumatized and bereaved youth.* Cambridge University Press.

Saltzman, W. R., Pynoos, R. S., Layne, C. M., Steinberg, A., & Aisenberg, E. (2001). Trauma/grief-focused intervention for adolescents exposed to community violence: Results of a school-based screening and group treatment protocol. *Group Dynamics: Theory, Research, and Practice, 5*, 291–303.

Saltzman, W. R., Pynoos, R. S., Lester, P., Layne, C. M., & Beardslee, W. R. (2013). Enhancing family resilience through family narrative co-construction. *Clinical Child and Family Psychology Review, 16*(3), 294–310. https://doi.org/10.1007/s10567-013-0142-2.

Sandler, I. N., Ayers, T. S., Wolchik, S. A. et al. (2003). The Family Bereavement Program: Efficacy evaluation of a theory-based prevention program for parentally

References

bereaved children and adolescents. *Journal of Consulting and Clinical Psychology, 71*(3), 587–600. https://doi.org/10.1037/0022-006X.71.3.587.

Sandler, I. N., Wolchik, S. A., Ayers, T. S., Tein, J., & Luecken, L. (2013). Family bereavement program (FBP) approach to promoting resilience following the death of a parent. *Family Science, 4*(1), 87–94. https://doi.org/10.1080/19424620.2013.821763.

Shapiro, D., Howell, K., & Kaplow, J. (2014). Associations among mother-child communication quality, childhood maladaptive grief, and depressive symptoms. *Death Studies, 35*, 172–178.

Silverman, P. R., Nickman, S., & Worden, J. W. (1992). Detachment revisited: The child's reconstruction of a dead parent. *American Journal of Orthopsychiatry, 62*, 494–503.

Stroebe, M., Schut, H., & Finkenauer, C. (2013). Parents coping with the death of their child: From individual to interpersonal to interactive perspectives. *Family Science, 4*(1), 28–36. https://doi.org/10.1080/19424620.2013.819229.

Walsh, H. C. (2008). Caring for bereaved people 1: Models of bereavement. *Nursing Times, 103*(51), 26–27.

Wardecker, B. M., Kaplow, J. B., Layne, C. M., & Edelstein, R. S. (2017). Caregivers' positive emotional expression and children's psychological functioning after parental loss. *Journal of Child and Family Studies, 26*, 3490–3501.

Warren, J. S., Brown, C. R., Layne, C. M., & Nelson, P. L. (2011). Parenting self-efficacy as a predictor of child psychotherapy outcomes in usual care: A multi-dimensional approach. *Psychotherapy Research, 21*, 112–123.

West, S. G., Sandler, I., Pillow, D. R., Baca, L., & Gersten, J. C. (1991). The use of structural equation modeling in generative research: Toward the design of a preventive intervention for bereaved children. *American Journal of Community Psychology, 19*(4), 459–480. https://doi.org/10.1007/bf00937987.

Wolfelt, A. (1996). *Healing the bereaved child*. Routledge.

Wolfenstein, M. (1969). Loss, rage, and repetition. *Psychoanalytic Study of the Child, 24*, 432–460.

Worden, J. W., & Silverman, P. R. (1996). Parental death and the adjustment of school-age children. *Omega: Journal of Death and Dying, 33*, 91–102.

World Health Organization. (2019). *International statistical classification of diseases and related health problems*, 11th ed. (ICD-11). https://icd.who.int/.

MGT Session

Grief Psychoeducation
What Is Grief?

How to Begin

MGT is a manualized treatment that is designed to be flexible with regard to the specific practice exercises used within each session. We like to use the phrase "flexibility within fidelity," meaning that you are not required to incorporate every practice element listed in each session into each meeting with the child. Rather, you can pick and choose which practice elements will resonate the most with your particular client and focus on those (e.g., you may decide that the caregiver is not ready to provide support and to therefore eliminate the caregiver/child grief facilitation exercises). Alternatively, you may decide to use all the practice elements in each session. We have tried to be as accurate as possible in estimating that most sessions should typically take only one to two meetings to complete, but some may require two to three separate meetings if you plan to incorporate all practice elements. We encourage you to use your own clinical judgment when deciding which practice elements to incorporate.

Note: Throughout the text, any words in *italics* are to be spoken out loud to the client.

Session Objectives

Increase the client's ability:

1. To identify grief reactions as healthy and universal; and understand there is no right or wrong way to grieve
2. To understand their own personal grief reactions
3. To distinguish between grief-related myths and facts
4. To develop their vocabulary for labeling and expressing grief reactions based upon multidimensional grief theory
5. To communicate effectively with caregiver(s) about their grief

Section Number	Session Overview
1	Check In
2	Grief Psychoeducation: What Is Grief?
3	Activity 1: The True/False Grief Game
4	Grief Psychoeducation: Different Ways of Grieving
5	Activity 2: Identifying Grief Reactions
6	Rating My Grief Reactions
7	Grief Goals
8	Check Out

Session Materials

- Grief statement cards and true/false cards (Handout 1.1)
- Grief character cartoons and grief reaction cards (Handout 1.2)
- Rating My Grief Reactions (Handout 1.3)
- Grief Goals (Handout 1.4)

1 Check In

- *Did anything happen that you feel good about since we saw each other at our feedback meeting?*
- *Is anything going on that may make it hard for you to pay attention in session today?*

2 Grief Psychoeducation: What Is Grief?

Cover the general points below in your own words.

Almost everyone will have someone close to them die at some point in their lives.

For many people, the death of someone they really love is one of the hardest things they ever have to go through. Even years after it happened, there are still times when it feels as if their family member or friend died just yesterday, and they miss them with all their heart.

*Let's start by talking about different words people use to describe these experiences. The first word is bereavement – what does the word bereavement mean to you? (Allow the client to tell you what they think this word means.) This is a word that is often used to describe the experience of having someone we care about die. People will often use two other words to describe how we react to bereavement including their private (personal) and public (shared) reactions to bereavement – these are **grief** and **mourning**.*

What does the word grief mean to you? (Allow the client to tell you what they think this word means). The word grief is about the private part of how people react to the death. Grief reactions are often things we keep to ourselves. They include our thoughts, feelings, dreams, and even physical feelings that we have inside our own bodies, like feeling our hearts ache, feeling a sinking feeling in our stomachs, or feeling empty inside. Grief can also include personal prayers for the person who died. It can also include comforting memories and warm feelings, like remembering good times you shared or how much you like doing things that would make them proud.

What does the word "mourning" mean to you? (Allow the client to tell you what they think this word means). The word mourning is about the more public part of how people react to a death (the part we share with other people). Examples of mourning include attending wakes, funerals and memorial services, candle-lighting ceremonies with others, creating memorials or shrines, wearing special clothes (like a T-shirt with their name or picture on it, or wearing all black), and posting about them on social media to let others know how important the person who died is to us.

Both the personal (grief) and public (mourning) parts can help you deal with the death of a loved one. You can use our time together as a safe place, so that as you start to feel more comfortable, you may want to share things that you've been keeping to yourself as part of your own personal grief reactions. Whether you choose to share, and when you choose to share it, is up to you. But sharing can feel good, it can help you get the support you need and help you to make sense of the feelings you're having.

3 Activity 1 The True/False Grief Game

Purpose:

- To distinguish between grief-related myths and facts

Materials: Grief statement cards and true/false cards (Handout 1.1). Alternatively, the statements can be read aloud and discussed.

Directions: Using your professional judgment, select statements (numbered below) you consider most relevant to your client and the caregiver. You do not have to use them all – choose only as many statements as you can cover in the time available.

Read each statement aloud and have the caregiver and child say and/or hold up their true/false cards simultaneously.

As each statement is read and responded to, encourage the caregiver and child to discuss their answers together and reinforce correct answers. When the client selects an incorrect answer, normalize it (e.g., "A lot of people think that, but in fact … "). Ask them to share their thoughts on why it's true or false. Then, fill in the remaining facts as appropriate.

You can tell the client that because bereavement and grief are things that we don't often talk about, there is a lot of misinformation about grief, and it's often hard to tell the difference between what's true and what's made up.

I'd like to read you some statements about grief and then ask you and your mom/dad/caregiver to tell me whether you think the statement is true or false by showing me the answer on your card (provide client and caregiver with the true and false cards).

Note: This activity is designed to be conducted with the client and caregiver together, if at all possible. However, if the caregiver is not able to support the client in this way (e.g., still feeling stuck in their own grief, unable to handle open discussions about the death) or the client is apprehensive or resistant to including their caregiver in the session (e.g., intense anger or mistrust towards the caregiver(s) or fear of upsetting them), this exercise can be done with just the client and therapist. Alternatively, the therapist can play this game with the client alone at first and then jointly with the caregiver, during which the child "quizzes" the caregiver by asking the caregiver to respond to the true/false statements. This can often help to lighten the mood and empower the client by ensuring that they already know the correct answers.

Helpful Hint: This activity should move along quickly. The lengthy, italicized passages after each question are there to help you prepare beforehand, so you can explain the concepts in your own words. You do not need to read every statement out loud. You can simply pick the ones you think are most relevant to your client and even add statements that are not included here.

1. **"It is normal to have many different types of grief-related feelings (for example, sad, angry, worried) at the same time."**

Answer: True

(Only as needed): *Most types of grief reactions are normal. Those strong feelings are signs that we are missing the person who has died or having trouble picturing life without them. These feelings can be healthy over time because they help us to adjust and create a new sense of normal. Even though some grief-related feelings can be painful and upsetting, they can also be comforting, reassuring, and they can even help us to feel relief over time, such as when we have a good cry or have a happy memory of a loved one. In our work together, we are not going to try to make your grief* go away, but instead we will try to make the more painful feelings easier to cope with. We will also try to increase the types of grief reactions that are most helpful to you, and decrease those that are less helpful to you.

2. **"After someone they care about dies, ALL kids get over their painful feelings after about 6–12 months."**

Answer: False

(Only as needed): *People grieve in different ways. There is no normal time limit when grief is supposed to be over. Many grieving kids talk about their very strong feelings of sadness or anger decreasing more and more over time, so that as time passes, the painful feelings are replaced by more helpful or positive feelings. But grief itself never goes away completely. We may also miss the person in different ways as we get older and our lives change. For example, we may miss different things about them when we face important life decisions or important events (like graduation, marriage, etc.). So there is no time limit for grieving. People grieve for as long as they continue to miss the person, and that's ok.*

3. **"It is best not to talk about the person who died – that way, it will be easier to move on with our life."**

Answer: False

(Only as needed): *Actually, talking about the person who died and sharing our feelings about the person or their death is one of the best ways to help each other through painful feelings of grief. Sometimes people who are having the hardest time after a death are working really hard to not think or talk about the death. Trying to hide our strong feelings, or staying away from others who might want to talk about it, can make it harder to grieve in helpful ways. Being alone with our strong feelings can also make us feel more lonely, sad, angry, or confused. On the other hand, it can feel good to share when you are in a safe place with someone who is ready to listen – like here.*

4. **"Grief reactions always stay the same over time."**

Answer: False

(Only as needed): *Grief reactions can change from day to day, year to year, or even moment to moment. Some kids may not have very strong grief reactions right after the death, but may start to have them as more time passes. For other kids, their grief reactions may be strongest right after the death, but then become less strong over time. Grief is different for everyone and may go up and down over time, often when we are faced with loss reminders. We will be talking more about loss reminders in a later session, but running into a loss reminder – like hearing the person's name, being someplace they used to be, doing something they used to do, their birthday, or during holidays or graduations – can bring up strong grief reactions, like really missing them, feeling very sad, or feeling very angry.*

5. **"Healthy grieving means that we forget or stop thinking about our loved one who died."**

Answer: False

(Only as needed): *Healthy and helpful grieving will never mean that you forget about the person who died. Instead, our goal is to change our relationship with them. To change our relationship with them, we need to move them from this physical world where they used to be to a different world – a world that lives in our memories, our minds, or our hearts. For some of us, depending on our beliefs, this can also be a spiritual world where we feel like they are watching over us in a comforting way or protecting us. Moving them to this new place helps to make room for the important work of living, as we still have lots to do, like learning, growing, making new friends, and doing good things with our lives. Making room for these new things feels a bit like stretching a muscle – the more we practice stretching, the stronger that muscle becomes and the easier it gets.*

6. **"Everyone in the same family or group of close friends grieves in the same way."**

Answer: False

(Only as needed): *Different people in the same family or group of close friends can have very different reactions to the death, including how strong their feelings are or when they have these strong feelings the most. This can be because of how close they were to the actual death itself. For example, some kids may have seen the person die or were closer to the things that happened at the time of the death. People also have very different personalities and different ways of coping that can affect how they grieve. These differences between family members or friends can cause stress and can sometimes make it harder to get along with each other. Family members and close friends often need to talk with each other more after a death so they can understand each other's grief reactions and learn how to better support each other.*

7. **"After someone we feel close to dies, we can still be happy and enjoy our lives."**

Answer: True

(Only as needed): *Although it may feel like you and/or your life are very different now because of the death, it is still possible to live a happy life. The death of a loved can change our lives because some things are truly different after a death. But the changes it brings aren't always bad ones. Sometimes the death of a loved one can teach us important life lessons, like what things really matter in life. Sometimes kids learn something good about the person who died that they admire and want to carry with them, like the person's sense of humor or their kindness. Learning important life lessons or holding onto good things about the person who died can make our lives better by helping us to feel happy or grateful for the time that we had with that person.*

Grief Psychoeducation

8. **"If we do not have a strong reaction to a death, it means we did not care about the person who died."**

Answer: False

(Only as needed): *Reactions to a death depend on many things. Sometimes, people who cared a lot about the person who died don't show strong reactions. This can be due to their personality, or just that it may be too painful right now to even think about the person. Reactions can also appear later when we are faced with certain loss reminders.*

9. **"Sometimes we may feel relieved when a person dies."**

Answer: True

(Only as needed): *People who had a hard or difficult relationship with the person who died, or had upsetting memories of the person who died, can sometimes feel relief or even some feelings of happiness after they die. People who feel relieved about the death may also feel ashamed or guilty about these feelings and try to hide them. Kids can also feel relief after someone dies if the person had been suffering from an illness like cancer for a long time. They might have thoughts like "I'm glad he/she doesn't have to suffer anymore," or "I'm glad it's finally over, so I don't have to keep worrying and wondering about when it's going to happen." These thoughts are completely normal, and although they may be hard to talk about, many, many people have them after a death.*

At the end of the game, thank the caregiver for participating in the true/false game and have the client and caregiver briefly discuss what it was like to play the game together.

---

4 Grief Psychoeducation: Different Ways of Grieving

5 Activity 2 Identifying Grief Reactions

Purpose:
- To identify which grief reactions are helpful versus harmful
- To gain more control over grief-related thoughts by recognizing them as they are happening

Materials: Grief character cartoons and grief reaction cards (Handout 1.2).

Directions: Introduce the idea that people have very different reactions to a death and that these reactions change over time.

Now that we've learned a little more about grief, let's look at some specific thoughts, feelings, and behaviors some people may have after someone dies. I'm going to be showing you some cartoons and I'd like for you to tell me which cartoon character may have said each of these things. It's important to know that we can have both gloomy and good grief reactions going on at the same time.

Introduce each of the grief characters and describe some of their associated cognitions. It is easiest for youth to grasp the concepts of maladaptive/adaptive grief reactions if you pair a "gloomy" grief character with his/her opposing "good" grief character. For example, the following characters should be paired together: Majorly Missing Them Mindy with Creating Connections Cora; Lost and Lonely Laurence with Meaning Making Marcus; and What Made Them Die Wendy with Leaving a Legacy Lorraine.

After you introduce each pair of characters, give the client the stack of grief reactions cards that pertain only to those two characters and ask him or her which one may have made that particular statement. Encourage the client to talk about their own reactions and whether they can relate to any of the cards. After you go through each pair of characters (all six characters in total), ask if the client has any other grief reactions that you haven't talked about and how they might categorize those reactions.

Note: This activity is for the child only.

Majorly Missing Them Mindy

- Missing the person so much I feel like crying
- Wishing we were back together again
- Wanting to go look for them
- Wanting to cry for them
- Feeling angry that we aren't together
- Avoiding reminders that they are gone
- Feeling afraid to get close to other people because I could lose them too
- Feeling bad (regretful or guilty) that I didn't treat the person better while they were alive

46

Grief Psychoeducation

Optional Additional Comments

Many grieving kids want to

- cry;
- search for the person who died or be on the lookout for them to show up, such as imagining that it's them whenever they hear the front door open;
- stay away from people, places, or things that can be loss reminders (things that remind them that the person is gone).

Some grieving kids also have what they might call "weird" experiences, such as

- feeling like the person is nearby, even though they don't see them;
- seeming to see or hear them, such as catching a glimpse of their face in a crowd.

Actually, these supposedly weird experiences are very normal, especially soon after the loss. These experiences can mean different things to different kids, depending on their specific beliefs and ideas. For example, when this happens, it may be telling us how much we wish that our loved one didn't really die and that we wish they would come back to us. Or some people believe that the spirit of the person who died can still visit us from time to time to let us know that they are still around to comfort or protect us. Whatever feels the most helpful to you is the best way to think about it.

- Enjoying talking about them
- Enjoying looking at pictures or videos of them
- Having comforting or special dreams about them
- Feeling like I can still have a special relationship with them, even though it's very different than it used to be
- Finding ways that I am similar to them

Optional Additional Comments

Grieving kids may also feel like they can still have a positive connection with the person who died even though the person is no longer there physically.

It is often easy to feel like two different people at once (e.g. Mindy and Cora) because we can have both helpful and unhelpful grief-related thoughts at the same time.

Lost and Lonely Laurence

Creating Connections Cora

- Feeling like they are watching over me and/or looking out for me
- Wanting to do the same things they used to do

- Feeling like part of me died with them
- Feeling lost without them
- Not knowing what to do without them
- Losing hope that I can still have a good life
- Feeling bored, like nothing matters
- Not caring what happens to me anymore

Optional Additional Comments

Grieving kids may also change the way they act around other people. They may

- be less interested in keeping up with their friendships or making new friends;
- feel bored with life;

- get easily mad, angry, or critical of others;
- stay away from other people, even though it leaves them feeling lonely or bored.

the death, either about themselves or about the world around them. They may even feel more spiritual or religious and have a greater sense of what they want to do with their lives – like they are here for an important reason. Some find it helpful to get involved in volunteer opportunities where they can reach out to others who are suffering.

Meaning Making Marcus

What Made Them Die Wendy

- Wanting to live the kind of life that my person would have wanted for me
- Wanting to help other people who are going through hard times
- Understanding other people's sadness better
- Feeling confident that I can still lead a happy life
- Feeling like I can make it through almost anything now
- Feeling like I care even more now about other people
- Wanting to take good care of myself so I can live a long life

- Feeling angry about the way they died
- Feeling guilty that I didn't do more to stop them from dying
- Being so upset over how they died that it's hard to remember the good times
- Wanting revenge on whoever or whatever I think is responsible
- Having scary thoughts or feelings about how they died
- Wondering about whether the death was scary or upsetting for them

Optional Additional Comments

Sometimes, grieving kids may feel like their life has more meaning after the death of someone they love. Usually this doesn't happen right away, but over time, kids may take life a little more seriously than before or may appreciate their lives more. They may feel like they learned something from

Optional Additional Comments

- *Many people describe feeling angry about the death. Sometimes, they also feel guilty or ashamed over what happened, especially when the person died in a violent, sudden, or very upsetting way. We'll focus on these difficult feelings in later sessions.*

- *People who have someone die violently or in very scary ways can have upsetting pictures in their minds of how the person died. These thoughts can be so upsetting that it makes it hard to hold onto happy memories about them. Thoughts of how the person died can be so upsetting that people may try to stop thinking or talking about the special person who died. This can make it much harder to grieve in a healthy way.*

Leaving a Legacy Lorraine

- Doing my part to keep others from dying in similar ways
- Knowing in my heart that there is nothing I could have done to save them
- Focusing on things about their death that bring me comfort (like whether I was able to say what I wanted to say to them)
- Feeling comfortable talking about the way they died
- Feeling comfortable thinking about the way they died

Optional Additional Comments

After someone we love dies, it can take a long time before we are able to think about the death in a different way and learn how to change our upsetting thoughts and feelings about how the person died into something that we can do to help other people. In fact, a lot of time may pass before we're able to make meaning in this way. For example, later in life, we may want to try and raise money for a special charity that will prevent similar types of deaths. Or we may want to volunteer to work with other kids or families who have lost loved ones in similar ways. We can explore what this might look like later in our work together.

Helpful Hint: The idea of meaning making, although sophisticated, can still be taught to grieving children, but this can often take more time based upon the child's developmental level, the amount of time that has passed since the death, the child's relationship to the person who died, and the ability of surviving caregivers to support and facilitate this work. It is important to note that most children must make sense of the death prior to making meaning of the death. In other words, they often have to understand the facts related to how the person died as a first step. For this reason, it is important to not push the child too much to come up with ways of making meaning of the death before they're truly ready.

6 Rating My Grief Reactions

Introduce the grief thermometers and have the child rate his/her own grief reactions using Handout 1.3. You can explain that this will be used every time he/she comes to see you as a way of monitoring his/her grief reactions over time. Note that each of the grief thermometers reflects one of each of the dimensions of grief (both adaptive and maladaptive).

7 Grief Goals

Introduce the Grief Goals worksheet (Handout 1.4) and have the child fill out the worksheet.

Now that we've learned all about different grief reactions and your own personal grief reactions, this worksheet will help us to set specific goals about your own grief. In other words, this worksheet can help us to make sure that the treatment is working to address your specific grief-related goals and keep us on track as treatment progresses.

This activity can also be assigned as a practice exercise to be reviewed during the next session if time is limited.

8 Check Out

- *How are you feeling now?*
- *What did you learn about yourself today?*

Grief Psychoeducation

Adolescent Adaptation

Learning about Different Grief Reactions

Below are optional lists of grief reactions that can be used in place of the cartoons for older children/adolescents. You can have the client circle which grief-related thoughts they have been experiencing lately and rate the "top three thoughts/feelings" that they would like to change (have more of or less of).

Separation Distress

- Missing the person so much I want to cry
- Feeling sad that we are no longer physically together
- Wishing we could be together again
- Feeling my heart ache inside for them
- Sighing a lot
- Wanting to go search for them in places where they used to be
- Feeling angry or frustrated that we aren't together
- Thinking of where they are now; wondering whether I'll ever see them again
- Thinking I can see them (like their face in a crowd) or feeling their presence nearby
- Feeling like they are watching over me and looking out for me
- Wanting to do positive things he or she used to do that I admired

Existential/Identity Distress

- Feeling like part of myself died with them
- Feeling lost without them
- Not knowing what to do with myself without them
- Losing hope that I can still have a good life without having them here
- Not caring what happens to me anymore since they died
- Feeling bored, like nothing matters anymore since they died
- Losing my desire to work hard to have a good life
- Wanting to live the kind of life that he or she would have wanted for me
- Wanting to help other people who are going through very hard times

Circumstance-Related Distress

- Feeling angry about the way they died (thinking their death was unfair)
- Feeling guilty or angry at myself that I didn't do more to keep them from dying
- Feeling ashamed over how I acted at the time of their death
- Feeling angry at other people for not doing more to keep them from dying
- Being so upset over how they died that it's hard to remember the good times
- Wanting to get revenge on whoever is responsible
- Wanting to do positive things that keep other people from dying the way my loved one died

Handout 1.1

Grief Statement Cards and True/False Cards

It is normal to have many different types of grief-related feelings (for example, sad, angry, worried) at the same time.

After someone we care about dies, all kids get over their painful feelings after about 6–12 months.

It is best not to talk about the person who died – that way, it will be easier to move on with your life.

Grief reactions always stay the same over time.

Healthy grieving means that we forget or stop thinking about our loved one who died.

Everyone in the same family or group of close friends grieves in the same way.

After someone we feel close to dies, we can still be happy and enjoy our lives.

If we do not have a strong reaction to a death, it means we did not care about the person who died.

Sometimes we may feel relieved when a person dies.

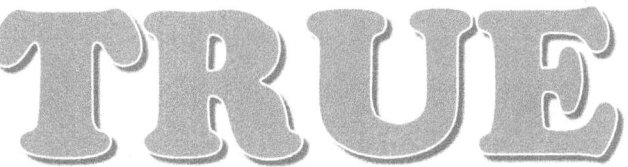

Grief Psychoeducation

Handout 1.2

Grief Character Cartoons and Grief Reaction Cards

Grief Psychoeducation

Grief Psychoeducation

Grief Psychoeducation

I have dreams about my person that help me to feel better

I can sometimes feel my person nearby like he/she is protecting me and looking out for me

I like to do the positive things my person used to do that I really liked and admired

Grief Psychoeducation

59

Grief Psychoeducation

Grief Psychoeducation

> I do my best to do and say things that would make my person proud

> Even though my person is gone, I know I can still have a good life

> Because of what I've been through, it's so much easier now to understand other people who are going through tough times

Grief Psychoeducation

Grief Psychoeducation

- I have a hard time thinking and talking about my person because of the way they died

- Things that remind me of my person bring up bad memories of the way that they died

- Sometimes, I feel guilty that I didn't do more to keep my person from dying

Grief Psychoeducation

Grief Psychoeducation

I want to spend time with other people who lost a loved one the way I did

I know there was nothing more I could have done to keep my person from dying

Grief Psychoeducation

Handout 1.3

Rating My Grief Reactions

Directions: Write one number (from 1 to 10) in the line next to each thermometer to show how strongly you are feeling each grief reaction.

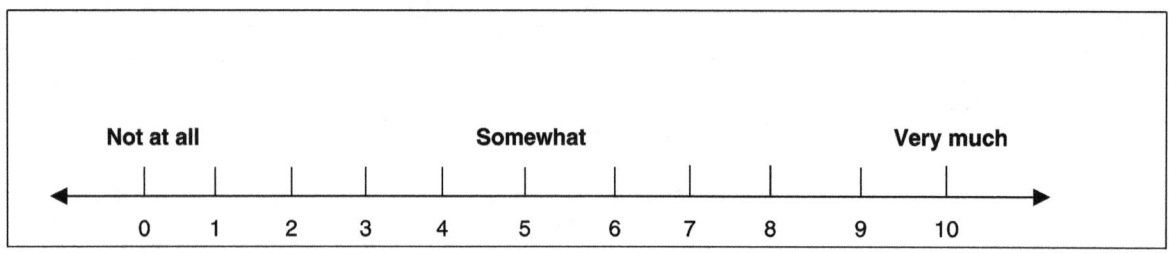

 **Missing the person a lot**

_____

 **Feeling like they're watching over me in a comforting way**

_____

 **Feeling lost without them**

_____

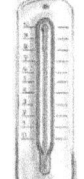 **Wanting to live the kind of life they would want me to have**

_____

 **Feeling so upset about the way that they died, that it's hard to remember the good times**

_____

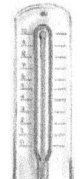 **Wanting to make the world safer so other people don't die in tragic ways**

_____

 **Feeling afraid of forgetting important things about them**

_____

 **Wanting to avoid things that remind me of the way they died (trauma reminders)**

_____

 **Wanting to avoid things that remind me they are no longer here physically (loss reminders)**

_____

 **Feeling like they are still an important part of my life**

_____

A PDF version of this handout is available for download on Cambridge Core and via www.cambridge.org/MGT

Handout 1.4

Grief Goals Worksheet

Please check **all of the boxes** that are true for you.
By the end of this treatment,

I want to feel *less*: (check all that apply)				
☐ Angry	☐ Sad	☐ Alone	☐ Scared	☐ Nervous
☐ Confused	☐ Guilty	☐ Different from other kids	☐ Other _____	
I want to feel *more*: (check all that apply)				
☐ Calm	☐ Happy	☐ Hopeful	☐ Confident	☐ Close to others
☐ Understood	☐ In Control	☐ Cared For	☐ Other _____	

I want to change the way I do things, the way I think about things, or the way I feel about things in the following way(s): (check all that apply)

- ☐ Be able to calm myself down when I get upset
- ☐ Be able to understand my thoughts and feelings about the person who died a little better
- ☐ Feel more connected to the person who died, even though they are no longer here physically
- ☐ Know what to do when my grief feels overwhelming
- ☐ Be able to think or talk about the person who died without getting upset
- ☐ Stop staying away from things that remind me that the person died
- ☐ Stop staying away from things that remind me of **the way** the person died (or what caused them to die)
- ☐ Have an easier time dealing with strong or confusing feelings about the death
- ☐ Feel like I can live the kind of life that the person would have wanted for me
- ☐ Have an easier time talking to family members about the death
- ☐ Have an easier time talking to friends about the death
- ☐ Have a better idea of what to do or say when other kids find out about the death
- ☐ Feel like I can still have a good future even though this death has happened
- ☐ Other:

MGT Session

2 Emotion Psychoeducation and Identification

What Am I Feeling and Why?

Session Objectives

Increase the client's ability:

1. To describe feelings and emotions
2. To track emotions by becoming aware of how they are experienced in the body
3. To regulate emotions by experiencing feelings within the moderate range of intensity (rather than bouncing between 0 and 10) on the feelings thermometer
4. To recognize emotions expressed by others and respond appropriately
5. To tolerate (rather than avoid, suppress, or deny) painful emotions

Section Number	Session Overview
1	Check In with Grief Thermometers
2	Emotion Psychoeducation: What Are Feelings?
3	Learning to Name and Measure My Feelings
4	Activity 1: Feelings Charades (Guess What I'm Feeling)
5	Activity 2: Feelings Selfie
6	Activity 3: Color Your Body
7	Assign Practice Exercise: Monitoring Changes in My Mood and Feelings
8	Check Out

Session Materials

- Rating My Grief Reactions (Handout 1.3)
- Feelings Thermometer (Handout 2.1)
- Feelings Faces (Handout 2.2)
- Feelings Selfie (Handout 2.3)
- Color Your Body (Handout 2.4)
- Monitoring Changes in My Mood or Feelings (Handout 2.5)

1 Check In with Grief Thermometers

Have child complete Rating My Grief Reactions (Handout 1.3) and explore current snapshot of grief experience. The following are some sample prompts:

- *How are you feeling on your grief thermometers?*
- *How did your grief thermometers change from last week?*

Additional check-in prompts may be appropriate:

- *Did anything happen since we saw each other last that you feel good about?*
- *Was there anything we talked about in our last session that you thought about this week or that stuck with you?*
- *Is anything going on that may make it hard for you to focus during our session today?*

2 Emotion Psychoeducation: What Are Feelings?

Cover the general points below in your own words.

Last time we met, we talked about different kinds of grief reactions we can have when someone dies, and we met each of the different grief characters. Today we are going to talk about some other feelings that people can have when someone dies. There are some important things to remember about feelings after a death:

- *Some people may not have any feelings at all, or they may feel numb inside.*
- *Others may try not to have any feelings by pushing them away or trying not to think about those feelings.*
- *Some people may be afraid to face their feelings because they seem too big to handle.*
- *Some people may have really big or strong feelings much of the time, like anger or sadness or fear.*
- *Some people may go back and forth between having lots of very strong feelings and not feeling much of anything.*

Our feelings and moods can change a lot throughout the day. We may feel happy, sad, angry, and excited at different times of the day, or even feel a different mix of these feelings at different times of the day. To get better at controlling our feelings, we need to practice paying attention to what we are feeling, especially to strong emotions like fear, sadness, or anger. It may be tempting to ignore our strong upsetting feelings, such as by stuffing our feelings inside, trying to not feel them, or telling ourselves that we don't feel them. But when we push our feelings away, this is usually not very helpful, especially in the long run. Here are some important things to remember:

- *Even though upsetting feelings don't feel good, it is important to stay with them long enough to be able to recognize and name them.*
- *All emotions are OK, even unpleasant ones. Everyone has them. It is what you do with your emotions that matters.*
- *Remember that when people are stressed out or upset, they sometimes forget to pay attention to the good things they are feeling. It helps to recognize these good feelings, even if they're mixed in with upsetting feelings.*
- *People who have had someone die may feel guilty if they start to have happy feelings again. Remember that it's normal and healthy to be happy at times, even after someone we love has died.*

Last time we met, we talked about measuring our grief reactions using the grief thermometers. We can also use the feelings thermometer to better understand (1) what it is we're feeling; and (2) how strong that feeling is. For example, right now, what feeling do you have? And can you tell me how strong it is according to the feelings thermometer?

Ask the Client to Share What Feeling Words They Know.

Can you tell me how many feeling words you know?

The therapist can make this into a game and have the client list as many feeling words as they can in one minute. You can also use the Feelings Faces handout (Handout 2.2) to help increase the number and types of feelings that the client can identify. Then ask the client to choose one or two of the feelings that they tend to have the most and share how they experience those feelings.

- *How do you show this feeling?*
- *How could I tell if you were really sad or really mad about something?*
- *Where do you have this feeling in your body? How do you know when you're having this feeling?*
- *Do you ever have a really strong feeling and wonder where it came from? Like not really knowing how or why you feel that way?*

We sometimes believe that our feelings are out of our own control, but there are things we can do to take charge of our own emotions. To do this, we need to be able to name our feelings and to talk about them, both to ourselves (knowing what it is we're feeling) and with others (knowing how to explain what we're feeling).

First, let's practice naming our feelings. Sometimes it can be hard for people to figure out what they're actually feeling in the moment, especially when those feelings are so strong. For example, people who have had a loved one die may be reminded of the person or the way that they died, and these reminders can bring up strong feelings. This can happen even when we're not expecting it.

You may all of a sudden, feel sad, scared, or angry and have no idea why you feel that way because nothing seems to be going on that would cause that feeling. But it may be that something or someone around you has reminded you of the person who died, or the way that they died, or how much things have changed since they died. At other times, you may feel suddenly happy because something – a special song or the smell of something cooking in the oven – reminds you of a happy time you shared in the past with the person who died.

When we ask people how they are feeling, they usually use just a word or two: "good," "not bad," "I'm cool," "nervous," "great," "could be worse," and so on. Actually, people often feel more than one emotion at a time, especially after a death. For example, people can feel a mixture of happy and upsetting emotions at the same time, like happily remembering the good times with the person who died while also feeling really sad that they're no longer with us.

3 Learning to Name and Measure My Feelings

Note: Depending on the time available, you may wish to select only two or three of the activities below. Choose those activities that best meet the developmental level and needs of your client.

Emotion Psychoeducation and Identification

4 Activity 1 Feelings Charades (Guess What I'm Feeling)

Purpose:

- To learn how emotions register and are expressed on people's face, including their own
- To enhance clients' ability to interpret the body language of other people

Gaining control of our emotions doesn't just depend on being able to recognize our own feelings. It also depends on recognizing how other people are feeling. Sometimes people may say they feel a certain way, but you can tell from the look on their face or their body language that they don't really mean what they're saying. Sometimes it's helpful to learn more about what different emotions can look like in others so that we're better able to understand what they might be feeling.

Directions: Create a stack of cards with both feelings and situations that tend to evoke strong emotions. Take turns with the client picking a card and acting out the feeling or acting out how you might feel in the situation. Whoever is the observer should identify the feeling. Sometimes it is helpful if the therapist goes first to break the ice. You or the client will then try to guess the feeling.

5 Activity 2 Feelings Selfie

Purpose:

- To increase understanding of client's own emotions at the time of their loved one's death
- To reinforce the notion that multiple emotions can be felt at once

Materials: Feelings Selfie handout (Handout 2.3).

Directions: Give the client colored markers and/or crayons and introduce the Feelings Selfie handout.

The next activity is kind of like taking a selfie snapshot of all the emotions you may feel about the death of _____. When you think about your person's death, what feelings come up for you? Pick three or four emotions that come to mind. Pick a color for each feeling and write the name of that feeling in that color on the blank lines of the Feelings Selfie worksheet. You can use the Feelings Faces handout if you need some ideas. Next, color in the Feelings Selfie showing how much you are feeling each emotion. So if you are a half hopeful, a quarter sad, and a quarter worried, then color half the circle with your color for hopeful, a quarter with your color for sad, and a quarter with your color for worried.

Invite your client to discuss their feelings selfie. Validate and normalize as appropriate. Emphasize the following points:

- Our feelings selfies can change from moment to moment and from one situation to the next.
- Different people have different feelings after a death, even people within the same family, or people who were there when the death happened (e.g., the same car crash).
- Even when people feel the same emotions, they often feel them differently. One person might feel a certain emotion strongly, another medium, and another only a little bit.
- When we recognize our feelings better and find the right words to describe those feelings, this can help us to understand ourselves and each other better, help us to talk through those feelings, and help us to support each other.

6 Activity 3 Color Your Body

Purpose:

- To learn how thoughts are experienced in the mind and feelings are experienced in the body
- To explore, on an experiential level, how emotions differ from thoughts
- To become more aware of their own physical cues, and to use those cues to identify the emotions they are feeling at the moment

Materials: Color Your Body handout (Handout 2.4).

Directions: Use the Color Your Body handout. Ask the client to use the same three or four emotions they identified in their feelings selfie and the same color key.

When we start to notice changes in our feelings and understand where they are coming from, it can help us to gain more control over those feelings. Our bodies are sending us important signals all the time about what we are feeling. If we learn to tune in and listen carefully to our body's signals, we will get better at understanding what we are feeling and why. This is a very important step towards gaining control over how we are feeling.

Take one emotion at a time and ask the client to tell you where in his or her body they feel that emotion. Have the client fill in the color on the gingerbread figure where he or she feels different emotions in his/her body.

For example:

- *You may get a knot in your stomach, sweaty hands, or shaky legs when you are feeling anxious or afraid.*
- *You may feel anger in your jaw, or your fists, or your forehead.*
- *When you are feeling sad, you may feel an emptiness down in the bottom of your stomach, or your heart might hurt.*
- *When you are feeling happy, your face may feel energetic around your eyes and your mouth.*
- *An important thing to keep in mind is that everybody's body is different and gives us different types of signals.*

Apply these insights by asking the client to imagine a time (either now or in the past) when they felt each emotion. Have them remember the situation as best as they can, and where they felt each emotion in their body.

Note: Because this exercise covers several emotions, the gingerbread figure will most likely end up layered with many colors in certain parts of the body, such as the face or heart areas.

7 Assign Practice Exercise: Monitoring Changes in My Mood and Feelings

Purpose:

- To become more aware of their own feelings
- To better understand what might be happening "on the outside" that can influence their feelings or mood

Materials: Monitoring Changes in My Mood and Feelings worksheet (Handout 2.5).

Directions: *During this session we talked about different feelings people have. To help control our feelings, it is important to pay attention to when we begin to feel strong feelings. Pick one time this week during which you notice a sudden change for the worse in your mood. When you notice this change, write down your feeling and how much you were feeling that way using your feelings thermometer. Then, write a brief description of what was happening outside of you at the time. Where were you and what were you doing when you started to feel bad? For example, were you talking to someone? Reading? Watching TV? Listening to the radio? Alone by yourself? Pay attention to where you are and what just happened, then write it down.*

I look forward to hearing what you have learned!

8 Check Out

- *How are you feeling now?* (Use feelings thermometer ratings)
- *What did you learn about yourself today?*

End of Session

Handout 2.1

Feelings Thermometer

Sometimes we feel a feeling just a little bit, and other times we feel a feeling so strongly that we think we might burst with that feeling! You can rate or measure your feelings, just like a thermometer measures temperature. The number tells how intense the feeling is.

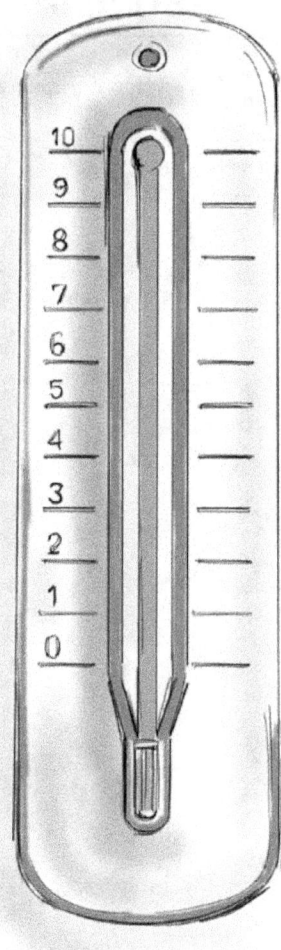

What distressful feelings are you having right now? How would you rate each of these feelings (on a scale of 0 to 10)?

A PDF version of this handout is available for download on Cambridge Core and via www.cambridge.org/MGT

Handout 2.2

Feelings Faces

Emotion Psychoeducation and Identification

Handout 2.3

Feelings Selfie

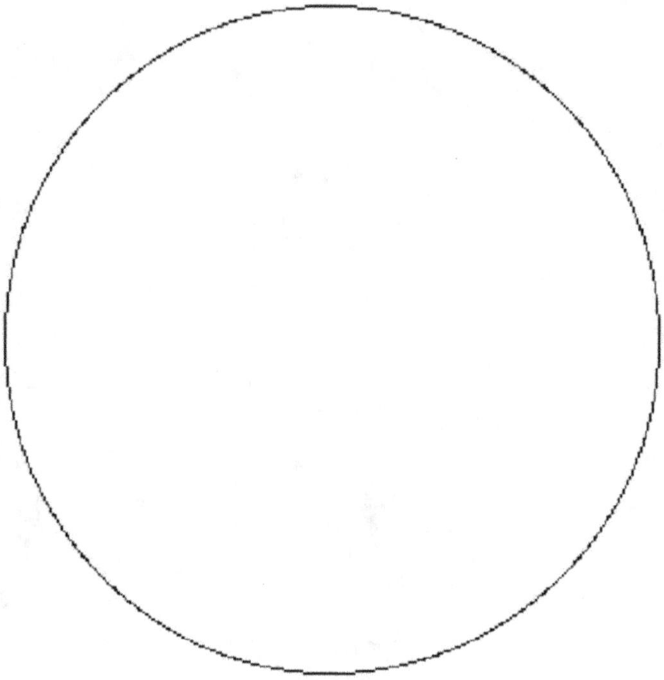

☐ _____

☐ _____

☐ _____

☐ _____

☐ _____

☐ _____

A PDF version of this handout is available for download on Cambridge Core and via www.cambridge.org/MGT

Emotion Psychoeducation and Identification

Handout 2.4

Color Your Body

A PDF version of this handout is available for download on Cambridge Core and via www.cambridge.org/MGT

Handout 2.5

Monitoring Changes in My Mood or Feelings

Directions: Pick one time this week when you noticed your mood change for the worse. When this happens, write down one or two feelings you have, and rate each feeling on your thermometer from 0 to 10. Then, write a brief description of what was happening outside of you.

What were you feeling?
_____

How much were you feeling that way (using your feelings thermometer from 0 to 10)?
_____ (choose a number from 0 to 10)

What was <u>happening</u> outside of you at the time?
_____
_____
_____
_____

A PDF version of this handout is available for download on Cambridge Core and via www.cambridge.org/MGT

MGT Session

Grief Psychoeducation Continued
How Has My Grief Changed Over Time?

Session Objectives

Increase the client's ability:

1. To normalize and validate grief reactions as healthy and universal
2. To expand their understanding of how grief reactions can change and fluctuate over time
3. To explore healthy ways in which they can feel connected to the deceased and potentially reduce grief-related distress
4. To explore their grief reactions over time, and share them with caregiver(s) to facilitate mutual understanding of family members' grief experiences

Section Number	Session Overview
1	Check In with Grief Thermometers
2	Review Practice Exercise: Measuring My Feelings
3	Grief Psychoeducation Continued: How Does Grief Change over Time?
4	Activity 1: Exploring My Waves of Grief
5	Activity 2: Introduction to The Good Grief Jar
6	Sharing with Caregiver (optional)
7	Assign Practice Exercise: Riding the Waves of Grief
8	Check Out

Session Materials

- Rating My Grief Reactions (Handout 1.3)
- Riding the Waves of Grief (Handout 3.1)
- Good Grief Jar

1 Check In with Grief Thermometers

Have child complete Rating My Grief Reactions (Handout 1.3) and explore current snapshot of grief experience. The following are some sample prompts:

- *How are you feeling on your grief thermometers?*
- *How did your grief thermometers change from last week?*

Additional check-in prompts may be appropriate:

- *Did anything happen since we saw each other last that you feel good about?*
- *Was there anything we talked about in our last session that you thought about this week or that stuck with you?*
- *Is anything going on that may make it hard for you to focus during our session today?*

2 Review Practice Exercise: Measuring My Feelings

- *How did your practice go last week?*
- *Did you notice any mood changes?*
- *What were you feeling on the inside? And what was going on for you on the outside?*

The more we practice noticing our own feelings, and the situations that make us feel a certain way, the more we can take charge of those feelings and learn to cope with them better.

3 Grief Psychoeducation Continued: How Does Grief Change over Time?

If you remember in our first session, we talked about different grief characters (like Majorly Missing Them Mindy or Leaving a Legacy Lorraine) and the different kinds of grief reactions they each have. We know that we can have lots of different kinds of grief feelings at the same time (like really missing the person while also feeling proud of the things we have in common with them).

In our second session, we talked about other feelings we might have after someone we love dies. We may feel angry, sad, or scared, but we may also feel happy when we think about fun things we did with the person. We also know that these feelings can change week by week, day by day, or even minute by minute.

It can help to think of our grief and related feelings like waves in the ocean. Waves come and go, and they can be strong (sometimes even as strong as a tsunami), medium, or weak. One minute you can be swept up by a big wave of anger, and then after a while it becomes smaller, and then you can be swept up by a big wave of guilt or sadness (use the client's predominant emotions as examples). *Today we are going to be exploring what your own grief waves have looked like over time.*

4 Activity 1 Exploring My Waves of Grief

Purpose:

- To examine the client's own waves of grief and how they may have changed over time

Materials: Waves of Grief worksheet (Handout 3.1).

Directions: Using the Waves of Grief worksheet, introduce the exercise. Cover the general points in your own words.

This activity helps us think about different types of feelings we had in the very beginning, right after the person died (like in the first few weeks after the death) and how those feelings might have changed over time. This activity also helps us to think about anything that was happening on the outside that made us feel a certain way during that period of time (for example, going to the cemetery or looking at photos of the person). You'll see a thermometer on the left side of this graph. Similar to our feelings thermometer, this tells us how strong the feeling (or wave) is.

Have the client choose three different colored markers, pencils, or crayons (they may want to use the same colors and feelings they used in the previous session) and provide the following directions.

I'd like you to choose three different colored markers (or pencils/crayons) that represent three feelings you had within the first few weeks after the person died (e.g., red = angry; blue = sad; purple = guilty). Then, using each of the markers and the thermometer on the handout as a guide, I'd like you to draw a wave for each feeling, showing how that feeling may have changed over time. For example, you may have felt really angry right after the death, then that wave may have gone down a little, but maybe it went up again after your graduation ceremony two weeks ago. Or maybe there has been no wave at all, and the feeling you had right after the death has stayed the same over time. There is no right or wrong way to grieve, so everyone's waves may look different. Even people in the same family can have very different waves of grief.

Have the client draw their three feeling waves and describe how intense the feelings were (lower along the thermometer = less intense; higher on the thermometer = more intense) in the beginning (right after the death) and over time. Note that it may be helpful to use the Feelings Faces handout if the client has trouble identifying feelings. If the client has focused primarily on distressing feelings, encourage them to plot a fourth feeling that is more positive, such as happy, hopeful, or grateful, and describe how that feeling may also have changed over time. Explore what may have been happening "outside of me" (including loss reminders such as important events, lost opportunities, hearing the person's name, etc.) as the waves went higher or lower over time. As you review and comment on more versus less intense feelings, explore what each feeling was like to experience at each time point and what they did with those feelings at the time (e.g., How did they cope? What did they do?).

After the exercise is completed, ask the client what it was like to do the exercise – what thoughts or feelings might have come up? Remembering how they felt soon after the death can pull up strong emotions, even now. Youth may have different reactions, including becoming quiet, withdrawn, anxious, or even animated. Create a safe space where they can share their current emotions and validate their feelings.

5 Activity 2 Introduction to The Good Grief Jar

Purpose:

- To help the client find healthy ways of feeling connected to the person who died

Materials: Clear mason jar, markers or colored pencils, two strips of paper, and stickers or other decorations for the jar.

Directions: Cover the following general points in your own words.

Just as certain people, places, things or situations (called loss reminders) can make painful feelings stronger, other reminders, like happy memories of the person, can bring us comfort and make it a bit easier to deal with our more upsetting feelings. When we have strong waves of grief, sometimes it can help to think about things we loved about the person (like his/her sense of humor), things we did together that were really fun (like going to a concert or playing games), or even things that we have in common with the person (like how much you both loved animals, enjoyed cooking, etc.). This jar is going to be an important tool as we continue our work together. It's called a Good Grief Jar because we will be adding happy memories and positive thoughts about the person at the end of each session. When we're all done with treatment, this is a jar that you'll be able to keep to remind yourself of these happy memories whenever you need them.

Using the prior Waves of Grief exercise, ask the client to identify two happy memories, thoughts, or images of the deceased person that could make the waves of grief feel less painful. Have the client write each of those memories/thoughts on two strips of paper and put them in the jar. You can then have them decorate the jar using stickers or other craft materials. You can explain that you will be adding to the jar after each session as you move forward with treatment together.

6 Sharing with Caregiver (optional)

As with most of the exercises in MGT, it is often helpful to have the client share with one or both caregivers some of the content from the session. This provides an opportunity for the client to share more about their own personal grief process and open the door to further communication between family members. This sharing can also help to reduce the child's sense of being alone with their painful thoughts, feelings, and memories and reinforce the idea that talking about grief can actually be helpful. However, there are some situations in which it may be counterproductive to involve the parent/caregiver:

- The caregiver is so emotionally distressed or overwhelmed by their own grief that they cannot be fully present to support the child.
- The child does not feel comfortable sharing any of the material with the caregiver.

In many cases, this sharing activity will require some one-on-one coaching with the caregiver beforehand (e.g., a phone call prior to the session or a brief meeting before the session) to help them understand how they can be most supportive during the activity. For example, you may need to remind the caregiver that the most important and helpful thing they can do is listen and praise the child for opening up and sharing their feelings. This is not the time to correct the child's memory or interpretation of events. It is also inherently difficult for parents to bear witness to their child's pain. For this reason, they may make minimizing comments (e.g., "I'm sure you didn't really feel like you wanted to die") or try to instantly fix or problem solve. In this exercise it is important for the parents to simply listen with an open heart. Prompts can be given during the sharing to keep the caregiver on track, and you, as the therapist, can help to model active listening and positive reinforcement.

Directions for Child-Caregiver Sharing (as appropriate): If the client feels comfortable, invite the caregiver into the last part of the session (usually the last 20 minutes) to discuss the Waves of Grief activity.

First, have the client show the caregiver his/her own waves of grief graph. Once the youth shares their feelings and how they may have changed over time, the caregiver can be guided to plot the very same feelings that the client identified on their own waves of grief graph, showing the caregiver's own grief experience during the same time period. Focusing only on the specific feelings that the client identified helps to ensure that the discussion remains centered on the client. This can involve having the caregiver complete their own waves of grief chart (again, using the same feelings as the client) or simply talking about how they felt. They can discuss how their own waves were similar or different from the client's. This can be a teachable moment regarding how it may be hard to communicate with and understand each other when we are feeling different grief waves than our other family members. Reinforce the idea that there is no right or wrong way to grieve and that each person in the family can have their own unique waves of grief. Help the caregiver and child reflect on the change in their feelings over time. In most cases there will be a general trend towards less intensity of the same emotions. You can discuss this in a hopeful manner in that grief is always changing and the strength of those powerful feelings tends to diminish over time.

Throughout this sharing activity, it will be important to help the caregiver maintain appropriate boundaries with regard to not oversharing their own personal grief reactions that could be perceived as distressing or overwhelming to the child (e.g., "I really wasn't sure how I would ever go on living without your dad"). You might prompt them to share if they knew how the other was feeling at that time. Very often, parents will not have known the intensity of their child's feelings at that time. This provides a healing opportunity for the parent to acknowledge how difficult or lonely that must have been for the child. You can help the parent to validate the client's feelings and reassure the child that this is information that the parent wants to hear.

End by praising them for their courage and willingness to do this work. You might also explore with them how, going forward, they can continue to check in with each other and find ways to tell each other when their grief-related feelings go up or down.

7 Assign Practice Exercise: Riding the Waves of Grief

Refer the client to the practice exercise Riding the Waves of Grief. Go through the directions on the sheet with them.

8 Check Out

- *How are you feeling now?* (Use feelings thermometer ratings)
- If caregiver sharing was done: *What was it like to talk about your waves together? Is this something you would be comfortable discussing together at home (outside of this office)? What would make that easier for you?*
- *What did you learn about yourself today?*

**End of Session **

HANDOUT 3.1

Riding the Waves of Grief

Directions: Learning how to recognize your grief reactions, and the situations that cause them, can help you to take charge of your grief so you don't feel overwhelmed or out of control.

First, pick a specific grief reaction or feeling that you would like to focus on this week. You can either focus on difficult feelings (like feeling sad, angry, or guilty) that keep bothering you or more positive feelings that you want to have more frequently. Write the feeling you have chosen to focus on in the space below.

The grief reaction I want to focus on is: _____.

Second, learn about your own grief reactions by circling, for each day, a number from 1 to 10 to show how strongly you felt that feeling. Is the feeling steady (like a flat line) from day to day? Or does it instead go up and down, coming and going, like a wave?

At the end of each day, mark the strongest you felt the feeling that day by circling a number (from 1 = not at all, to 10 = extremely strong) for that day. For example, if it is the end of the day on Friday, and you decide that the strongest you felt the grief reaction was medium, then you would circle the number "5" under Friday. **At the end of the week, draw a line to connect the marks.**

	Sunday	Monday	Tuesday	Wednesday	Thursday	Friday	Saturday
How Strong Was the Feeling? (circle a number from 1 to 10)	10 9 8 7 6 5 4 3 2 1	10 9 8 7 6 5 4 3 2 1	10 9 8 7 6 5 4 3 2 1	10 9 8 7 6 5 4 3 2 1	10 9 8 7 6 5 4 3 2 1	10 9 8 7 6 5 4 3 2 1	10 9 8 7 6 5 4 3 2 1

Third, pay attention to the **situations** where you feel this grief reaction most strongly. What types of situations does it occur in? What was happening on the outside right before you had the feeling?

_____

_____

Describe what kind of support from others would be most helpful when you have upsetting grief reactions. Or if you chose a more positive feeling, what helped you to feel that way?

_____

_____

A PDF version of this handout is available for download on Cambridge Core and via www.cambridge.org/MGT

MGT Session

4 Understanding Caregivers as Key Grief Facilitators

What Can My Caregiver Do to Support Me?

Session Objectives

Increase the client's ability:

1. To view the caregiver (and family) as a resource with the understanding that "I don't have to do this alone"
2. To identify specific actions that caregivers and family members can take when the client experiences painful grief reactions
3. To openly communicate with their caregiver regarding which specific behaviors and activities at home are most helpful to the client, and which are least helpful
4. To identify and share healthy ways of feeling connected to the deceased, both individually and with the caregiver

Section Number	Session Overview
1	Check In with Grief Thermometers
2	Review Practice Exercise: Riding the Waves of Grief
3	Introduction/Understanding Caregivers as Key Grief Facilitators: What Can My Caregiver Do to Support Me?
4	Activity 1: The Grief Facilitation Inventory and What Helps Me Grieve
5	Activity 2: Sharing with the Caregiver (optional)
6	Activity 3: The Good Grief Game (optional)
7	Assign Practice Exercise: Sharing Positive Memories
8	Check Out

Session Materials

- Rating My Grief Reactions (Handout 1.3)
- Grief Facilitation Inventory (Handout 4.1)
- What Helps Me Grieve (Handout 4.2)
- Parent/Caregiver Guidance (Handout 4.3)
- The Good Grief Game (Handout 4.4)

1 Check In with Grief Thermometers

Have the child complete Rating My Grief Reactions (Handout 1.3) and explore current ratings of grief. Sample prompts:

- *How are you feeling on your grief thermometers?*
- *How did your grief thermometers change from last week?*

Additional check-in prompts as appropriate:

- *Did anything happen since we saw each other last that you feel good about?*
- *Was there anything we talked about in our last session that you thought about this week or that stuck with you?*
- *Is anything going on that may make it hard for you to focus during our session today?*

2 Review Practice Exercise: Riding the Waves of Grief

- *How did your practice go last week?*
- *Which grief reaction did you choose to focus on?*
- *Did your grief reaction change during the week? If it did, what was going on on the outside that made it go up or down (like a wave)?*

As we talked about last week, the more we practice noticing our own grief reactions, and the situations that make us feel a certain way, the more we can take charge of those feelings and learn to cope with them better.

3 Introduction/Understanding Caregivers as Key Grief Facilitators: What Can My Caregiver Do to Support Me?

In our last session, we talked about how things that may be going on around us can make our grief waves feel stronger or, on the other hand, can help our grief waves calm down so that we feel more in control (of our thoughts, feelings, and behaviors). We know that the things we do with caregivers or family members, such as a fun activity, sharing memories, or simply talking about our loved one, can sometimes help us feel better. But at other times, we may not feel like talking about our loved one and may end up feeling worse if we do.

Today, we are going to be talking about the things that your caregiver or family members do that feel most helpful to you, as well as the things they do that may be unhelpful. There are no right or wrong answers, and you don't need to worry about getting your caregiver in trouble for telling me your honest answers. We know that not everyone in the same family grieves in the same way. What helps you to feel better might not be the same things that make your caregiver or other family members feel better. For example, some caregivers may really like when people talk about their loved one who died, so they might assume you feel the same way and bring them up often, which may or may not be helpful to you. This is why it's so important for caregivers to know what kinds of things help you to feel better. As we go through the activity today, we will be thinking about what it would be like to share these things with your caregiver. As always, we will only share as much or as little of this information as you'd like. In fact, we don't have to share any of it at all if that's what you prefer. You are in charge of how much information we share with your family members, and you can make that choice at the end of our conversation after you've had a chance to think it over.

4 Activity 1 The Grief Facilitation Inventory and What Helps Me Grieve

Purpose:

- To help families better understand the specific behaviors that caregivers may or may not be engaging in that can help their children to grieve in healthy ways

Materials: Grief Facilitation Inventory (GFI; Kaplow & Layne, 2012) (Handout 4.1); What Helps Me Grieve worksheet (Handout 4.2).

Directions:

1. **Provide initial prompt (as follows) exploring the client's current perceptions of their caregiver's grief facilitation.**

Prior to administering the GFI, begin the conversation by informally asking the client to think about times with caregivers or family members in which their family member's actions helped the client feel better, feel less alone or sad, or even feel lighter and more hopeful. Your objective is to begin to flesh out the idea that the things that people do around your client can have a positive impact and, even more important, that your client can influence the types of support they receive by (1) asking for what feels better and what is most helpful, and (2) providing feedback about what is not helpful and when.

Towards the end of the general conversation on what helps and what doesn't, you can introduce the idea that we can learn more specifically what is most helpful by answering questions on a special survey, called the GFI, made for kids who have experienced the death of a loved one.

2. **Administer the GFI (Handout 4.1).**

The GFI (Alvis et al., 2020; Kaplow & Layne, 2012) is an assessment tool designed to help clinicians and families better understand the specific behaviors that caregivers may or may not be engaging in that can help their children to grieve in adaptive and healthy ways. The GFI can be used with children and adolescents, aged 7 to 18, and usually takes about 10 minutes to administer. The GFI can be used as a clinical interview, as opposed to simply having the client fill out the questionnaire on his/her own. For example, you can ask the client each question out loud and record their response on the GFI, while also probing for more information or details when necessary. This can be a very effective way of better understanding how the caregiver and child may be interacting at home, specifically surrounding the death of their loved one. This is also an opportunity to learn more about what the client perceives to be most helpful with regard to their caregiver's behaviors.

3. **Complete the What Helps Me Grieve Worksheet (Handout 4.2).**

After administering the GFI, it can be helpful to summarize what you learned from the client about which caregivers' behaviors were seen as the most versus least helpful. You can summarize this information using the What Helps Me Grieve worksheet located at the end of this session. This worksheet was created with the intention of sharing the information with the caregiver and was designed to allow the client to pick and choose what they felt most comfortable sharing. You can explain this part of the activity in the following way.

I really appreciate you telling me your honest answers about the things that _____ (caregiver name) does at home that feel helpful, as well as the things that they do at home that may not be as helpful. What I'd like to do now is to make sure we understand exactly what things they do that are most helpful to you, and also what things they do that may make things harder for you. Let's first take a look at the most helpful behaviors. Based on the questionnaire we just filled out, what would you say are the top five favorite things that you really like your caregiver to do with you?

Using the information you just gathered from the GFI, have the client identify the top five behaviors that seemed to be most helpful to them and write those down on the What Helps Me Grieve worksheet.

Next, you can say, *"Now that we know what your top five favorite things are, what are the top five things that make grieving harder that you wish your caregiver would do more of or less of?"* Using the same What Helps Me Grieve worksheet, write down specific things the child would like the caregiver to do more or less frequently.

To conclude this activity, review the What Helps Me Grieve worksheet and ask the client what they feel comfortable sharing with their caregiver. Note that sometimes caregivers may not even be aware of the things they're doing at home that either make it harder or easier to grieve in ways that feel comforting and helpful. If the client doesn't feel comfortable sharing all of the information on the worksheet, you can ask if they might feel more comfortable sharing just one or two of the things listed. The client may be most comfortable with you sharing the activity with the caregiver while the client and caregiver are both in the room together. It is important to gently encourage the client to share, while also acknowledging and validating that this may not be the right time for them to share and they can always come back to the worksheet and share more at a later date, if they wish.

As part of this exercise, you can encourage the client to write down two of the "most helpful" behaviors that they identified on the What Helps Me Grieve worksheet and add those two pieces of paper to their Good Grief Jar. This provides them with additional coping tools/strategies that they can call upon when needed.

5 Activity 2 Sharing with the Caregiver (optional)

Purpose:

- To facilitate a discussion with the caregiver(s) regarding behaviors the child identified as being most helpful and not so helpful
- To positively reinforce those specific behaviors that the child endorses as helpful and praise ongoing, open communication between the child and caregiver(s)

Materials: Completed What Helps Me Grieve worksheet (Handout 4.2).

Directions: As with last week's activity, prior to including the caregiver in this session, it will be important to understand the caregiver's own capacity to provide support to the client and offer positive reinforcement. It may be helpful to meet briefly with the caregiver prior to the session to help them understand the purpose of this activity: to better understand the things they can do at home to help their child grieve in adaptive and healthy ways (see Chapter 4 for a more detailed explanation of how to work with caregivers prior to joint sessions). The most important thing the caregiver can do is listen to their child and validate their experience. You may want to provide the caregiver with specific statements they can make during the activity to show their support (e.g., "I'm so glad you're sharing this with me"; "It really helps me to know what I can do to support you"; "I'm proud of how much you've been able to tell me – I know this is hard to talk about"). This information is also contained in Handout 4.3, which you can provide to the caregiver prior to the sharing session.

When you have both the caregiver(s) and child together in the room, you can introduce this activity in the following way.

As we talked about last week, people grieve in different ways, and even people in the same family can have very different grief reactions. We also know that some things that feel good and helpful to one family member can feel not so helpful to another family member. This exercise is designed to help caregivers better understand the things that they might be doing at home that feel really good to their child as well as some of the things that their child would like to change at home. These conversations are so important to have because we know that caregivers want what's best for their child, but it's often hard to know what is most helpful if we don't talk about it openly.

At this point, you can guide the client and review the What Helps Me Grieve worksheet with the caregiver, first starting with the column "I Like It When," noting all of the behaviors that feel helpful to the client. Next, you can review the "I Wish I Could Change" column. This may require some additional guidance on your part to ensure that the conversation feels informative and constructive rather than accusatory in any way. After reviewing the entire worksheet, you can ask the client what it felt like to share that information with the caregiver, and what it was like for the caregiver to receive the information. You can also ask the caregiver if it feels doable to try and engage in more of the behaviors that the child finds helpful.

6 Activity 3 The Good Grief Game (optional)

Purpose:

- To further facilitate open communication between the caregiver and child, specifically related to reducing separation distress and finding healthy ways of feeling connected to the deceased

Materials: The Good Grief Game handout (Handout 4.4)

Directions: It is often the case that caregivers may avoid talking about the deceased person because they do not want to upset their child(ren) by doing so. In addition, caregivers are often confused about what to talk about. This activity provides prompts for the caregiver and child to engage in a helpful discussion about the deceased, including topics that are meant to foster a healthy connection with the deceased person and reduce separation distress.

To begin the activity, you can ask the caregiver and child to sit across from each other. Each should have a notepad and pencil/pen. You can then use the Good Grief Game handout as your guide and ask them each to write their answers to the questions (one by one) on the notepad without looking at each other's responses. You can then have them share their responses with each other after each question. You do not have to ask them all of the questions. You can simply choose the questions that may be the most relevant/helpful. At the end of this activity, you can ask the client and the caregiver to describe what it was like for them to talk about their person in this way. Is this something they could envision doing at home?

7 Assign Practice Exercise: Sharing Positive Memories

Using the What Helps Me Grieve worksheet as the foundation for this practice exercise, you can ask the caregiver and child to brainstorm about one or two activities they plan to engage in together this week that can enable healthy or adaptive grieving (e.g., looking at photos of the deceased person, reading condolence cards, watching videos of the deceased person together). You can ask them to report back to you about how that activity went when you see each other next week.

8 Check Out

- *How are you feeling now?* (Use feelings thermometer rating)
- If caregiver sharing was done, you can ask the caregiver: *What was shared today that was either surprising or helpful?*
- *What did you learn about yourself today?*

End of Session

Handout 4.1

Grief Facilitation Inventory (GFI) – Child Version

Child's Initials: _____   Child's Date of Birth: _____

Directions: I'm going to be describing different things that caregivers* may say or do with their child after someone their child cared about has died. Some caregivers say and do these things often, and others may not do them at all. After I describe each thing, I'll ask you to show me how often it happened during the last month (help the child select a date marker for one month ago) by choosing one of these cups (show drawings of the cups). You can choose between not at all during the past month, a little during the past month, sometimes, a lot, or almost always during the past month.

Remember: We are talking about your caregiver and things he/she may have said or done since your _____ (name of the deceased) died. Also remember that caregivers may say or do lots of different things after someone dies, and there are no right or wrong answers here. Are you ready to begin?

*Interviewer may substitute "Mom," "Dad," "Grandma," etc., as appropriate for "caregiver" throughout.

In the last month, how often has this happened?	Not at all	A little	Sometimes	A lot	All the time
1. My *caregiver* talks with me about my _____.	0	1	2	3	4
2. My *caregiver* tells me how he/she is feeling about my _____'s death (e.g., "I'm really missing _____ right now" or "I feel sad that _____ isn't here").	0	1	2	3	4
3. My *caregiver* shares his/her thoughts with me about _____'s death (e.g., "Things seem really different without _____ here" or "Sometimes it's hard to believe _____ is really gone").	0	1	2	3	4
4. My *caregiver* does things with me to help me remember my _____ (like looking together at photo albums, watching videos of _____ together, reading sympathy cards together, etc.).	0	1	2	3	4
5. My *caregiver* tries to help me get my mind off of my _____'s death when I start to get really upset about it (like telling me to read a book, to watch TV, or to do one of my hobbies; telling jokes; or changing the subject when my _____'s name comes up).	0	1	2	3	4
6. My *caregiver* cries about my _____ in front of me.	0	1	2	3	4

A PDF version of this handout is available for download on Cambridge Core and via www.cambridge.org/MGT

In the last month, how often has this happened?	Not at all	A little	Sometimes	A lot	All the time
7. My *caregiver* does his/her best to help me <u>understand the facts</u> about what it means to die (e.g., your heart stops beating, you can't feel any pain, you don't come back to life, etc.)	0	1	2	3	4
8. My *caregiver* encourages me to form <u>new relationships</u> with other adults or to start spending more time with other adults already in my life (like a friend's parent or a school counselor, relatives, or teachers or coaches at school).	0	1	2	3	4
9. My *caregiver* tries hard <u>not</u> to show how upset he/she is about my _____'s death.	0	1	2	3	4
10. My *caregiver* <u>tells me about good things</u> my _____ used to say or do, or important things that he/she accomplished.	0	1	2	3	4
11. My *caregiver* <u>shares good memories with me</u> about things that my _____ did with me.	0	1	2	3	4
12. My *caregiver* <u>shares comforting spiritual beliefs</u> with me about my _____ (like, _____ is in a better place now, like heaven or with God; _____ is watching over me; or I will see _____ again someday). What does your caregiver say that is most helpful to you? _____ _____	0	1	2	3	4
13. My *caregiver* does things with me to <u>help keep my _____'s memory alive</u> (like doing things that my _____ used to do or doing things that my _____ believed in, like donating to a charity in their memory).	0	1	2	3	4
14. My *caregiver* <u>tries not to mention</u> my _____'s name or his/her death.	0	1	2	3	4

In the last month, how often has this happened?	Not at all	A little	Sometimes	A lot	All the time
15. My *caregiver* encourages me to <u>talk</u> with him/her whenever I'm feeling sad or missing my _____.	0	1	2	3	4
16. My *caregiver* encourages me to <u>keep doing the things I liked to do before</u> my _____ died (like spending time with friends, playing games, doing after-school activities, etc.).	0	1	2	3	4
17. My *caregiver* encourages me to <u>talk</u> with him/her about parts of my _____'s <u>death</u> that upset me or are hard to think about (like things that made me angry, or were scary or gross).	0	1	2	3	4
18. My *caregiver* encourages me to <u>do things I really liked or admired</u> about my _____ (like picking up on some of my _____'s good habits or talents, standing up for things that my _____ really believed in, etc.).	0	1	2	3	4
19. My *caregiver* lets me know that even though my _____'s death is hard to handle, <u>good things</u> have still come into our lives because of the death (like learning important lessons about what really matters, learning how strong we are as a family, or learning good things about my _____).	0	1	2	3	4
20. My *caregiver* tells me <u>not to talk about how my</u> _____ <u>died</u> with people outside of my family.	0	1	2	3	4
21. My *caregiver* helps or encourages me to <u>do things that help me feel closer</u> to my _____ (like keeping a picture of him/her nearby, wearing something he/she used to wear, or lighting a candle).	0	1	2	3	4
22. My *caregiver* <u>does most things the same way we used to before</u> my _____ died (like eating the same kind of breakfast, waking up around the same time, getting ready for bed in the same way, etc.).	0	1	2	3	4

In the last month, how often has this happened?	Not at all	A little	Sometimes	A lot	All the time
23. My *caregiver* lets me know that he/she <u>doesn't believe</u> in God or heaven or an afterlife.	0	1	2	3	4
24. My *caregiver* lets me know that it's <u>not OK</u> to cry.	0	1	2	3	4
25. My *caregiver* encourages me to <u>do things that will help me have the kind of life that my</u> _____ <u>would want for me</u> (like doing my best in school, making good friends, making good choices, etc.)	0	1	2	3	4
26. My caregiver lets me know that he/she <u>isn't really the best person</u> to talk to about my _____'s death.	0	1	2	3	4
27. My *caregiver* <u>reminds me</u> of all the people in my life who care about me.	0	1	2	3	4
28. My *caregiver* tells me about some of the things my _____ did that <u>weren't so good</u> (like reminding me about some of my _____'s bad habits or bad decisions he/she made).	0	1	2	3	4
29. My *caregiver* lets me know there will <u>always</u> be someone around to take care of me.	0	1	2	3	4
30. My *caregiver* gives me hugs and kisses, cuddles me, tickles me, or wrestles with me in a <u>loving or caring</u> way.	0	1	2	3	4
31. My *caregiver* tells me everything that I want to know about what caused _____ to die (like what happened and the things that led up to it). What did your *caregiver* tell you about what caused _____ to die? _____ _____	0	1	2	3	4
32. My *caregiver* tells me he/she <u>loves</u> me.	0	1	2	3	4

In the last month, how often has this happened?	Not at all	A little	Sometimes	A lot	All the time
33. My *caregiver* lets me know that my _____ loved me.	0	1	2	3	4
34. My *caregiver* tells me about <u>good things I have in common</u> with my _____ (like his/her good looks, athletic ability, sense of humor, intelligence, etc.).	0	1	2	3	4
35. My *caregiver* starts to act <u>uncomfortable or strangely</u> when the topic of my _____'s death comes up.	0	1	2	3	4
36. My *caregiver* lets me know <u>I can still have a good life</u> even though my _____ has died (like I can still have a happy, successful, and normal life).	0	1	2	3	4

Rating Scale

How much of the time did it happen during the past month?

Directions: Below are five pictures of cups that show your different answer choices. For each question, point to the cup that shows how often you have had that thought or feeling in the last month.

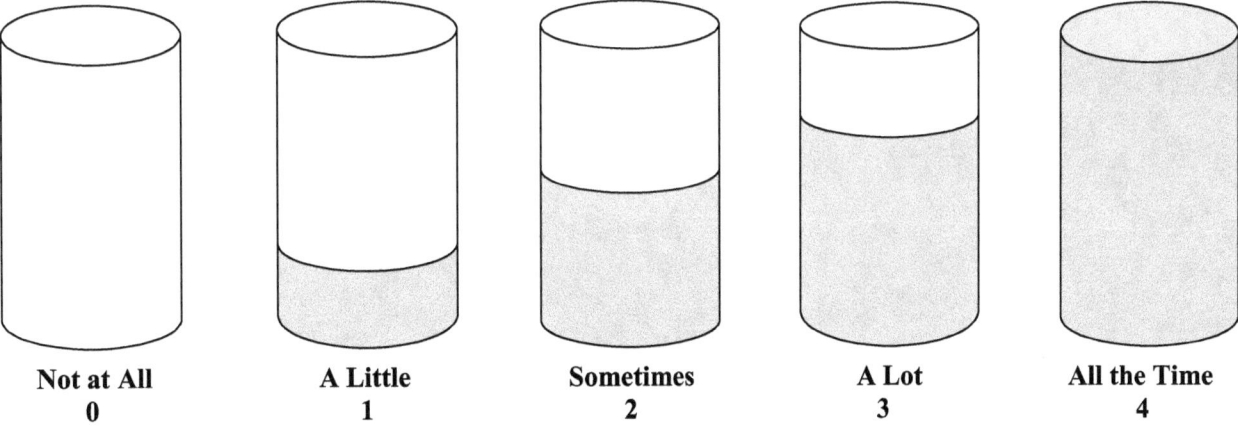

| Not at All | A Little | Sometimes | A Lot | All the Time |
| 0 | 1 | 2 | 3 | 4 |

Handout 4.2

What Helps Me Grieve

Directions: Using the results of the Grief Facilitation Inventory, write down the client's top five choices of caregiver behaviors that they feel are most helpful. Next, write down the client's top five choices of caregiver behaviors that make good grieving harder that they would like to have *more of* or *less of*. You can then use this worksheet to have an open discussion between the client and caregiver.

I Like It When:	I Wish I Could Change:
1.	1.
2.	2.
3.	3.
4.	4.
5.	5.

A PDF version of this handout is available for download on Cambridge Core and via www.cambridge.org/MGT

Handout 4.3

Parent/Caregiver Guidance

Guidelines for Parents and Caregivers: What to Say and Do to Help Your Child in Session and at Home

You may be called into a session with your child to review their work, practice skills learned, or share and discuss your own thoughts or feelings. Given that most children experience some concerns about talking with their parent or caregiver about the death (e.g., not wanting to upset them), how you respond in session can reduce some of this anxiety and increase the likelihood of more open communication at home. When you are also grieving, communicating with your child about the death and their experience can be even more challenging. For this reason, it can be helpful to prepare for these conversations ahead of time. Here are some tips (called the five Ss) that can be useful to remember, whether you are part of a therapy session or communicating with your child at home:

1. **Show that you are listening by normalizing and validating their experience.** If ever at a loss for words or caught off guard, statements such as "I can understand why you would feel that way," "I am so glad you felt comfortable sharing that with me," or (if true) "I feel/have felt the same way too" can help your child to feel heard and understood. Even nonverbal behaviors, like making good eye contact, leaning toward them, smiling at them, or nodding, can send the same important message. Another way to encourage open communication and create a comfortable environment is to allow them uninterrupted time to express their feelings and to praise your child's motivation in session with statements like "I am so proud of all of the work you have done here," "You have made such great progress," or "I know how challenging talking and sharing about this can be."

2. **Be sensitive to your individual child's unique needs.** Children express their grief in different ways. Some children may want to talk about their deceased loved one, and other children may not want to talk at all. Their individual needs may also change over time. The work we do in session can help to guide your child through their own grief process, but that can look different depending on what feels most comfortable to your child. Having an open door policy at home (e.g., "I'm here to listen whenever you want to talk") can provide a safe space for your child to share their feelings with you if/when they are ready to do so.

3. **Separate caregiver grief from child grief.** Caregivers often believe that their children have very similar grief reactions and grief-related needs as they do, but we have found that this is usually not the case. This assumption can lead to misunderstandings (i.e., what is helpful to the caregiver is also helpful to the child) or even conflict in families. For example, a caregiver may believe that their child wants to hold onto certain holiday traditions after a death, but the child may actually find those family traditions to be too painful. Accepting the different ways in which you and your child may be grieving can help to ease communication, whether in session or at home. At the same time, it is important to recognize when you may need support. Caregivers are often so worried about their children that they forget to care for themselves. Getting the support you need is just as critical as caring for your children.

4. **Keep it simple and straightforward.** Most children will have lots of questions about the events leading up to the death or the death itself, although they may not always feel comfortable asking those questions. Keeping language about the death simple and straightforward involves meeting children where they are, providing simple facts, and allowing them to guide the conversation whenever possible. Children are almost always aware of parent's attempts to hide important information about a death. Even when caregivers have the best of intentions by hiding certain

A PDF version of this handout is available for download on Cambridge Core and via www.cambridge.org/MGT

pieces of information, this can often do more harm than good, especially if the child is left to fill in the blanks with their imagination. Providing age-appropriate information about the death of a loved one is an important part of helping children grieve in adaptive ways. For example, you might say: "I always want to be open and honest with you. If you have questions about how _____ died, I will try my best to answer them honestly, and I will give you as much information as you need."

There may be times when you find yourself wanting to correct something your child says in session. For example, they may say something about the deceased person or about the way that they died that is factually incorrect. Before correcting them, ask yourself whether the information is important. Will the information be helpful to your child? If not, it's best to just let them continue with their story without interruption. On the other hand, if the information will be critical for helping your child to make sense or meaning of the death, you might say something like "I'm so glad we're talking about this because I have some more information that might be helpful for you to hear."

5. **Stay connected to the deceased.** One of the most important tasks for children who are grieving is to find healthy ways of feeling connected to the deceased. There are a number of things that caregivers can do to help with this process. Sharing stories about the person, looking at pictures, or doing an activity to honor their memory are wonderful ways for children to express their feelings and feel connected to their loved one. The following are examples of what you might say to initiate these actions:

- *Is there anything you would like to do on the day _____ died/on their birthday/on special holidays?*
- *There is a special walk to support _____. Would you be interested in walking in honor of _____? If not, that is okay too.*
- *I have been going through some of _____ things. Is there anything of his/hers you might want to keep for yourself?*

One of the most challenging yet most rewarding things that you can do to help your grieving child is to be fully present. This means listening with an open heart and open mind and letting them know that you're there whenever they need you.

Handout 4.4

The Good Grief Game

Directions: The clinician should ask the parent and child to sit across from each other. Each should have a notepad and pencil/pen. The clinician should ask them each to write their answers to the following questions (one by one, read aloud by the clinician) on the notepad and then share with each other after each question. The clinician does not have to use all of the questions below. They can choose the questions that may be the most relevant/helpful.

- Name three good things the child has in common with _____ (person who died). These can be positive behaviors, habits, things they enjoy doing, how they look, etc.
- What was the child's favorite thing to do with _____ (person who died)?
- What did _____ (person who died) love about the child?
- What advice would _____ (person who died) give the child if he/she was feeling down or sad?
- What was _____'s (person who died) favorite memory of the child?
- What was _____ (person who died) most proud of about the child?
- What things did _____ (person who died) think the child was most good at?
- What did _____ (person who died) think the child would be when he/she grows up?

A PDF version of this handout is available for download on Cambridge Core and via www.cambridge.org/MGT

MGT Session

5 Understanding Loss Reminders and Trauma Reminders

What Reminds Me That They're No Longer Here or about How They Died?

Session Objectives

Increase the client's ability:

1. To understand loss reminders and trauma reminders
2. To identify their own personal loss reminders and trauma reminders
3. To understand the ways in which specific loss reminders and trauma reminders affect the way they grieve and adjust to a death
4. To cope with different types of reminders, including anticipating reminders, learning to regulate intense emotions, and taking proactive steps to remove or reduce certain unhelpful reminders

Section Number	Session Overview
1	Check In with Grief Thermometers
2	What Are Reminders?
3	Introduction to Reminders (loss reminders and trauma reminders)
4	Learning about My Loss Reminders and Trauma Reminders
5	Activity 1: Reminders Card Sorting Game
6	Activity 2: My Reminders
7	Activity 3: Coping with Reminders
8	Activity 4: Sharing with Caregiver
9	Assign Practice Exercise: My Coping Toolkit
10	Check Out

Session Materials

- Rating My Grief Reactions (Handout 1.3)
- Reminders Card Sorting Game (Handout 5.1)
- Reminders Assessment Tool (Handout 5.2)
- My Reminders (Handout 5.3)
- My Coping Toolkit (Handout 5.4)

1 Check In with Grief Thermometers

Have the child complete Rating My Grief Reactions (Handout 1.3) and explore current ratings of grief reactions. Sample prompts include the following:

- *How are you feeling on your grief thermometers?*
- *How did your grief thermometers change from last week?*
- *How did you feel those changes during the week?*

Additional check-in prompts as appropriate:

- *Did anything happen since we saw each other last that you feel good about?*
- *Was there anything we talked about in our last session that you thought about this week or that "stuck" with you?*
- *Is anything going on that may make it hard for you to focus during our session today?*

2 What Are Reminders?

Cover the general points below in your own words.

Sometimes, it may feel as though we don't have any control over how or when we start to really miss our person. For example, sometimes memories or thoughts of the person just seem to pop into our heads and make us really wish they were there with us. Sometimes we may be reminded of the way the person died and feel really sad or angry.

Although these thoughts and feelings may seem like they come up suddenly or out of the blue, they are often pretty easy to understand or predict. This brings us to the topic of reminders. Understanding what reminders are and how they work can help us to make sense of why we react to certain situations the way we do, such as feeling sad, angry, lost, or lonely. Learning what our personal reminders are and how we react to them not only helps us to understand ourselves and our reactions better. It can also help us to predict when reminders will come up and prepare to deal with them. Being aware and prepared will help us to gain more control over how we think, feel, and behave.

3 Introduction to Reminders (loss reminders and trauma reminders)

To create an entry point to discussing loss and trauma reminders, you can simply ask your client whether they notice any specific times or situations during which they tend to experience grief-related feelings or have thoughts about their person. Most youth are able to describe common situations, such as specific times of the day, activities or settings associated with the person, and so forth. In the process of normalizing and validating these experiences, you can begin to provide psychoeducation about what loss reminders and trauma reminders are and how they work.

Cover the general points below in your own words.

Today, we will talk about two types of reminders – loss reminders and trauma reminders.

What Are Loss Reminders?

Anyone who has experienced the death of a loved one will be faced with loss reminders, no matter how that person died – even a peaceful death at an old age.

Loss reminders are people, places, things, sounds, tastes, smells, or situations that remind us that our person is no longer with us physically. Loss reminders can bring up difficult feelings like sadness, really missing our person, or wanting more than anything to be with our person. Loss reminders can be **things outside of you:**

- *A person (someone who looks like the person who died)*
- *A place (their favorite restaurant)*
- *A thing (the chair they used to always sit in)*
- *A sound (someone's laugh that sounds like your person's laugh)*
- *A taste (the apple pie they used to make)*
- *A smell (the smell of your person's perfume or shampoo)*
- *A situation (things you used to enjoy doing with your person)*
- *A specific time/date (when you wish your person was there with you, e.g. your birthday)*

Loss reminders can also be **things inside of you:**

- *Something you feel inside your body (when your person was usually there with you to help you, e.g. butterflies on the first day of school)*
- *An emotion or feeling (especially if those emotions remind you of happy memories of your person, e.g. excitement or even joy)*
- *A thought (wondering what your person would say in a certain situation)*

Loss reminders can also be about **how things have changed since your person's death.** *These reminders of how things have changed can be things you don't necessarily like. For example:*

- *Worries about money or a parent getting a new job*
- *Being separated from friends*
- *Living with a parent or caregiver who is gone a lot more or is having a hard time*

But they can also be things you don't mind or that are even helpful. They just remind you that things have changed because your loved one has died. For example:

- *Moving to a new place*
- *Starting a new school*
- *Making new friends*

Something important to know about loss reminders is that even if they are painful now, they can become easier to cope with as time goes on and may even become comforting. For example, a song on the radio, your person's belongings, or their favorite chair can bring up strong feelings of sadness at first. But over time, these loss reminders can remind us of them in comforting and even enjoyable ways, like remembering fun times with the person or things the person did that made you laugh.

What Are Trauma Reminders?

It is important to understand what trauma reminders are, especially if your loved one died in a very upsetting or scary way. Similar to loss reminders, trauma reminders can also be people, places, things, sounds, tastes, smells, or situations, but instead of reminding us that our person is no longer with us, they remind us of the WAY the person died. Trauma reminders can bring up difficult memories or feelings about our person's death like fear, guilt, or anger. Trauma reminders can be **things outside of you:**

- *A person (someone who told you that your loved one had died)*
- *A place (the place where they died)*
- *A thing (the shirt they were wearing at the time of their death)*
- *A sound (the sound of a gunshot or fireworks)*
- *A taste (what you were eating for dinner on the night they died)*
- *A smell (the smell of a hospital or ambulance)*
- *A situation (a look of fear or distress on your parent's face)*

Understanding Loss Reminders and Trauma Reminders

- *A specific time/date (the anniversary of the person's death)*

*Trauma reminders can also be **things inside of you** that feel similar to how you felt when your person died:*

- *A physical sensation that you feel inside your body (like your heart pounding or butterflies in your stomach – similar to how you felt at the time)*
- *An emotion or feeling (like feeling scared or anxious, or any other emotions you felt around the time your person died)*
- *A thought (like thinking about what they looked like right before they died)*

People whose loved ones died in very upsetting or scary ways can experience both loss reminders and trauma reminders. This is because they are not only reminded that their loved one is no longer with them physically, but they can also be reminded of how their loved one died. Dealing with both loss reminders and trauma reminders all at once is one reason why having a loved one die in a very scary or upsetting way can make it more difficult to grieve and requires extra support, like what we are doing now.

4 Learning about My Loss Reminders and Trauma Reminders

5 Activity 1 Reminders Card Sorting Game

Purpose:

- To help clients identify and gain understanding of their personal loss reminders and trauma reminders

Materials: The Reminders Card Sorting game (Handout 5.1).

Directions: Using the Reminders Card Sorting game, cut the different loss reminders and trauma reminders into squares.

- Remind the client of the definition of loss reminders: Things that remind us that the person is no longer physically with us in our lives.
- Start with the loss reminder cards by having the client sort the loss reminders cards into "Yes" or "No" piles, meaning "Yes, this is a loss reminder for me" or "No, this is not a loss reminder for me."
- Identify and label the client's own personal loss reminders, how often and where they encounter them.
- Explore and label the types of feelings they have when they encounter a loss reminder (e.g., separation distress) (look for both distressing and comforting grief reactions – loss reminders can evoke both types)
- Explore how they usually cope with their reactions to loss reminders – what do they do?
- Remind the client of the definition of trauma reminders: Things that remind us of the very upsetting or terrifying way that the person died.
- Next, as appropriate (if the way the person died may be a significant source of distress), have the client sort the trauma reminders cards into "Yes" or "No" piles, meaning "Yes, this is a trauma reminder for me" or "No, this is not a trauma reminder for me."
- Identify and label the client's own personal trauma reminders, and how often and where they encounter them.
- Explore and label the types of feelings they have when they encounter a trauma reminder (look for circumstance-related distress, PTSD)
- Explore how they usually cope with their reactions to trauma reminders – what do they do?

Optional for Adolescents: Instead of using the Card Sorting Activity, have the client complete the Reminders Assessment Tool (see Handout 5.2). This can be administered as more of a semi-structured clinical interview, rather than having the client just complete the measure without any discussion. This can be used as an opportunity to take a "deeper dive" into the client's personal loss reminders and trauma reminders, especially their frequency and intensity.

6 Activity 2 My Reminders

Purpose:

- To identify the client's "top five" loss reminders (reminders of the physical absence of the person) and trauma reminders (reminders of the upsetting way in which the person died). These should represent the reminders that typically cause the client the most distress.
- To share this information with the caregiver, as appropriate.

Materials: My Reminders worksheet (Handout 5.3).

Directions: Have the client identify their top five loss reminders and, if appropriate, top five trauma reminders, based on the results of Activity 1. Use this as an opportunity to talk about the importance of identifying loss reminders and trauma reminders as a way of predicting how the client might react in certain situations. After completing the worksheet, you can ask the client what they feel comfortable sharing with their caregiver. Note that sometimes caregivers may not even be aware of specific loss or trauma reminders that the client is encountering at home that make it harder to grieve in ways that feel comforting and helpful. If the client doesn't feel comfortable sharing all of the information on the worksheet, you can ask if they might want to share just one or two of the reminders listed. They may even be most comfortable with you sharing the activity while they are in the room.

As part of this exercise, you can encourage the client to write down two loss reminders that may be helpful or comforting and add those two pieces of paper to their Good Grief Jar. This provides them with additional coping tools/strategies that they can call upon when needed.

7 Activity 3 Coping with Reminders

Purpose:

- To identify coping strategies that the client can use when encountering painful loss or trauma reminders
- To share this information with the caregiver, as appropriate

Directions: You can use each of the coping strategies below as points of discussion by asking questions about each strategy. For example, is this something they have tried before? Has it worked? Can they envision using this coping strategy? You do not have to review each and every strategy (this list is simply meant to provide different options based on the needs and strengths of individual clients): simply choose those that you think may resonate the most with your client.

You can describe this activity by stating: *"When we are faced with a loss reminder or trauma reminder and begin to feel upset, there are a number of things we can do to help ourselves feel calmer and in control. To begin, what are some things you do to make yourself feel better when you are reminded of your person or the way that they died?"*

Praise any proactive coping strategies they describe. If they list some potentially maladaptive or unhelpful coping strategies, comment that some strategies can be more helpful than others, and that you can review these at a later time. But for now, you can build on their positive coping skills by considering some potential new ones. Then, introduce techniques (listed below) they are not already using that may be helpful to them. You can say: *"You've done a great job identifying some strategies that are helpful to you. Maybe we can review some more coping strategies together that you may not have used before, so you have a good set of tools to use when you're facing painful reminders."*

1. Breathing Exercises and/or Physical Activity

First, it is important to understand that when our bodies are relaxed, it is practically impossible for our minds to be stressed. That's why some of the best ways to cope with loss or trauma reminders involve exercises that we can do to relax our bodies.

For younger children: It can be helpful to have them place a stuffed animal on their stomach and watch the stuffed animal rise and fall as they breathe in and out. Use this as an opportunity to discuss how their body may feel different or more relaxed when they change their breathing (e.g., how can they make the stuffed animal rise and fall more slowly?).

Another breathing exercise that can be used with younger children is the chocolate chip cookie breathing exercise. Have the client pretend that they are holding a fresh-out-of-the-oven chocolate chip cookie and imagine that they are smelling the cookie (breathing in through their nose), followed by blowing on the cookie to cool it off (blowing out through their mouth).

You can also instruct your client to pretend to be an "uncooked noodle" (standing up straight and tall) versus a "cooked noodle" (with all muscles relaxed and loose). Ask them to describe what their body feels like under both conditions. Which "noodle" helps them to feel more relaxed?

For adolescents: There are a number of breathing techniques that can help to relax the body and regulate emotions. One technique is the 4, 7, 8 breathing exercise. This involves breathing in through your nose for the count of four, holding that breath for the count of seven, and then blowing out through your mouth for the count of eight. You can practice this together to demonstrate. Research shows that this particular technique can slow down heart rate and lower blood pressure, creating a calming sensation.

Other activities that can help to reduce distress in response to loss reminders or trauma reminders include exercise, yoga, dancing, sports, or singing.

2. Calming Self-Talk

Introduce the idea of calming self-talk by covering the points below in your own words.

Sometimes it can help to have statements that we say to ourselves that can calm us down when we are facing an upsetting reminder. The following are some examples of calming self-talk:

- *"I can get through this."*
- *"This feeling won't last forever."*
- *"These are just thoughts – I can let them go."*
- *"I'm safe now."*
- *"I know I'm going to be OK."*

If the client describes being reminded of past events by trauma reminders (e.g., "Hearing people screaming makes me think of that night he died"), then calming self-talk focusing on contextual discrimination (distinguishing between the past event and the present reminder) may also help to calm them down:

- *"That was then, this is now."*
- *"What's the same?"* (Identify what is the same between the past event and the current reminder, so they can understand what is happening and why. They can then reassure themselves by saying: "Of course I get upset when I'm reminded of that night. It was a terrible night.").
- *"What's different?"* (Identify three to five things in the present situation that are different than the traumatic situation – different time, different place, different people, etc.). They can then use these to help bring themselves back to the present and focus on the "here and now."

Have the client write down one or two phrases that can help them when they feel overwhelmed or upset by reminders.

3. Prepare for Loss Reminders and/or Trauma Reminders

Once clients can identify and understand their own personal reminders, they can better prepare for situations in which these reminders are unavoidable (e.g., family reunions, the anniversary of their loved one's death, graduation, etc.). Have your client plan ahead by noting what they can do in those situations to help themselves, whether it's reaching out to a friend ahead of time, memorializing their person that day in their own special way, or coping strategies that they find most helpful (e.g., listening to music, going for a walk).

4. Connect with Friends or Family

Social support is one of the most powerful protective factors for youth in the aftermath of a loss. Even if it is just knowing who they can call if they need a listening ear or someone to validate their experience, you can help your client to create a list of the people they can turn to for support. Different people may serve as a support person in different ways. For example, is there someone in their life who is a really good listener? What about someone who can distract them and make them laugh? Or someone who knew their loved one really well, who could share positive memories with them? This is also a list that they can keep in their Good Grief Jar, so they can remember just how many people in their life care about them and are there to support them.

5. Engage in Fun Activities

What are some of the things your client enjoys doing the most? You can help them to create a list of fun, healthy, and safe activities that can help to lift their spirits when faced with loss or trauma reminders. These can include physical activities (walking outside, playing basketball, riding a bike, dancing) or quiet, peaceful activities like listening to music, reading a book, or watching their favorite movie.

6. Write in a Journal

Evidence suggests that writing about painful experiences can have a powerful healing effect, in that it can reduce symptoms of posttraumatic stress and depression. You can have your client create a journal that they can use to describe how they are feeling each day, memories that they have of their person, things they are grateful for, or even potential loss and/or trauma reminders that they encountered that day and how they were able to cope with them. This journal should not be seen as work; rather it should be used as another outlet to process their feelings and to learn how to cope with distressing situations.

8 Activity 4 Sharing with the Caregiver (optional)

Purpose:

- To facilitate a discussion with the caregiver(s) regarding loss or trauma reminders that the client may be encountering and about coping strategies that the client feels are most helpful
- To positively reinforce and encourage ongoing, open communication between the child and caregiver(s)

Materials: My Reminders worksheet (completed during Activity 2).

Directions: As with last week's activity, prior to including the caregiver in this session, it will be important to understand the caregiver's own capacity to provide support to the client and offer positive reinforcement. It may be helpful to meet briefly with the caregiver prior to the session to help them understand the purpose of this activity: to better understand the loss and trauma reminders that may lead to distress in their child (see Chapter 4 for a more detailed explanation of how to work with caregivers prior to joint sessions). This is important information for the caregiver to understand, as they may not be attuned to the fact that the client may be encountering certain personal reminders regularly, which can result in emotional and/or behavioral dysregulation (e.g., "acting out," avoidance, tearfulness, etc.). This can lead to important discussions about what caregivers can do at home to either reduce or eliminate reminders that feel "unhelpful" in the environment. You may want to provide the caregiver with specific statements they can make during the activity to show their support (e.g., "I'm so glad you're sharing this with me"; "It really helps me to know what reminders you're experiencing at home"; "I'm proud of how much you've been able to tell me – I know this is hard to talk about").

When you have both the caregiver(s) and child together in the room, you can introduce this activity by saying: *As we talked about last week, just as people grieve in different ways, people in the same family can have different loss reminders (things that remind them of the person's absence) or trauma reminders (things that remind them of the way their person died). We also know that some reminders that feel helpful or comforting to one family member can feel not so helpful to another family member. This exercise is designed to help caregivers better understand their child's own personal loss and trauma reminders, and different coping strategies that their child has identified as most helpful when they're faced with those reminders at home or elsewhere.*

At this point, you can guide the client and review the My Reminders worksheet with the caregiver. After reviewing the worksheet, you can ask the client what it felt like to share that information with the caregiver, and likewise, what it was like for the caregiver to receive the information. You can also ask the caregiver if there were any reminders that they were unaware of and if there are things they can do as a family to help reduce distressing reminders and identify potentially helpful or positive reminders.

9 Assign Practice Exercise: My Coping Toolkit

Introduce My Coping toolkit (Handout 5.4).

10 Check Out

- *How are you feeling now?* (Use feelings thermometer rating)
- *What did you learn about yourself today?* (For example, identifying positive loss reminders, support people, or positive memories)

End of Session

Handout 5.1

Reminders Card Sorting Game

Potential Loss Reminders

Hearing _____'s name

Certain dates or times of the year (anniversaries, birthdays, etc.)

Certain smells, sounds, or tastes

_____'s belongings

Pictures or videos of _____

Activities we used to do together

Things that _____ used to do (their job, hobbies, etc.)

Seeing someone who looks like _____

Happy or special times that you want to share with _____

Hard times when you want to turn to _____ for support

Places where _____ used to be

Seeing or being with ____'s family or friends

Being around family members or social gatherings

Other things that remind you ____ is not here physically

Potential Trauma Reminders

The place where _____ died

People who were there when it happened

People who told you about the death

Certain smells or tastes

Certain sounds (alarms, loud noises, etc.)

Things connected to how you learned about the death (phone, news, etc.)

Emergency workers (ambulances, firefighters, etc.)

Certain dates or times of the year (anniversaries, birthdays, etc.)

Things connected to the military (medals, uniforms, rifles, etc.)

Videos or movies that remind you of the way _____ died

Things connected to law enforcement (police, sirens, etc.)

Things connected to medicine (pills, hospitals, equipment, etc.) or things _____ needed when they were sick

Symbols/pictures of organizations that focus on the way _____ died

Other things that remind you about the way _____ died

Handout 5.2

Reminders Assessment Tool

Loss Reminders: *Now I'd like to ask you about things that may be on your mind because they keep reminding you of _____ or that _____ is <u>no longer physically here</u>. These may be reminders for some people, but not others. Remember that these are only suggestions and that there are no right or wrong answers.*

In the last month, how often has this happened?	Not at all	A little	Sometimes	A lot	All the time
1. Hearing _____'s name ☐ N/A					
1a. How much does this reminder make you feel happy, comforted, or grateful for the good times you had with _____?	0	1	2	3	4
1b. How much does this reminder make you feel sad, angry, lonely, or very upset that _____ isn't here (physically) any more?	0	1	2	3	4
2. Certain smells or sounds (like the smell of _____'s perfume or a type of food he/she used to make, hearing an instrument _____ used to play, etc.) ☐ N/A					
2a. How much does this reminder make you feel happy, comforted, or grateful for the good times you had with _____?	0	1	2	3	4
2b. How much does this reminder make you feel sad, angry, lonely, or very upset that _____ isn't here (physically) any more?	0	1	2	3	4
3. _____'s belongings (like clothes, hats, books, tools, jewelry) ☐ N/A					
3a. How much does this reminder make you feel happy, comforted, or grateful for the good times you had with _____?	0	1	2	3	4
3b. How much does this reminder make you feel sad, angry, lonely, or very upset that _____ isn't here (physically) any more?	0	1	2	3	4
4. Pictures or videotapes of _____ ☐ N/A					
4a. How much does this reminder make you feel happy, comforted, or grateful for the good times you had with _____?	0	1	2	3	4
4b. How much does this reminder make you feel sad, angry, lonely, or very upset that _____ isn't here (physically) any more?	0	1	2	3	4
5. Activities or things that _____ used to do (like his/her work, hobbies, favorite food, or favorite music) ☐ N/A					
5a. How much does this reminder make you feel happy, comforted, or grateful for the good times you had with _____?	0	1	2	3	4
5b. How much does this reminder make you feel sad, angry, lonely, or very upset that _____ isn't here (physically) any more?	0	1	2	3	4

A PDF version of this handout is available for download on Cambridge Core and via www.cambridge.org/MGT

6. Seeing someone who looks like _____ ☐ N/A					
6a. How much does this reminder make you feel happy, comforted, or grateful for the good times you had with _____?	0	1	2	3	4
6b. How much does this reminder make you feel sad, angry, lonely, or very upset that _____ isn't here (physically) any more?	0	1	2	3	4
7. Happy times that you want to share with _____. ☐ N/A					
7a. How much does this reminder make you feel happy, comforted, or grateful for the good times you had with _____?	0	1	2	3	4
7b. How much does this reminder make you feel sad, angry, lonely, or very upset that _____ isn't here (physically) any more?	0	1	2	3	4
8. Hard times when you want to turn to _____ for support ☐ N/A					
8a. How much does this reminder make you feel happy, comforted, or grateful for the good times you had with _____?	0	1	2	3	4
8b. How much does this reminder make you feel sad, angry, lonely, or very upset that _____ isn't here (physically) any more?	0	1	2	3	4
9. Places _____ used to be in (like their bedroom, favorite chair, chair at the kitchen table, home office, or other places they used to hang out in) ☐ N/A					
9a. How much does this reminder make you feel happy, comforted, or grateful for the good times you had with _____?	0	1	2	3	4
9b. How much does this reminder make you feel sad, angry, lonely, or very upset that _____ isn't here (physically) any more?	0	1	2	3	4
10. Seeing or being with _____'s family or friends ☐ N/A					
10a. How much does this reminder make you feel happy, comforted, or grateful for the good times you had with _____?	0	1	2	3	4
10b. How much does this reminder make you feel sad, angry, lonely, or very upset that _____ isn't here (physically) any more?	0	1	2	3	4
11. Family or social gatherings (like mealtimes, parties, weddings, or holidays) ☐ N/A					
11a. How much does this reminder make you feel happy, comforted, or grateful for the good times you had with _____?	0	1	2	3	4
11b. How much does this reminder make you feel sad, angry, lonely, or very upset that _____ isn't here (physically) any more?	0	1	2	3	4

12. Are there other things I have not mentioned that remind you that _____ is no longer here physically? If yes, can you tell me what those things are? ☐ N/A		

12a. How much does this reminder make you feel happy, comforted, or grateful for the good times you had with _____?	0	1	2	3	4
12b. How much does this reminder make you feel sad, angry, lonely, or very upset that _____ isn't here (physically) any more?	0	1	2	3	4

Note: Only ask the child the next set of questions if he/she is able to describe <u>how</u> the person died (even if it's only a guess)

Trauma Reminders: *Next I'd like to ask you about things that may still bother you or be on your mind because they keep reminding you of <u>the way</u> that _____ died. Just like before, these may be reminders for some people, but not others. How much does each of these things <u>make you feel sad, afraid, or upset</u>?* (Interviewer should specify the exact cause of the person's death)

In the last month, how much does this make you feel sad, afraid, or upset?	Not at all	A little	Sometimes	A lot	All the time
13. The <u>place</u> where _____ died	0	1	2	3	4
14. Certain <u>smells or sounds</u> (like the smell of the hospital, the sound of an ambulance, or the sound of someone screaming)	0	1	2	3	4
15. <u>Emergency workers</u> (seeing ambulance workers, firefighters, doctors, nurses, or police)	0	1	2	3	4
16. <u>Videos or movies</u> that show the way _____ died (like a movie about someone who dies in a car accident, a documentary about someone having cancer, a film shown in school about what happens when someone has a heart attack, etc.)	0	1	2	3	4
17. <u>Symbols or pictures of organizations</u> that focus on the way _____ died (like a pink ribbon for breast cancer, the American flag for a military death, etc.)	0	1	2	3	4
18. <u>Medical equipment, medication</u> (like pill bottles), or things _____ needed when he/she was getting treatment (like a wig, a walker, or a wheelchair)	0	1	2	3	4
19. The same type of <u>objects or things or events</u> that caused _____ to die (e.g., a gun, pills, a car accident, etc.)	0	1	2	3	4

20. Are there <u>other things</u> that remind you of the <u>way</u> that _____ died that I have not mentioned? If yes, can you tell me what those things are? _____ _____ 20a. *(If the child provides a response to 20, then ask)* Please pick the one thing that makes you the most upset about the way _____ died and tell me <u>how much</u> it makes you upset. What is it? *(describe):* _____ _____ _____	0	1	2	3	4
21. Was there <u>media coverage</u> of _____'s death (like a <u>news story</u> on TV, the radio, in the newspaper, internet, etc.)? *(Interviewer circles "Yes" or "No")* **Yes** **No** If yes, continue to 21a. If no, go to 22. 21a. How much did this make you feel sad, afraid, or upset about _____'s death? *(choose a number)*	0	1	2	3	4
22. After _____ died, did you <u>see or hear people</u> making mean comments about _____ or their death (like hearing classmates or neighbors gossip about the way _____ died, seeing mean or hurtful postings about _____'s death on Facebook, or having people say mean things about _____ to your face)? *(Interviewer circles "Yes" or "No")* **Yes** **No** If yes, continue to 22a and 22b. If no, go to 23. 22a. Please describe: _____					
22b. How much did this make you feel sad, afraid, or upset? *(record number on the scale)*	0	1	2	3	4
23. After _____ died, did you <u>see or hear people</u> saying unkind or mean things about <u>you</u> or how you're handling _____'s death (like hearing classmates or friends say that you're "just trying to get attention" or "being too sensitive")? *(Interviewer circles "Yes" or "No")* **Yes** **No** If yes, continue to 23a and 23b. 23a. Please describe: _____					
23b. How much did this make you feel sad, afraid, or upset? *(record number on the scale)*	0	1	2	3	4

Handout 5.3

My Reminders

My Loss Reminders
(Things that remind me my person is gone)

1.

　　　+　 −

2.

　　　+　 −

3.

　　　+　 −

4.

　　　+　 −

5.

　　　+　 −

Note: Have child circle whether the loss reminder results in positive (happy) feelings or negative (sad) feelings.

My Trauma Reminders
(Things that remind me of the way my person died)

1.

2.

3.

4.

5.

A PDF version of this handout is available for download on Cambridge Core and via www.cambridge.org/MGT

Handout 5.4

My Coping Toolkit

During this session we talked about loss reminders and trauma reminders and how they can affect us. We also talked about different coping strategies we can use to help us when we are faced with our own personal reminders.

Directions: Pick one time this week when you faced a loss reminder or trauma reminder. What was it and how did it make you feel?

_____
_____
_____
_____

Using the table below, place a checkmark next to the coping strategy that you used when faced with a loss or trauma reminder this week. Next, rate how helpful that coping strategy was on a scale from 0 (not at all helpful) to 3 (very helpful).

Coping Strategy	Used	0 = Not at all helpful	1 = A little bit helpful	2 = Pretty helpful	3 = Very helpful
Breathing Exercises					
Calming Self-Talk					
Preparing for Loss or Trauma Reminders					
Connecting with Friends or Family					
Doing Fun Activities					
Writing in a Journal					
Other					

A PDF version of this handout is available for download on Cambridge Core and via www.cambridge.org/MGT

MGT Session

6 Sizing Up a Situation

How Can Our Thoughts Change the Way We Feel or Act?

Session Objectives

Increase the client's ability:

1. To distinguish between situations, thoughts, feelings, and behaviors
2. To understand links between situations, thoughts, feelings, and behaviors
3. To understand how situations involving loss or trauma reminders can lead to specific bereavement-related thoughts, feelings, or behaviors
4. To identify their own helpful or hurtful thoughts and ways to manage them

Section Number	Session Overview
1	Check In with Grief Thermometers
2	Review Practice Exercise from Last Week
3	What Are Thoughts, Feelings, and Behaviors?
4	Activity 1: Sizing Up a Situation Card Game
5	Activity 2: Practice Sizing Up a Situation
6	Activity 3: Helping Out a Friend Exercise
7	Assign Practice Exercise
8	Check Out

Session Materials

- Rating My Grief Reactions (Handout 1.3)
- Sizing Up a Situation (Handout 6.1)
- Sizing Up a Situation card game (Handout 6.2)
- Situation, Thoughts, Feelings, and Behaviors (STFB) (Handout 6.3)
- Illustrations 1–3 (Handouts 6.4, 6.5, and 6.6)
- Sketches (for the Helping Out a Friend exercise), Situations 1–15

1 Check In with Grief Thermometers

Have the client complete Rating My Grief Reactions (Handout 1.3) and explore current ratings of grief reactions. Sample prompts include the following:

- *How are you feeling on your grief thermometers?*
- *How did your grief thermometers change from last week?*
- *How did you feel those changes during the week?*

Additional check-in prompts as appropriate:

- *Did anything happen since we saw each other last that you feel good about?*
- *Was there anything we talked about in our last session that you thought about this week or that stuck with you?*
- *Is anything going on that may make it hard for you to focus during our session today?*

2 Review Practice Exercise from Last Week

- Last week we learned about loss reminders, trauma reminders, and coping strategies we can use to help us feel better.

Using the My Coping Toolkit from last week, ask the following questions:

- Were you able to identify a loss or trauma reminder? Can you describe it for me?
- What coping strategy did you use to handle it?
- Do you think that particular strategy was helpful? Why or why not?
- Would you do the same thing next time? If not, what might you do differently?

3 What Are Thoughts, Feelings, and Behaviors?

Cover the general points below in your own words. Refer to Figure 6.1, as needed.

*Today we are going to talk about how **thoughts** change what you **feel**, and then what you **do**. What we think about can make us feel a certain way. For example, if you think about a bright sunny day, or your favorite dessert, or your favorite color, how does that make you feel? Just like certain thoughts can make us feel happy or excited, other thoughts can make us feel sad or angry, like thoughts about a sad movie or a friend who may have done something hurtful. It's also important to know that how we feel can make us act in certain ways. For example, if we're thinking about something that makes us feel happy, we might smile or laugh. Sad or angry feelings can make us act in certain ways too, like they can make us cry, or yell, or go into our rooms and not talk to anyone. The important thing to remember is that we have the power to control our thoughts. And by controlling our thoughts, we can also control how we feel and how we act.*

Before we talk about how to control our own thoughts, first we need to make sure we understand the differences between situations, thoughts, feelings, and behaviors.

What is a situation? (Have the client generate ideas about what a "situation" is.)

A situation is something that happens to us or something that is going on around us.

What is a thought? (Have the client generate ideas about what a "thought" is.)

A thought is an idea that comes up in our mind or something we tell ourselves. Sometimes a thought might just pop into our head because of a reminder, or we might spend a lot of time thinking about something on purpose, like when we're trying to solve a problem or because something is really bothering us. People talk to themselves (in their thoughts) all day. Do you ever catch yourself doing that? Everybody does it, but most of the time we don't even know we are doing it.

What is a feeling? (Have the client generate ideas about what a "feeling" is.)

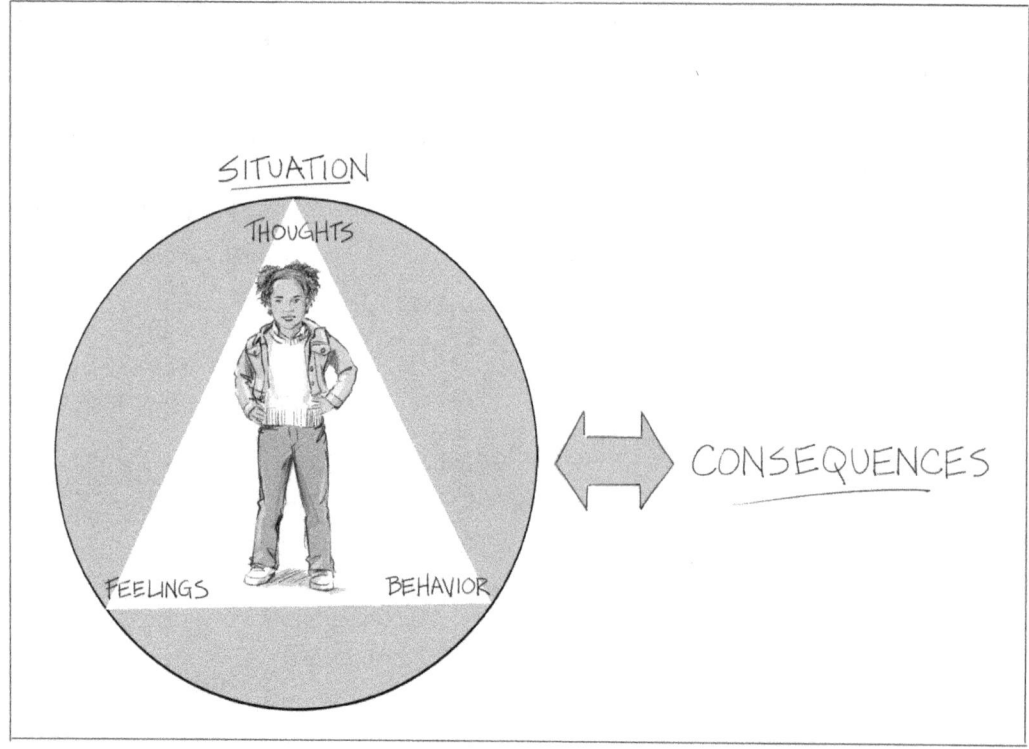

Figure 6.1 Sizing Up a Situation

A feeling or emotion is a reaction to a thought. Most emotions can be felt in our body, like our heart racing if we're nervous, or feeling light on our feet if we are happy. Unlike thoughts, feelings can usually be described in just one word (e.g., happy, sad, scared, excited).

What is a behavior? (Have the client generate ideas about what a "behavior" is.)

A behavior is the way that we act or what we do, usually because of a feeling we're having.

Let's practice sorting out the differences between situations, thoughts, feelings, and our own behaviors using a game.

4 Activity 1 Sizing Up a Situation Card Game

Purpose:

- To help clients distinguish between situations, thoughts, feelings, and behaviors

Materials: Sizing up a Situation card game (Handout 6.2).

Directions: Using the Sizing Up a Situation card game, cut the different items into separate squares. On four different pieces of paper, write the words, "Situation," "Thought," "Feeling," and "Behavior." Introduce this activity by saying: *"Sometimes it can get tricky figuring out if something is a thought or a feeling. Similarly, it can be hard to know the difference between a behavior and a situation. This card game will help us to better understand those differences."*

- Ask the client to choose a card and place it on the paper that shows the correct category.
- You can continue to do this with each card.
- For cards that seem to be more challenging, have a discussion about what makes that particular card tricky.

Optional for Adolescents: Instead of using the Sizing Up a Situation card game, you can just use the Situation-Thought-Feeling-Behavior Quiz (see below) by reading each item out loud and asking the client to identify which category it belongs in.

Situation-Thought-Feeling-Behavior Quiz
S = Situation; T = Thought; F = Feeling; B = Behavior

1.	Irritated	F
2.	Someone knocks at the door	S
3.	You work hard on homework	B
4.	I can't do it	T
5.	Frustrated	F
6.	You hit someone	B
7.	I've got to get even	T
8.	Someone hits you	S
9.	A teacher yells at you	S
10.	Scared	F
11.	A police car passes by with a siren	S
12.	I'll always be alone	T
13.	Surprised	F
14.	I can do it	T
15.	It's my fault	T
16.	My sister is the favorite	T
17.	A teacher praises you	S
18.	You yell at someone	B
19.	Things will never get better	T
20.	You share a treat with someone	B
21.	Happy	F

5 Activity 2 Practice Sizing Up a Situation

Purpose:

- To help clients to better understand links between situations, thoughts, feelings, and behaviors

Materials: STFB handout (Handout 6.3) and Illustrations 1–3 (Handouts 6.4, 6.5, and 6.6).

Directions: Using the STFB handout (Handout 6.3), have the client identify the situation, thought, feeling, and behavior in each of the illustrations (see Handouts 6.4, 6.5, and 6.6) referred to in Steps 1–3.

Now let's look at a couple of examples showing how thoughts can change how we feel and what we do.

Step 1: View Illustration 1 and the STFB handout to explore the situation, thought, feeling, etc.

Let's say Joe bumps into Mike and knocks his books down. Mike might think to himself, "He did that on purpose!" How would Mike feel if he had this thought? What would he do as a result? What are the consequences likely to be if he does that?

Lead the client through the situation (Joe knocks down Mike's books), the thought (Mike thinks Joe did that on purpose), how Mike is feeling (most youth will name "angry" as the feeling, endorsing a 9 or 10 on the feelings thermometer), Mike's behavior in response to that feeling (Mike may yell at Joe or get into a fight with Joe), and the likely consequences (someone might get hurt, school suspension/expulsion).

Step 2: View Illustration 2 and the STFB handout to explore the situation, thought, feeling, etc.

"But what if Mike thinks instead, "I guess he wasn't watching where he was going." How might Mike feel if he had this thought? What might he do as a result? What will the consequences probably be if he does that?"

The client may still say that Mike will be irritated, but not at a 9 or 10 on the feeling thermometer (more like a 2 or 3), so Mike is unlikely to be very angry and push Joe and get himself into trouble for his behavior.

Step 3: View Illustration 3 and the STFB handout to trace the feelings, behaviors, and consequences the three students are likely to have when they respond with three different thoughts to the same test.

Sizing Up a Situation

What is Andy likely to be feeling when he tells himself, "I am so stupid" and can't do the test? What will he do? What about Erica in the back, who thinks, "He never said this would be on the test"? What about Bill, who tells himself, "OK, I will do the best I can"? How will their behaviors and the consequences be different between the three students?

Summarize this activity with the following points:

- *Hurtful thoughts can lead to upsetting feelings.*
- *We can catch ourselves when we're having a hurtful thought and change it into a more helpful thought.*
- *When we replace a hurtful thought with a helpful thought, we usually feel better.*
- *When we feel better, we do better (that is, we behave better).*
- *When we behave better, it usually brings better consequences.*

6 Activity 3 Helping Out a Friend Exercise

Purpose:

- To help clients identify loss reminders that can bring up strong grief-related thoughts, feelings, behaviors, and potentially problematic consequences
- To help clients to generate helpful thoughts to replace more hurtful thoughts in response to various bereavement-related challenges

Materials: Sizing up a Situation handout (Handout 6.1); Sketches, Situations 1–15.

Directions: Our own research (Kaplow, Wardecker, et al., 2018) has shown us that children who talk about and describe their own bereavement-related challenges in the third person (like a fly on the wall) exhibit less psychological distress and better coping strategies. This exercise allows youth to project their own hurtful or helpful thoughts onto their "friend" in the drawing. This "best friend" stance helps to create a protective psychological distance while allowing clients to practice empathy, learn about different ways in which grief can express itself, and problem solve and practice constructive coping responses to many different stressful situations. To begin this activity, follow the steps below in sequence.

1. Each of the sketches for this activity illustrates a particular bereavement-related challenge associated with a specific grief domain (as reviewed in Session 1). You can select two or three sketches for this exercise depending on the time available and the needs of your client based on their particular grief profile (i.e., separation distress, existential distress, or circumstance-related distress), their developmental stage, culture, and other factors. Clients are not expected to go over each and every sketch. These sketches depict a broad age range (from younger children to older adolescents), circumstances of the death, relationship to the deceased, and prominent grief reactions. This rich variety of choices helps you to flexibly tailor MGT for the particular grief profile and life circumstances of each client. Rely on your assessment profile and on the lens of multidimensional grief theory to guide your decisions about which sketches to use.

2. Show one of the sketches to the client and ask them to imagine that the child or adolescent in the sketch is a close friend who is having a hard time after someone they really cared about has died, and they're turning to your client for help. Your client's job is to give their very best advice and support to their friend by helping to identify links between situations (e.g., loss reminders), thoughts, feelings, behaviors, and consequences, and by changing hurtful thoughts into more helpful thoughts that will likely lead to better consequences.

3. Have the client refer to Handout 6.1 to help identify the specific elements of each sketch and problem solve how to think, feel, and behave in a more helpful way. You can say: *"The goal is to help your friend identify their hurtful thought, figure out why it's hurtful, and come up with a helpful thought instead. The key to beating hurtful thoughts is to understand that for every hurtful thought, there is at least one helpful thought that you can replace it with."*

4. Begin with the first selected sketch. Using the guide for that particular sketch, ask the following questions:

   - *What is the stressful situation (or what is the loss reminder)?*
   - *What is the main hurtful thought the person is having (see the thought bubble in the sketch)?*
   - *What upsetting feeling(s) might the thought bring up?*
   - *What might the person do if he/she is thinking/feeling that way?*
   - *What are some likely negative consequences of behaving in that way?*
   - *Can you help your friend in the sketch to think differently about the situation? Are there more helpful thoughts they can use to replace the hurtful thought(s)?*

This session contains fifteen sketches of various stressful or challenging situations that may be used to discuss how to cope with each of them. They are listed as Situation 1 through Situation 15. Guidelines for how to structure the discussion for each of the sketches are provided below in the boxes and anything written in italics (e.g., the description of the situation, questions following the description) should be read aloud to the client. Review each of the sketches and pick two to three that you think would be most relevant to your client.

Sketches for Children (ages 7 to 11)

Situation 1: Distress/Anger over "Replacing" Loved One

Missing Them (separation distress)

Dinner Table

Description: *This girl's father died about a year ago, and her mother recently started dating someone. The girl thinks that her mother's new boyfriend will try to replace her father. Seeing him sitting in her father's chair is a strong loss reminder and makes her miss her father even more.*

What is the <u>situation</u>? A girl is sitting at the dinner table with her mom on her right looking lovingly at her new boyfriend, who is sitting to the girl's left. Mom's boyfriend is sitting in Dad's former chair at the head of the table, smiling.

What is her <u>hurtful thought</u>? That's Dad's chair. Who does he think he is? He will NEVER be my dad.

How might she be <u>feeling</u> if she is thinking this way? (Angry, sad, lonely, hopeless, empty, feeling misunderstood, worried that people might forget her dad or how important he was to her)

What <u>behaviors</u> might she be tempted to engage in if she is thinking and feeling this way? (Acting like she doesn't want anything to do with her mom's boyfriend, avoiding fun activities that involve the boyfriend, isolating herself in her room, missing out on forming a new, healthy relationship, becoming aggressive toward her mother's boyfriend)

What might be some <u>negative consequences</u> of thinking, feeling, and behaving this way? (Becoming isolated, feeling lonely, leading a boring life, getting into trouble for being rude or mean, feeling depressed or even suicidal)

What <u>helpful thoughts</u> could you suggest as replacements?

- Even if I start spending time with Mom's boyfriend, it doesn't mean I loved my dad any less.
- I know Dad would want me to have fun and do things as a family. He'd want Mom to be happy too.
- I can still hold on to my favorite memories of Dad and how much he meant to me – those memories will always be mine to remember and keep.
- It may feel sad to do activities without Dad now, but I might start to enjoy spending time with Mom's boyfriend once I get to know him.
- I can talk about Dad and share things about him with Mom's boyfriend so that he gets to know me and can understand me better. It may help to let him know how much I still love my dad and how important he still is to me.

Sizing Up a Situation

- I can have new fun experiences with other people while still remembering all of my fun times with Dad and still feeling connected to him.

(As appropriate): *Could you believe these thoughts if you were in her situation?*

How could choosing to think about the situation in these ways change how she feels and behaves?

If she changes how she feels and behaves, what might happen next? Could something good come from those more helpful thoughts, feelings, and behaviors?

Situation 2: Distress/Frustration over Others Experiencing Joy

Missing Them (separation distress); Feeling Lost without Them (existential/identity distress)

Holiday Dinner

Description: *This boy's grandmother died three months ago, and he's watching as his family gathers for a holiday meal. He is having a hard time understanding how they can seem so happy, when he is still grieving the loss of his grandmother. The big holiday dinner*

120

serves as a strong loss reminder – this will be the first time in his life that his grandmother won't be with him for the holiday.

What is the <u>situation</u>? A boy is standing in the doorway of the family dining room where his large extended family has gathered for a holiday dinner. The boy is looking in the doorway at his family members, surprised that they appear to be enjoying themselves.

What is his <u>hurtful thought</u>? How can they all be laughing and smiling and having a good time, when Grandma just died three months ago? They must not have loved her the way I did.

How might he be <u>feeling</u> if he is thinking this way? (Confused, lonely, sad, resentful that others can have a good time, worried that others may have forgotten how important his grandmother was to the family, feeling angry that they seem disloyal)

What <u>behaviors</u> might he be tempted to engage in if he is thinking and feeling this way? (Avoiding family activities, isolating himself, getting into arguments or fights with family members)

What might be some <u>negative consequences</u> of thinking, feeling, and behaving this way? (Becoming isolated, feeling misunderstood and all alone in his grief, missing out on fun family activities that could help him feel better, feeling depressed or even suicidal)

What <u>helpful thoughts</u> could you suggest as replacements?

- You can be sad and really miss the person who died, while also being able to celebrate with family and experience happiness. It is possible to be both happy and sad at the same time.
- Everyone grieves in different ways – some family members may feel better celebrating Grandma's life by having fun and being together, while others may want to spend time alone.
- Family gatherings were so important to Grandma – I know she would want me to be happy and join the group.
- It may feel really sad to have a holiday dinner without Grandma now, but there are ways we can remember her when we're all together (like making her favorite apple pie or placing a photo of her on the dinner table). Maybe we can take a moment to remember her or to share a favorite memory.
- Being around other people who knew and loved Grandma and sharing family memories can help me to feel more connected to her.
- Just because I'm having fun or laughing doesn't mean that I loved Grandma any less.

(As appropriate): *Could <u>you</u> believe these thoughts if you were in his situation?*

How could choosing to <u>think about the situation</u> in these ways change how he <u>feels</u> and <u>behaves</u>?

And if he changes how he <u>feels</u> and <u>behaves</u>, what might <u>happen next</u>? Could something good come from those more helpful thoughts, feelings, and behaviors?

Situation 3: Feeling "Weird" or Different from Other Kids

Feeling Lost without Them (existential/identity distress)

Mother's Day

Description: *This girl's mother died, and her elementary school teacher has just given the class an assignment to make Mother's Day cards. The other students seem excited and happy about the assignment, while this girl is dreading it. She is trying to be invisible so that the other students don't notice that she is not making her own card. The class assignment serves as a strong loss reminder that her mom will not be there for Mother's Day this year.*

What is the <u>situation</u>? A girl whose mother has died becomes upset when her teacher tells the class that their assignment is to create Mother's Day cards to bring home to their moms.

What is her <u>hurtful thought</u>? Not again! I hate having to tell people my mom died. I know the teacher is just going to feel bad, and the other kids are going to look at me weird. I just wish I could be like everyone else.

How might she be <u>feeling</u> if she is thinking this way? (Self-conscious, sad, lonely, confused, angry, embarrassed, worried about not fitting in, feeling awkward and the center of unwanted attention)

What <u>behaviors</u> might she be tempted to engage in if she is thinking and feeling this way? (Avoiding talking to the other kids, isolating herself, complaining that she doesn't feel well so she can go home or not come to school tomorrow, avoiding making new friends so she doesn't have to answer questions about her mom)

What might be some <u>negative consequences</u> of thinking, feeling, and behaving this way? (Becoming isolated, feeling lonely, having no one to talk to, feeling depressed, not being able to form new relationships)

What <u>helpful thoughts</u> could you suggest as replacements?

- Even if kids find out that my mom died, that doesn't mean they won't want to be my friend.
- I still have other things in common with kids in my class.
- I can still write a Mother's Day card for my mom to honor her memory, or I could write one for my grandma or my aunt instead.
- If I tell the teacher that I'm having a hard time, I'm sure she'll understand and help me think of something else I can do for this assignment.
- Sometimes sharing personal things, like telling someone in my class that my mom died, can make people feel closer to you.
- True friends will care about me no matter what I've been through.
- All families have difficult problems to deal with – I'm sure other kids have had upsetting things happen to them, too, so maybe we're not that different.

(As appropriate): *Could <u>you</u> believe these thoughts if you were in her situation?*

How could choosing to <u>think about the situation</u> in these ways change how she <u>feels</u> and <u>behaves</u>?

Sizing Up a Situation

And if she changes how she <u>feels</u> and <u>behaves</u>, what might <u>happen next</u>? Could something good come from those more helpful thoughts, feelings, and behaviors?

Situation 4: Struggling to Address Parents' Own Grief While Meeting Their Own Needs

Feeling Lost without Them (existential/identity distress)

Birthday Party Invitation

Description: *This girl's father died several months ago. She just started a new school and was recently invited to a friend's birthday party this coming weekend. Although she wants to go to the party and see her new friends, she feels guilty leaving her mom, who has been struggling with her own grief. The girl feels responsible for supporting her mother and cheering her up. She feels very torn between doing what she wants to do versus doing what she thinks she should do – helping her mom cope with the death of her father.*

What is the <u>situation</u>? A girl sits across from her mother, holding an invitation to a friend's party. Her mother looks depressed and overwhelmed. The girl feels very torn about whether to attend the party or stay home with her mom.

What is her <u>hurtful thought</u>? How can I leave her like this? Dad always used to be the one to make her laugh and cheer her up. Without him here, I'm all she has left.

How might she be <u>feeling</u> if she is thinking this way? (Confused, frustrated, angry, sad, worried about her mom, worried that she might miss out on making new friends, resentful that she has to give up normal things that kids her age do)

What <u>behaviors</u> might she be tempted to engage in if she is thinking and feeling this way? (Saying no to invitations or

social events with friends, becoming isolated, getting into arguments with her mom, not being able to focus in school)

What might be some <u>negative consequences</u> of these thoughts and feelings and behaviors? (Having a hard time making or keeping good friends, doing poorly in school because of low grades, feeling isolated and depressed, missing out on fun and exciting experiences, maybe wanting to hurt herself)

What <u>helpful thoughts</u> could you suggest as replacements?

- I know that my mom is sad about my dad's death, but it's not my job to make her happy.
- I can find ways of being there for my mom while also not giving up on fun activities or time with friends.
- My dad would have wanted me to be social and enjoy time with friends. He would not have wanted me to give up on those things to take care of my mom.
- It makes my mom happy to know that I'm doing OK. Maybe she'll feel better when she sees that I'm still able to have fun with friends.
- If I go to the party, I can come home and share what happened with my mom. It can cheer her up to know that I'm doing OK and making new friends.
- My mom is an adult and can find lots of ways to get the support she needs. She doesn't need to rely on me for that.

(As appropriate): *Could <u>you</u> believe these thoughts if you were in her situation?*

How could choosing to <u>think about the situation</u> in these ways change how she <u>feels</u> and <u>behaves</u>?

And if she changes how she <u>feels</u> and <u>behaves</u>, what might <u>happen next</u>? Could something good come from those more helpful thoughts, feelings, and behaviors?

Sizing Up a Situation

Situation 5: Difficulty Reminiscing Due to Upsetting Thoughts/Images

Emotional Pain over the Way They Died (circumstance-related distress)

Sister's Death

Description: *This girl's sister died of cancer two years ago after going through chemotherapy and other invasive treatments. Although she wants to enjoy happy memories, any reminder of her (like seeing her picture or hearing her name) seems to bring up upsetting feelings about how much her sister suffered while she was sick.*

What is the <u>situation</u>? A girl is looking through a photo album and is focused on a photo of her and her sister on a hiking trail with their arms around each other. They are both smiling in the photo, and her sister looks happy and healthy.

What is her <u>hurtful thought</u>? I wish I could remember her this way – healthy and happy. But all I see when I think of her now are those tubes that helped her to breathe and how thin and weak she looked at the end.

How might she be <u>feeling</u> if she is thinking this way? (Sad, frustrated, hopeless, anxious, worried that she won't be able to remember her sister in the way she wants to, guilty that she had to suffer so much)

What <u>behaviors</u> might she be tempted to engage in if she is thinking and feeling this way? (Trying not to think about her sister at all, staying away from anything that reminds her of her sister – including friends and family – not being able to concentrate in school, isolating herself)

What might be some <u>negative consequences</u> of these thoughts and feelings and behaviors? (Having trouble making or keeping friends, struggling in school because

of her difficulties concentrating, wanting to hurt herself or actually doing something to harm herself)

What helpful thoughts could you suggest as replacements?

- Maybe I just have to accept that it might be hard right now to picture my sister when she was healthy and happy, but it won't be this difficult forever.
- My sister would want me to remember all of the great things about her and not focus on the upsetting way that she died.
- I can try to live my best life for my sister, including focusing on all of the positive things that she taught me and believed in.
- I can work in therapy to talk about my thoughts and feelings about the way she died so that I don't get overwhelmed every time I'm reminded, and I can start to enjoy good memories of her.

(As appropriate): *Could you believe these thoughts if you were in her situation?*
How could choosing to think about the situation in these ways change how she feels and behaves?
And if she changes how she feels and behaves, what might happen next? Could something good come from those more helpful thoughts, feelings, and behaviors?

Situation 6: Distress over COVID-Related Death

Emotional Pain over the Way They Died (circumstance-related distress)

COVID Death

Description: *This girl is attending her father's funeral with only a small number of people in the funeral parlor, all with masks on due to the COVID-19 pandemic. She is sitting in the front row with her mother and younger brother. They are all seated with a closed*

Sizing Up a Situation

casket in front of them while the minister is giving the eulogy. The girl is crying.

What is the situation? The girl's father recently died of COVID-19, and she is attending his funeral. They had to limit the number of people in attendance due to social distancing regulations. She is there with her mother and brother.

What is her hurtful thought? Why did he have to die this way – all alone in the hospital? I wonder what he must have been thinking at the time. I can't believe we didn't even get to say goodbye.

How might she be feeling if she is thinking this way? (Sad, frustrated, hopeless, anxious, worried that her father might have felt scared and alone at the time of his death, guilty that she didn't have a chance to say goodbye, angry at whoever she believes may have transmitted the virus to her father)

What behaviors might she be tempted to engage in if she is thinking and feeling this way? (Trying not to think about her father at all, staying away from anything that reminds her of her father including friends and family, staying away from anything that reminds her of the way that he died, not being able to concentrate in school, getting into arguments with people who had not been taking precautions seriously during the pandemic)

What might be some negative consequences of these thoughts and feelings and behaviors? (Having trouble making and keeping friends, doing poorly in school because of her problems concentrating, wanting to hurt herself)

What helpful thoughts could you suggest as replacements?

- Maybe I just have to accept that I'm going to feel mad and sad for a long time, but that doesn't mean I'll feel this way forever.
- My dad would want me to remember him as the great person he was and not by the upsetting way he died.
- I can try to live my best life for both my dad and myself, including focusing on all of the positive things that he taught me and believed in.
- Even though I didn't have a chance to say goodbye, my dad knew how much I loved him and how important he was to me. He would have known how much I wanted to be with him.
- I can work in therapy on coming to terms with what happened to my dad, so that I don't get overwhelmed by it every time I get reminded and I can start to enjoy good memories of him.

(As appropriate): *Could you believe these thoughts if you were in her situation?*

How could choosing to think about the situation in these ways change how she feels and behaves?

And if she changes how she feels and behaves, what might happen next? Could something good come from those more helpful thoughts, feelings, and behaviors?

Situation 7: Distress over an Ambiguous Loss

Emotional Pain over the Way They Died (circumstance-related distress)

Ambiguous Loss

Description: *This boy's brother died recently, and he is still struggling to figure out how he died. Although he was told it was "an accident" that killed his brother, he has a strong feeling that his family is not telling him the whole story. He can't stop thinking about what might have really happened. He wishes someone would tell him everything so that he can stop wondering.*

What is the situation? A boy is standing in the doorway and overhears his mother talking to a friend about his brother's recent death. He is trying to listen carefully, hoping to hear more information that might help him understand what really happened to his brother.

What is his hurtful thought? Why won't anyone tell me how he really died? They all keep saying it was "an accident," but I know they're not telling me everything. It drives me crazy not knowing what really happened to him.

How might he be feeling if he is thinking this way? (Confused, frustrated, angry, lonely, sad, worried that he'll never know the truth)

What behaviors might he be tempted to engage in if he is thinking and feeling this way? (Getting into arguments with family members who he thinks may be "hiding something," distancing himself from friends or family, trying not to think about his brother at all, not being able to concentrate in school, not caring about life anymore)

What might be some negative consequences of these thoughts and feelings and behaviors? (Having trouble keeping friends or having close relationships with family, not trusting other people, failing out of school because of poor concentration and low grades, feeling angry and irritable all the time)

What helpful thoughts could you suggest as replacements?

- I can find the right time to ask one of my family members if they could tell me everything they know about how my brother died. Maybe if I ask them directly, they'll give me a direct answer.
- I can still hold onto positive memories of my brother, even if I don't know exactly how he died.
- I understand that my mom and family members are not trying to make me upset – they probably just want to protect me by not telling me details they think will upset me.
- My brother would have wanted me to focus on all of the great things about him and our fun times together, and not be so worried about exactly how he died.

(As appropriate): *Could you believe these thoughts if you were in his situation?*

How could choosing to think about the situation in these ways change how he feels and behaves?

And if he changes how he feels and behaves, what might happen next? Could something good come from those more helpful thoughts, feelings, and behaviors?

Sizing Up a Situation

Sketches for Adolescents (ages 12 and up)

Situation 8: Avoiding Loss Reminders
Missing Them (separation distress)

Basketball Tickets
Description: *This teen's father died of a sudden heart attack three weeks ago. He and his dad used to do lots of fun things together, including going to basketball games. In fact, that was this teen's favorite activity to do with his dad. Now, going to any sports events, but particularly basketball games, serves as a strong loss reminder.*

What is the <u>situation</u>? Mother handing her teenage boy two season tickets to a basketball game, saying: "Your dad would want you to enjoy these tickets. Why don't we go to the game together?"

What is his <u>hurtful thought</u>? I can't ever go back there again. It won't ever be the same without him.

How might he be <u>feeling</u> if he is thinking this way? (Sad, empty, lost, bored, feeling like a big part of him died, hopeless)

What <u>behaviors</u> might he be tempted to engage in if he is thinking and feeling this way? (Acting like he doesn't care anymore, giving up activities that he used to enjoy,

127

Sizing Up a Situation

avoiding relationships that may remind him that his dad is gone, missing out on fun opportunities)

What might be some <u>negative consequences</u> of thinking, feeling, and behaving this way? (Becoming isolated, feeling lonely, leading a boring and unfulfilling life, feeling suicidal, engaging in more risk-taking behaviors)

What <u>helpful thoughts</u> could you suggest as replacements?

- It won't always hurt so bad. Waves of grief come and go, and I can get through them.
- I know Dad would want me to have fun and do the things we used to enjoy doing together. He'd want me to spend some time with Mom because he loved us both.
- Even though my life will be very different, it can still be a good life. I don't have to throw it all away or give up trying just because I'm feeling discouraged right now.
- It may feel sad to do activities without him now, but maybe there are other people who I could enjoy spending time with and doing fun things with.
- Instead of giving up hope that I can have a good life, I might want to become a doctor or nutritionist or physical trainer who works on preventing heart disease, so that other families don't have to go through the pain my family is going through.

(As appropriate): *Could <u>you</u> believe these thoughts if you were in his situation?*

How could choosing to <u>think about the situation</u> in these ways change how he <u>feels</u> and <u>behaves</u>?

And if he changes how he <u>feels</u> and <u>behaves</u>, what might <u>happen next</u>? Could something good come from those more helpful thoughts, feelings, and behaviors?

Situation 9: Reunification Fantasies

Missing Them and Feeling Lost without Them (separation distress and existential distress)

Reckless Driving

Description: *This teenager's closest friend died of a drug overdose, and she misses her every single day. They used to do everything together, including driving together, so driving alone is a loss reminder. To her, being alone and feeling lonely are painful loss reminders that keep reminding her that her friend is no longer there.*

What is the <u>situation</u>? Teenage girl driving fast in a car without her seat belt on, windows rolled down, wind in her hair, tears running down her cheeks, mournful expression on her face.

What is her <u>hurtful thought</u>? It doesn't matter if I live or die. If I crash, the bad news is I'm dead, but the good news is I get to see my friend again.

How might she be <u>feeling</u> if she is thinking this way? (Sad, empty, missing her friend, wanting to be back with her friend, feeling lost, feeling like a piece of her died, hopeless, helpless)

What <u>behaviors</u> might she be tempted to engage in if she is thinking and feeling this way? (What she is doing – driving recklessly without a seatbelt – or other risky behavior like neglecting her health, acting like she doesn't care about anything anymore, cutting off other important relationships, using drugs to escape her pain and to maybe feel closer to her friend who died from an overdose)

What might be some <u>negative consequences</u> of thinking, feeling, and behaving this way? (Crashing her car and hurting herself or other innocent people, dropping out of school, becoming socially isolated and lonely, getting an expensive traffic ticket, losing her insurance and then being unable to drive, getting arrested, becoming addicted to drugs, attempting suicide)

What <u>helpful thoughts</u> could you suggest as replacements?

- My friend wouldn't want me to die. She would want me to make the most of my life.
- I can do things with my life that would make her proud to call me her friend.
- I can use this experience to help other teens – maybe I can prevent other kids from ending their lives.
- I still have other people in my life who care about me.
- I'll never be able to replace her, and I would never want to. But I can form other relationships that will bring me and others some happiness.
- Bringing other special people and activities that I cherish into my life doesn't mean that I'm replacing her. I'll always keep a special place for her in my heart. But my heart can grow bigger.

(As appropriate): *Could you believe these helpful thoughts if you were in her situation?*

How could thinking about the situation in these ways change how she feels and behaves?

And if she changes how she <u>feels</u> and <u>behaves</u>, what might <u>happen next</u>? Could something good come from those more helpful thoughts, feelings, and behaviors?

Sizing Up a Situation

Situation 10: Social Withdrawal and Fear of Getting Close

Missing Them (separation distress)

Social Withdrawal

Description: *This teenage girl lost one of her closest friends when she was killed in a drunk driving accident several months ago. Ever since, she has been avoiding the other girls who made up their same circle of friends as they are strong loss reminders for her. Being in their company reminds her that her close friend who died is not there with them anymore.*

What is the <u>situation</u>? Teenage girl walking away from a small group of friends who are saying, "Hey, why don't you hang with us anymore?"

Sizing Up a Situation

What is her **hurtful thought**? It's better not to get too close to people. I don't want to feel the pain of losing someone else ever again.

How might she be **feeling** *if she is thinking this way?* (Sad, lonely, worried, scared)

What **behaviors** *might she be tempted to engage in if she is thinking and feeling this way?* (Pulling away from friends and other relationships, isolating herself, hurting herself to try to distract herself from negative feelings)

What are some likely **negative consequences** *of these behaviors?* (Being lonely all the time, missing out on fun opportunities, doing poorly in school, injuring herself, having suicidal thoughts or behaviors)

What **helpful thoughts** *could you suggest as replacements?*

- I'll bet they miss her, too, and we can support each other through this.
- Being close to other people can help me to deal with my grief – pulling away from them will just make it harder in the long run. We can remember and reminisce about our friend together.
- If I can open up to my friends about how I'm feeling, it will be easier for them to open up to me about difficult feelings they may be having. Helping each other creates good friendships.
- It's unlikely that I'll have to lose my other friends. What happened to my close friend was a terrible accident, but the chances of that happening again are highly unlikely.
- My friend would never want me to become isolated. She always wanted the best for me, including having good friends.
- It's better to have loved and lost then to never love at all. Even though I lost my friend way too soon, our friendship was worth the pain I'm feeling now.
- I can take one of her most positive qualities, like her friendly personality, and try to be more like her in that way. That way I can keep feeling close to her by enjoying her gift to me.

(As appropriate): *Could* **you** *believe these thoughts if you were in her situation?*

How could **thinking about the situation** *in these more positive ways change how she is* **feeling** *and* **behaving**?

And if she changes how she **feels** *and* **behaves**, *what might* **happen next**? *Could something good come from those more helpful thoughts, feelings, and behaviors?*

Situation 11: Giving Up on Future Plans

Feeling Lost without Them (existential distress)

Giving Up on Future Plans

Description: This teenage girl's father was killed as an innocent bystander in a drive-by shooting several months ago. He was very supportive of her staying in school and had high hopes that she would graduate from high school and go to college. She just found out she was accepted to her college of choice. But with her father's death, it's hard to feel excited about it. In fact, the college acceptance letter is as a strong loss reminder because she doesn't have her dad here to celebrate her acceptance with her. She knows that he won't be around to cheer her on during her studies, and he won't be there when she graduates.

What is the **situation**? A teenage girl is reading a college acceptance letter and throwing it in the trash.

What is her **hurtful thought**? I don't care about my future anymore if he's not going to be a part of it. He'll never see me graduate anyway, so what's the point?

How might she be **feeling** *if she is thinking this way?* (Sad, empty, lost, hopeless, feeling like a big part of her died, feeling like life has lost its meaning, feeling like nothing matters anymore, feeling like her life is over, feeling like it's not worth trying anymore)

What **behaviors** *might she be tempted to engage in if she is thinking and feeling this way?* (What she is doing now – throwing away an acceptance letter with a scholarship! – not trying to really make something of her life, giving up on her hopes for a good future, passing up valuable opportunities to succeed, acting like she doesn't care about anything anymore, not trying anymore, dropping out of school, hanging out with the wrong crowd, getting a boring low-paying job with no real opportunities for moving up)

What might be some **negative consequences** *of thinking, feeling, and behaving this way?* (Not making something out of her life, underachieving, feeling unsatisfied and unfulfilled, being bored, regretting having passed up big opportunities, losing a chance to make a positive difference in the world, dropping out of school, cutting off relationships with good friends who can help her keep her life on track, feeling suicidal because nothing seems worth it anymore)

What **helpful thoughts** *could you suggest as replacements?*

- I know Dad would want me to do good things with my life – he would have been thrilled that I got accepted, and so proud of me if I decided to go to college.
- Even though my life will be very different, it can still be a good life. I don't have to throw it all away just because I'm feeling discouraged right now. There is a big difference between having a life that's different than what I had planned and having a life that's not worth living.
- If I take advantage of this opportunity and actually go to college, maybe I could do something important with my life, like help other kids who have suffered the way I have.
- My spiritual beliefs tell me that Dad is watching over me and will see me succeed if I try.

(As appropriate): *Could* **you** *believe these thoughts if you were in her situation?*

How could choosing to **think about the situation** *in these ways change how she* **feels** *and* **behaves**?

And if she changes how she **feels** *and* **behaves**, *what might* **happen next**? *Could something good come from those more helpful thoughts, feelings, and behaviors?*

Sizing Up a Situation

Sizing Up a Situation

Situation 12: Shame over Circumstances of the Death

Emotional Pain over the Way They Died (circumstance-related distress)

Shame over Circumstances

Description: *This teenage girl recently started attending a new high school and is just beginning to make some new friends. Her new friends know that her dad died several months ago, but what they don't know is how he died (he died by suicide). She feels very self-conscious and a little ashamed, and she worries about what her new friends might do if they found out about the way he died. She thinks that it's best to just play it safe and not really get to know anyone, even though it will make her life very lonely and boring.*

What is the <u>situation</u>? Some teenage girls are sitting at a table in the high school cafeteria, gesturing to the bereaved girl to come sit with them.

What is her hurtful thought? They'll never want to hang out with me once they know the truth about how my dad died.
What might she be feeling? (Shame, embarrassment, anxiety, worry that the others won't like her or will judge her)
What behaviors might she be tempted to engage in if she is thinking and feeling this way? (Pulling away from friends and other new relationships, isolating herself)
What are some likely negative consequences of these behaviors? (Dropping out of school, injuring herself, having suicidal thoughts or behaviors)
What helpful thoughts could you suggest as replacements?

- If they're true friends, it won't put them off to know how my dad died.
- All families have difficult problems to deal with – I'm sure these girls have had upsetting things happen to them, too.
- Just because my dad had some mental health problems doesn't mean that I do, too.
- If I choose to talk one day about my dad's suicide and help people understand what causes it, I may be able to prevent other people from taking their own lives the way my dad did.
- My dad would have wanted me to have friends who cared about me and supported me, no matter what has happened in my family.
- If I choose to open up to new friends about what happened to my dad, it will be easier for them to open up to me about bad things that may have happened to them. That openness and trust is what helps to create lasting friendships.

(As appropriate): *Could you believe these new thoughts about what happened if you were in her situation?*
How could thinking about the situation in these ways change how she feels and behaves?
And if she changes how she feels and behaves, what might happen next? Could something good come from those more helpful thoughts, feelings, and behaviors?

Situation 13: "Can't Stop Thinking about the Way He Died"

Emotional Pain over the Way They Died (circumstance-related distress)

Can't Stop Thinking about the Way He Died
Description: *This girl's brother was killed in a gang fight a year ago. Although she wants to enjoy positive memories of him, any reminder of him (like seeing his picture or hearing his name) keeping bringing up upsetting feelings. They remind her he is no longer physically present in her life (a loss reminder). They also remind her of the terrible night he was killed (a trauma reminder) when everyone was screaming and crying. She wishes her family would put away their pictures of her brother and not talk about him. She* believes that if she doesn't think about him, she won't get overwhelmed with the pain she still feels about his death.

What is the situation? A girl sits on a couch next to a photo of her brother on an end table, a troubled expression on her face.
What is her hurtful thought? Every time I see his picture, I can't help thinking about the night he got killed. It gets me so mad that it's hard to remember the good times.
What might she be feeling? (Anger, frustration, rage, fear, sadness, desire for revenge, regret)
What behaviors might she be tempted to engage in if she is thinking and feeling this way? (Trying not to think about her brother at all, staying away from anything that reminds her of her brother – including his friends and family – thinking of getting revenge by hurting other people, not being able to concentrate in school, drinking or using drugs to try to make the pain go away)
What might be some negative consequences of these thoughts and feelings and behaviors? (Getting put in detention or suspended for fighting at school, dropping out of school because of low grades, getting in trouble with the law for hurting other people, having a hard time making and keeping good friends or going on dates, getting herself hurt or killed)
What helpful thoughts could you suggest as replacements?

- Maybe I just have to accept that I'm going to feel mad and sad for quite a long time. But that doesn't mean I'll feel this way forever.
- My brother would want me to remember him as the great person he was and not by the tragic way he died.
- Letting bad memories of his death go and letting good memories in does not mean that I think the way that he died is "acceptable." I can believe it is wrong, and I can always want justice to be served, but I don't have to let these things keep me from moving on with my life.
- If I get myself hurt or killed, then my family will lose two children, not one. I can do my best to live for my brother as well as for myself, to try to make up for the good his life would have brought.
- By not allowing myself to remember my brother the way he would want me to, it's like I'm letting the people who shot him and treated him like dirt win.
- I can work in therapy on coming to terms with what happened to my brother, so that I don't get overwhelmed by it every time I get reminded and I can start to enjoy good memories of him.

(As appropriate): *Could you believe these thoughts if you were in her situation?*
How could thinking about the situation in these ways change how she feels and behaves?
And if she changes how she feels and behaves, what might happen next? Could something good come from those more helpful thoughts, feelings, and behaviors?

Situation 14: Feeling Guilty about a Friend's Suicide

Emotional Pain over the Way They Died (circumstance-related distress)

Guilt over Death

Description: *A teenager is grieving the loss of his friend, who recently died by suicide.*

What is the <u>situation</u>? He's sitting next to a note she left behind, which says, "The pain is too much for me."

What is his <u>hurtful thought</u>? It's all my fault. If I'd have paid more attention to what was going on with her, this never would have happened.

What might he be <u>feeling</u>? (Guilt, regret, remorse, shame, depression)

*What **behaviors** might he be tempted to engage in if he is thinking and feeling this way?* (Getting angry and acting out, zoning out like a zombie, hurting himself, using drugs or alcohol to try to numb out)

*What are some likely **negative consequences** of these behaviors?* (Hurting himself, hurting someone else, hurting his family and friends, getting into trouble, failing at school)

*What **helpful thoughts** could you suggest as replacements?*

- No one knew this was going to happen, including me. You really can't predict the future, no matter how much you want to.
- I may feel very bad about what happened, but there have been many times when I was kind to her and showed that I cared about her.
- I may feel regret about what happened (wishing it had never happened; wishing I had known what was about to happen, so I could've done more to stop it), but I don't have to feel responsible and guilty for it. Regret and guilt are two very different things.
- Instead of torturing myself with guilt, which she wouldn't want and doesn't do anyone any good, I'll do my best to do something kind for someone she cares about, like her friends or family.
- I want to do something to help stop tragedies like this, like volunteering with at-risk kids.

(As appropriate): *Could **you** believe these thoughts if you were in his situation?*

How could thinking about the situation in these ways change how he feels and behaves?

*And if he changes how he **feels** and **behaves**, what might **happen next**? Could something good come from those more helpful thoughts, feelings, and behaviors?*

Situation 15: Blame for Not Preventing Brother's Death

Emotional Pain over the Way They Died (circumstance-related distress)

Blaming Doctors

Description: *This boy just lost his older brother in a tragic car accident. The doctor has just informed the family that he died. The boy is shocked and confused but mostly enraged at the doctor. He believes that the doctor could have done more to save his brother and probably just gave up on him too soon. He can't imagine trusting another doctor ever again. Now, doctors in white coats or the sound of an ambulance serve as trauma reminders.*

*What is the **situation**?* A boy is in the emergency room with his family when the doctor tells them that his brother has died.

*What is his **hurtful thought**?* I know they could have done more to save him. If they had just tried harder, he would still be alive. I'll never trust these people again.

*What might he be **feeling**?* (Anger, confusion, guilt)

*What **behaviors** might he be tempted to engage in if he is thinking and feeling this way?*
(Getting revenge on the doctors responsible by hurting them, hurting himself, becoming suicidal, using drugs to try to relieve his pain and anger, never seeing another doctor again)

*What might be some **negative consequences** of these thoughts and feelings and behaviors?*
(Going to jail or getting killed and then his family loses two sons, hurting the wrong people, physical pain and stress from carrying that much anger/rage, health problems from not seeing a doctor again)

*What **helpful thoughts** could you suggest as replacements?*

- Maybe the doctors really did do everything they could. They didn't want my brother to die, either. There was only so much they could do given how badly he was hurt.
- Just because I feel angry at them doesn't mean they are guilty.
- My brother wouldn't want me to get revenge and end up in jail.
- If I hurt or kill someone, it won't bring him back.
- If I did something like that it would break my mother's/father's/grandparents' heart.
- I have my whole life ahead of me – I know my brother would want me to make the most of it.
- My family already lost one son. I don't want to put them at risk for losing another (me) by not taking care of my health or by doing something stupid that could get me in jail.
- I want to become an emergency room doctor so I can try and save kids like my brother.

(As appropriate): *Could **you** believe these thoughts if you were in his situation?*

How could thinking about the situation in these ways change how he feels and behaves?

*And if he changes how he **feels** and **behaves**, what might **happen next**? Could something good come from those more helpful thoughts, feelings, and behaviors?*

Sizing Up a Situation

Process the "Helping Out a Good Friend" Exercise

- *If you can support a friend by giving him or her good advice about how to handle a stressful situation differently, then you can do the same thing to yourself. You can be a good friend to yourself, just like you are to other people. So practice being kind and helpful to yourself, just as you have been so kind and helpful to your good friend!*
- *The more you practice identifying your own hurtful thoughts and replacing them with more helpful thoughts, the easier it will become. Just like any other skill, this improves with practice.*
- *Whenever you're faced with a loss reminder or difficult situation, you now have the tools to figure out how that situation is making you think and feel, how it's affecting your behavior, and how you can change your thinking to lead to better outcomes.*
- *Is this something you think you could do the next time you're upset by a loss reminder? What might make that more challenging?*
- *Remember that you may run into both **loss reminders** and **trauma reminders** in connection with the same death, especially if your loved one died in a traumatic way. Trauma reminders can bring up upsetting feelings about how they died, and loss reminders can bring up upsetting feelings about them not being physically with you anymore. The skills we have just practiced can help you to cope with both of these sets of reactions.*

7 Assign Practice Exercise

- *This week, pay attention to any loss reminders or stressful situations that bring up strong thoughts or feelings for you. Practice being your own "best friend" by thinking of more helpful thoughts. If you're having trouble, think back to a couple of the situations that we reviewed today. Are there any helpful thoughts that you used today that could be helpful to you in your own situation?*

8 Check Out

- How are you feeling now? (Use feelings thermometer rating)
- What did you learn about yourself today?

Handout 6.1

Sizing Up a Situation

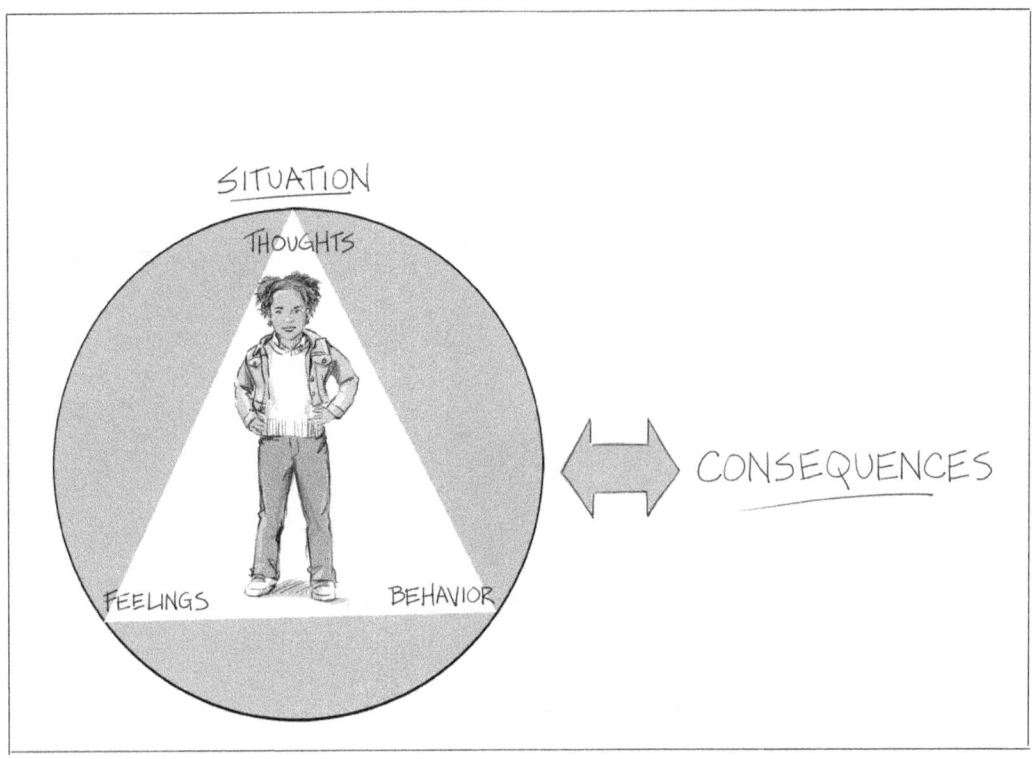

A PDF version of this handout is available for download on Cambridge Core and via www.cambridge.org/MGT

Handout 6.2

Sizing Up a Situation Card Game

Frustrated	I've got to get even	Someone hits you
Surprised	Scared	I can do it

A PDF version of this handout is available for download on Cambridge Core and via www.cambridge.org/MGT

Sizing Up a Situation

You yell at someone	You hit someone	Irritated
It's my fault	I'll always be alone	A teacher yells at you

Sizing Up a Situation

- A police car passes with a siren
- My sister is my favorite
- Someone knocks on the door
- A teacher praises you
- I can't do it
- Happy
- You work hard on homework
- You share a treat with someone

Handout 6.3

Situation, Thoughts, Feelings, and Behaviors

A PDF version of this handout is available for download on Cambridge Core and via www.cambridge.org/MGT

Handout 6.4

Illustration 1

A PDF version of this handout is available for download on Cambridge Core and via www.cambridge.org/MGT

Handout 6.5

Illustration 2

Sizing Up a Situation

Handout 6.6

Illustration 3

A PDF version of this handout is available for download on Cambridge Core and via www.cambridge.org/MGT

MGT Sessions

7–9 Loss Narrative

Telling the Story of My Person

Session Objectives

Increase the client's ability:

1. To identify and process three primary bereavement-related challenges, as defined by multidimensional grief theory
2. To find healthy ways of connecting with the deceased
3. To identify ways to carry on the legacy of the deceased
4. To make sense of, and ultimately, meaning of, the death of their loved one

Section Number	Session Overview
1	Check In with Grief Thermometers
2	Conceptual Background: What Is a Loss Narrative?
3	Activity 1: Creating the Loss Narrative
4	Activity 2: Preparing Caregivers
5	Activity 3: Sharing the Loss Narrative with Caregivers
6	Assign Practice Exercise
7	Check Out

Session Materials

- Rating My Grief Reactions (Handout 1.3)
- Notebook or laptop to create loss narrative
- Parent/Caregiver Guidance (Handout 4.3)

1 Check In with Grief Thermometers

Have the client complete Rating My Grief Reactions (Handout 1.3) and explore current ratings of grief reactions. Sample prompts include the following:

- *How are you feeling on your grief thermometers?*
- *How did your grief thermometers change from last week?*
- *How did you feel those changes during the week?*

Additional check-in prompts as appropriate:

- *Did anything happen since we saw each other last that you feel good about?*
- *Was there anything we talked about in our last session that you thought about this week or that stuck with you?*
- *Is anything going on that may make it hard for you to focus during our session today?*

2 Conceptual Background: What Is a Loss Narrative?

A number of evidence-based treatments for trauma and grief include helping children and adolescents to construct a trauma narrative that centers on processing the **circumstances** of the death. Constructing a trauma narrative typically progresses from a simple, fact-based account of "what happened" to a more in-depth unpacking of the experience over multiple sessions. Because trauma narratives focus predominantly on the circumstances of the death and on youths' reactions to what occurred, trauma narratives do not usually address the entire range of grief reactions evoked by the death (e.g., separation distress, identity-related challenges, or personal existential crises) (Kaplow, Layne, & Pynoos, 2019; Layne et al., 2017; Saltzman et al., 2017).

In contrast, MGT includes a loss narrative that not only focuses on the particular way the person died but also on other bereavement-related challenges and associated grief reactions that clients are likely to experience. The loss narrative covers each of the primary dimensions of grief, including both adaptive and maladaptive grief reactions, as described in multidimensional grief theory. Loss narratives in MGT can be flexibly tailored to address the specific dimensions of grief that are elevated in each client's assessment profile. As a general principle, bereaved children experiencing high levels of circumstance-related distress and/or PTSD often find it difficult to process other grief reactions (e.g., separation distress) effectively because of intrusive thoughts related to the death itself. Instead, these children often benefit from first processing their distressing preoccupations with the circumstances of the death (e.g., scary or gruesome images, concerns that the death was painful or upsetting for the person, confusion and ongoing questions about why and how the person died) (Kaplow, Layne, & Pynoos, 2019; Pynoos, 1992). This key insight is our primary reason why information about how the person died (Chapter 3 of the loss narrative) is processed near the beginning of the loss narrative.

The process of constructing and sharing the loss narrative in a safe and supportive setting carries multiple therapeutic benefits. Specifically, the loss narrative (1) increases tolerance for, and brings greater coherence to, memories and emotions that the client may have been avoiding; (2) reduces reactivity to painful memories; (3) provides insight into current loss and/or trauma reminders as well as associated unhelpful thoughts or behaviors; (4) enhances the client's ability to make sense and meaning of the death; and (5) when shared with caregivers, enhances understanding and communication between family members regarding the death. It is important to note that we encourage youth to complete their loss narrative in the third person (as if they are watching a movie of their life or as a fly on the wall) because our preliminary research shows that this facilitates greater insight, enhanced coping, and decreased psychological distress (Kaplow, Wardecker et al., 2018). Specifically, more self-distancing (but not avoidance) during the processing of thoughts and feelings creates emotional space for the material to feel less personal and/or threatening, allowing for greater flexibility and creativity in thinking.

How Is This Session Theoretically Grounded?

As discussed in Chapter 1, multidimensional grief theory covers a broad range of grief reactions and offers a flexible, individually tailored approach to both reducing unhelpful grief reactions and facilitating helpful grief reactions. The exercises in this session focus on the core coping tasks of each of the three conceptual domains – separation distress, existential/identity distress, and circumstance-related distress (Layne et al., 2017). Focusing on each domain will help you to provide a broad-spectrum, balanced, and wellness-focused intervention designed to both reduce distress and dysfunction, and increase your client's sense of comfort, hope, and positive adjustment.

Tips for Eliciting the Loss Narrative

Basic Knowledge about the Death. Prior to eliciting the narrative, it is important for you to have some basic knowledge about the circumstances and context surrounding the death. This information is usually gathered during the initial intake assessment with the caregiver (see Chapter 3). Examples of contextualizing types of information include:

- What was the client's relationship like with the deceased?
- Was the death sudden, violent, or the result of a long-term illness?
- What was the manner and intensity of the child's exposure to the death? Did it involve direct witnessing of violent, traumatic, or distressing aspects?
- If not witnessed, how was the child notified of the death, and what where they told?

This basic knowledge can help (1) to plan for the pacing and overall length of time needed for the narrative work; (2) to inform the type of prompts to use to elicit the narrative; and (3) to know when important material is being avoided.

The Process of Eliciting the Loss Narrative. Throughout narrative construction, a primary goal is to help the client feel safe, understood, and supported. Tools at your disposal include the quality of the therapeutic alliance, your comfort and familiarity with the activity, and your active listening skills (i.e., your ability to listen compassionately and to make your client feel heard and validated). This usually involves an ongoing process of reflecting and labeling the client's thoughts and feelings. Creating a safe and structured environment in which to develop the loss narrative helps clients to voice thoughts and feelings that may have been previously pushed away or avoided. In sum, the narrative process includes two equally important components: (1) the experience of verbally sharing their story and collaboratively processing it; and (2) creating an actual document (or book) that contains a written version of the narrative. This document can then be used for further processing, reflection, and sharing (see Activity 3: Sharing the Loss Narrative with Caregivers).

Timing. A complete loss narrative consists of nine chapters (or sections). The amount of time needed to complete each chapter can vary greatly depending on each client's age, developmental stage, and level of comfort with talking about the deceased person and the circumstances of the death. In most cases, you may complete two to three chapters per one-hour session. The process of eliciting the story of the actual death and its surrounding circumstances may take one or two sessions by itself.

Preparing the Client. It is generally helpful to introduce the loss narrative process during the session prior to beginning the actual work. Even with young clients, it is possible to provide a basic description of the process in a developmentally appropriate way. This description will help clients to better understand why narrative construction is helpful and help them to anticipate and prepare for what the process will involve. Examples of language that may be useful in constructing loss narratives are included in Activity 1: Creating the Loss Narrative.

Structure of the Loss Narrative

The first part of the loss narrative (Chapters 1 and 2) involves setting the stage, in which you explain the overall plan and the rationale for the narrative activities. This is done in a developmentally appropriate way at least one session before eliciting the child's experience. This stage setting is followed by a guided conversation in which you help to bring the deceased loved one to mind by helping the client share descriptions and memories of their person.

The second part of the narrative (Chapter 3) involves sharing the story of the death. You can help to support and guide the youth in recounting the specific circumstances and experiences leading up to the death, the death itself, and experiences following the death. As needed, this part of the narrative can involve helping the client to use their coping skills (e.g., deep breathing or other emotion regulation strategies) to talk through difficult parts of the death. The purpose is not simply to review what happened at the time of their person's death on a superficial level. Rather, it is to do a deeper dive into the client's thoughts and feelings connected to the death itself. A core assumption of this process is that if this narrative construction work is properly guided to ensure sufficient personal relevance (e.g., identifying the hardest parts to talk about), depth, and duration, clients will

- develop a greater capacity to tolerate painful grief-related memories and emotions;
- develop greater insight into their own personal loss and/or trauma reminders;
- experience a reduction in distressing reactions related to the circumstances of the death, including anger, guilt, shame, and/or posttraumatic stress reactions.

A key aspect of sharing the story of the person's death is to ensure that the client is within the working range of anxiety, which we define as falling between 5 and 8 on their feelings thermometer. Lower thermometer readings (e.g., 1 to 4) typically mean that the client is not engaging their thoughts and feelings sufficiently for adequate emotional processing. In contrast, higher readings (9 or 10) may be too overstimulating, overwhelming, and stressful for adequate emotional processing.

As a general guide, you should let the retelling of the story unfold without interruption unless you believe that the client is skipping over important moments or aspects of the experience (including difficult thoughts and feelings) (see Saltzman et al., 2017, Module 2). In recounting the death, youth will frequently skip over or move quickly through the most stressful or difficult parts of the experience. When you observe this, gently go back to that point in the story and slow down the description. Clients' wide-ranging experiences during this part of the narrative construction process – including moments when clients are actively verbalizing, silent moments of emotionally reacting to the content, or simply trying to put their experiences into words – can all be therapeutic if properly facilitated.

The third part of the narrative (Chapters 4 through 9) involves coping with the death. In this phase, you will lead a series of discussions designed to help the youth organize his or her internal experience of the death, cope with associated losses and adversities (including those they are likely to encounter in the future as a result of the death), and move forward along their very personal path of bereavement, grief, and mourning.

Traditional trauma narrative or exposure work usually focuses just on the second part of the process described above (i.e., sharing the story of the death). In contrast, we bookend this exposure work to the death itself by starting with setting the stage for narrative construction and ending with an extended set of structured discussions to help the client make sense and meaning of the death. Taken together, the loss narrative helps the client to develop practical skills and coping strategies to navigate daily life in the absence of their loved one.

3 Activity 1 Creating the Loss Narrative

Purpose:

- To help clients process a potentially broad range of grief reactions they are likely to experience as described by multidimensional grief theory

Directions: Cover the following general points in your own words.

Although we've had some time to talk about your loved one who died, sometimes it can be helpful to tell the whole story. This story will explain not just how they died, but who they were, and what they meant and continue to mean to you. This story will also help us to find ways for you to continue to feel connected to them, even though they are no longer here physically, as you move forward with creating a healthy, happy life for yourself. This special kind of story is called a "loss narrative." An important reason why we create loss narratives is that the more we're able to talk openly about the person who died, the less upset and overwhelmed we feel when we're reminded of the person or the way they died. And the less overwhelmed we feel when we think about our loved one and the way they died, the more we can grieve in comforting and helpful ways. But we are not going to be telling the story all at once. In fact, we're going to divide the story up over several sessions so that you can take your time, not feel rushed, and pay close attention to how you are feeling, both emotionally and in your body, as you tell the story.

Loss Narrative

For your story, I'd like you to imagine that you are watching a movie about yourself, and we'll be writing the story about _____ (client's name). This way of thinking can help us by allowing us take a step back and see things more clearly from a distance, like a fly on the wall. So let's imagine that someone is making a movie all about you, your person, and what happened after they died.

Follow the outline for the loss narrative to help the client create theirs. This can be done in several ways:

- The client can type the loss narrative on a computer.
- The client can write the loss narrative by hand on paper, including drawing out pictures.
- The client can dictate their thoughts/ideas to you, and you can type or write out the loss narrative as they speak. Of note, we have found the most success in using this method, as it allows the client to speak freely about their experience without getting caught up in the writing/typing. This also allows them to focus more explicitly on their thoughts and feelings and provide more detailed information. The loss narrative will likely take several sessions to complete.

Outline for the Loss Narrative

Title: _____'s (client's name) Story of Grief

(The client can also come up with a different title for their loss narrative.)

Chapter 1: All About _____'s (client's name) _____ (name/title of person who died; e.g., Mom, brother, etc.) (focus on separation distress)

Let's list things _____'s (client's name) thinks are important to know about their _____ (name/title of person who died). These can include serious things – like what they did for a living – as well as funny or personal things, like their sense of humor or little things they used to say. What were they like as a person? What were they like to be with?

Allow the client to generate their own facts about the deceased person but feel free to use any of the following prompts after they are done.

What was the person's

- *favorite food?*
- *favorite color?*
- *favorite TV show or movie?*
- *favorite hobby/activity?*
- *dislikes?*
- *place where they grew up?*
- *job?*
- *best characteristic/trait/behavior?*
- *quirky habit (e.g., favorite sayings)?*
- *other important fact/information?*

What do they want to remember most about their person (appearance, their voice, funny jokes, things they would say)?

If the client has specific questions about their loved one, have them generate a list of those questions and determine whom they could ask for the best answers.

If not done already, have the client bring a photo of their loved one to the next session to insert into the narrative.

As the client begins to describe their person's best characteristics, traits or behaviors, they can add those to their Good Grief Jar as appropriate.

Chapter 2: _____'s (client's name) Favorite Memories or Stories of _____ (name/title of person who died) (focus on separation distress)

What are some favorite memories or stories about _____? Allow the client to generate their own response and then feel free to use the following prompts:

- Certain activities they used to do together
- Funny things their person said or did
- Things their person did to support and help the client (homework, hobbies, school activities)
- Ways their person showed their love (hugs, kisses, fun teasing, smiles)
- Their companionship (hanging out, chatting online or on the phone)
- What it felt like to be around them (physical presence, smell, sound of voice)
- Helping the client to figure out how to handle problems (good advice their person used to give them)
- How they made the client feel about themselves (feeling needed and appreciated, believing in themselves)

The client can add comforting memories of the person to the Good Grief Jar as appropriate.

Chapter 3: How _____ Died (focus on circumstance-related distress)

Now, let's describe what is known about how _____ died. Sometimes it can be helpful if we describe the different experiences _____ (client's name) may have had before, during, and after the death itself.

For this section, first have the client generate their own response and then ask ALL questions below if they did not cover them all themselves.

- What was the client doing right before the person died (e.g., were they at home, at school, at a friend's house?)?
- How did the person die?
- What did the client witness/observe in terms of the death itself (if anything)? (It can be helpful to have them reflect upon their five senses at that time – what did they see, hear, smell, feel in their body, etc.)
- If the client wasn't present, how did they find out about the death? Who told them? What did that person say about what happened?
- What was the client thinking or feeling in the immediate aftermath of finding out about the death?
- What did the client do right after they found out about the death? How did they react?
- What was the hardest part about the person's death? The thing that has been hardest to deal with? (e.g., finding

out, seeing the person's body, seeing the coffin, seeing others upset, learning afterwards about what really happened, etc.)?
- Did the client have a chance to say anything to the person before they died?
  - If yes, what was it?
- Are there parts of the death that are still confusing to the client?
  - If so, what are they?
- Are there parts of what happened that the client still feels very angry about?
  - If so, what things still make them very angry?
- Are there parts of what happened that the client feels strong regret about, or really wishes hadn't happened?
  - If so, what things do they wish had been different?
- Are there parts of what happened that the client thinks are totally wrong or unfair (things they can't accept)?
  - If so, what things are unacceptable to them?

If the client still has questions about how the person died, have them generate a list of their questions and determine who they could ask for the answers. (This can include things to work on in future sessions.) If the cause of death is unclear to the whole family, what would the client like to know (even if no one can answer their questions definitively)? Emphasize that it is okay to have questions for which there are no good answers right now.

Chapter 4: How _____ (client's name) Can Stay Connected (focus on separation distress)

In Chapters 1 and 2, we talked about _____ (name/title of person who died), things that made them so special, and favorite memories of that person. Now, let's list any things _____ (client's name) does (activities, behaviors, rituals, etc.) to feel more connected to _____ (name of the person who died) even though they are not here with us physically.

Allow the client to generate their own responses. Then feel free to use the following prompts:

- Looking at photos or videos of them
- Looking at memorabilia/mementos (their person's belongings or things that were given to the client)
- Reading condolence cards from other people
- Going to places where they used to go
- Doing things they used to do together
- Wearing something that they used to wear
- Spending time with their family or friends
- Talking about the person
- Drawing pictures of the person
- Thinking or daydreaming about the person
- Dreaming about the person
- Doing good things they wanted the client to do or experience
- Praying for them
- Praying to them
- Other things they may want to do to feel more connected

Have the client add any positive connection items to the Good Grief Jar.

Optional Exercise for Chapter 4

(Focus on repairing the client's relationship with the deceased.) This optional exercise is helpful if the youth did not have an opportunity to say goodbye to their loved one and/or if they have unresolved thoughts or feelings that they wish they could have shared with the person (see Kaplow & Pincus, 2007, for examples of this exercise).

Now, let's pretend that _____ (client's name) decides to write a letter to their person telling them everything that they would like them to know. This could include things that are happening in _____'s (client's name) life, things that _____ (client's name) never had a chance to say to them, or anything else that _____ (client's name) wishes they could have done differently.

Next, let's pretend that _____ (person who died) is able to write a letter back to _____ (client's name). What would they say in response to _____'s (client's name) letter?

If appropriate, the client can include this letter in the Good Grief Jar.

Chapter 5: Where Are They Now? (this part of the narrative is optional based upon the client's/family's spiritual/religious beliefs) (focus on separation and/or existential/identity distress)

Let's describe _____'s (client's name) own thoughts/beliefs about death. What are some of their personal beliefs about what happens after someone dies? If the client seems unsure, you can ask, *"What would _____ (client's name) <u>like to believe</u> about what happens when someone dies?"*

Remind the client that there are no right or wrong answers. Allow them to generate their own responses, but then feel free to use the following prompts:

- Where do they believe the person's spirit or soul is now?
- If they believe in an afterlife, what is it like?
- What are some comforting spiritual beliefs that they may have (or wish to have) about the deceased person?
- Can they still feel the person nearby sometimes? What does that feel like? How can they still send love to the person? How can they receive love back from the person (e.g., visualization, prayers, meditation, holding onto something that the person owned)?

Have the client add comforting spiritual beliefs to the Good Grief Jar if appropriate.

Chapter 6: How Things Have Changed (focus on existential/identity distress)

After a loved one dies, some things may stay the same (for example, we may have the same friends or go to the same school), but other things can change. Let's work together to list ways in which things have changed, both inside as well as on the outside, in _____'s (client's name) life, since the person's death.

Allow the client to generate their own responses. Then feel free to use the following prompts to fill in what may have changed (note that not all changes have to be negative – some positive changes may have taken place, such as the family has grown closer):

- More quiet or withdrawn
- More nervous about getting close to other people
- More worried about the future without the person here (you can ask the client to expand on exactly what worries they may have that involve a future without their person here)
- More anxious or afraid about other people also dying
- More nervous about dying themselves
- Feeling self-conscious around other kids regarding the death
- Moved to a different home and/or school
- Needing to take on more responsibilities at home
- Feeling more distanced from relatives, friends, etc.
- More arguments or fights at home, school, with friend, peers, etc.
- Teased or bullied at school
- More difficulty concentrating in school
- Worrying more about money
- Worrying more about having people there to take care of them
- Difficulty falling asleep or staying asleep
- Eating more or less than they used to
- Feeling stronger than they did before
- Knowing who their true friends are
- Appreciating life more
- Having a clearer idea of what they want to do with their life

Have the client add positive or comforting changes to the Good Grief Jar if appropriate.

Chapter 7: Carrying on Their Legacy (focus on existential/identity distress and separation distress)

As we look to the future, one way that we can try to live our best life after a loved one has died is to recognize certain qualities of that person or behaviors they had that were healthy and helpful – ones that we can carry with us to make our own lives, and those of our loved ones, better.

We've already talked about some of those things that made the person so special. Let's focus again on the positive qualities or behaviors they had, but this time think of these qualities as a gift or legacy that the person is giving us and would want us to draw from as we move forward into our future life.

Allow the client to generate their own responses. Then feel free to use the following prompts:

- What are the good traits/behaviors/habits of the person that the client would like to keep with them? Have them list those that stand out.
- Does the client already share some of these good traits/behaviors/habits in common with the person?
- How can each of these traits or behaviors help make their own life better?
- How can the client use each positive quality to help other people in some way? (This can be something as simple as making use of the person's friendly smile and kindness by smiling at other people or giving someone a hug when they're having a tough time).
- Are there things the client can do personally to make their person's memory and positive influence live on?
- Where in their life do they still feel their influence?

Optional Exercise for Chapter 7

This optional exercise is designed for youth who may have ambivalent feelings about the person who died and/or a strained relationship. If this is the case, begin with one of the two optional exercises below *prior* to writing Chapter 7. Cover the general points below in your own words.

When someone dies, it's often easier to think and talk about things we loved or admired about them. But sometimes we may have mixed feelings about the person who died, including both memories of things we loved about the person and memories of things that are hard to think about or not so positive about the person, such as negative personality traits, behaviors, or habits that bothered us, or things they did that were difficult to deal with or hurtful. We may have even learned some of these unhelpful traits from our person.

It is perfectly normal to have lots of different feelings toward our person, including feelings of love and respect as well as feelings of anger or frustration. It can be helpful to remember that every single person has some things about them that are positive and negative, so it's normal to have both positive and negative feelings about your person at the same time.

It is up to us to choose which traits to focus on – we don't have to forget about their negative traits or things about them that bothered us, but we can choose to focus on, learn from, and cherish their positive traits. Learning to focus on a person's positive or helpful traits is an important life skill and can make it easier to get along with other people in your life. So as you think of the life of your loved one, you can ask yourself: "Which of their good traits or habits do I want to remember and bring with me into my future? And which not-so-good or unhelpful traits or habits can I outgrow and leave behind?"

We can often feel connected to people who have died by taking on certain qualities of that person or behaving in the same ways that they did when they were alive. This can be useful if those qualities or behaviors are healthy and helpful; but at the same time, we can create all sorts of problems for ourselves if we choose to carry on their unhelpful qualities or behaviors. The choice is ours.

With this in mind, our activity today will help us to think about and choose which of the person's positive qualities we value the most and would like to keep with us over time, almost like one of their gifts to us, and which qualities we would benefit from letting go.

Note that there are two options for this exercise: The first is preferred though it requires more materials (pens, popsicle sticks, stones, bowl, and water), whereas the second option is somewhat simpler and requires only purple and yellow construction paper and pens. Review both and decide which one is better for your setting.

Option 1 Sticks and Stones Exercise (promoting the positive, normalizing the negative)

Give the client a waterproof pen, three plain popsicle sticks (representing good attributes), and three stones (representing undesirable attributes). Place a large clear plastic bowl in the center of the table along with a pitcher of water.

I would like you to write down three of the positive or helpful qualities of your person on each of these popsicle sticks (these can be traits, characteristics, or behaviors that you really liked and still admire).

Next, I'd like you to write down three less helpful qualities of the person or things that were hard or you wished were different about that person on each of these stones (these may be things that bothered or upset you, or bad habits that caused problems for them or people around them). Feel free to write down whatever comes to mind.

First, invite the client to write three positive traits, habits, or behaviors that they admire on the popsicle sticks, one trait per stick. Next invite them to write three negative traits, habits, or behaviors that they do not admire or that created problems for the person on the stones, one per stone.

- Acknowledge that talking about not-so-positive parts of a deceased person's life can sometimes make people uncomfortable because it may feel wrong or disloyal in some way to say negative things about the deceased. However, you can remind the client that no one is perfect, and it's OK to remember those parts, too. Note that there may be cultural considerations to take into account when engaging in this part of the activity. For example, some cultures/religions prohibit speaking negatively about the deceased. Practicing cultural humility and being aware of one's own values and beliefs when addressing this issue will ensure that you are not pushing the client to engage in behaviors that are inconsistent with their own cultural and/or religious practices.
- If the client cannot identify any negative attributes that the person exhibited, you can remind them that no one is perfect and part of being human is that we all make mistakes at some point in our lives. This can also be an opportunity to explore what might make it hard to identify negative attributes (e.g., cultural and/or religious beliefs).
- Alternatively, if the client cannot identify any positive attributes that the person exhibited during their life, invite them to select characteristics or qualities that they personally wish that person had exhibited.
- Encourage the client to notice how each object (popsicle stick versus stone) feels. Note that the positive qualities are lighter and *easier to carry* with them. The more negative qualities are heavier and can *weigh them down*.

Second,

- Invite the client to share the things they admire about their loved one – those that they want to <u>keep</u> with them and incorporate into their own behavior/personality as they move forward with their lives.
- Next, invite the client to describe the person's traits, habits, or behavior that may have created problems for them in the past that they would prefer to leave behind.

After the client describes the positive and negative qualities of the person who died, they should first place the stones, followed by the popsicle sticks (i.e., with the popsicle sticks lying on top of the stones), in a large, clear plastic bowl in the middle of the table.

Third, summarize the following in your own words. *Thank you for sharing. The most important part of this exercise is to understand how we can bring those positive traits to the surface, so we can connect with them more easily, while letting those more negative or unhelpful traits become smaller and weigh us down less.*

You can then have the client pour a pitcher of water into the bowl. The popsicle sticks should rise to the top while the stones stay at the bottom of the bowl. You can then make waves in the water and ask the client to comment on what they observe.

Notice what happens to the popsicle sticks (or the positive qualities) and the stones (negative qualities) when we make waves in the water. The positive qualities stay afloat and ride the waves, kind of like the waves of grief that we've talked about. So when you're feeling a wave of grief coming on, if you're able to hold onto those positive traits and behaviors of the person who died, it will be easier for you to stay afloat even when waves of sadness or anger or loneliness wash over you. But what happens if you grab on to those negative traits or behaviors? They'll pull you down and you'll start sinking.

Also, notice how the popsicle sticks cluster together, almost forming a raft. So when we are able to make good use of all of the person's positive qualities, we can become even stronger, and this will help to carry us through tough times.

You can have the client add the popsicle sticks to the Good Grief Jar if appropriate.

Option 2: Yellow and Purple Paper Exercise (choosing what to keep and cherish, and what to let go)

Give your client a pen, three strips of yellow construction paper (representing good attributes of their deceased loved one), and three strips of purple construction paper (representing undesirable attributes of their deceased loved one).

Loss Narrative

I'd like you to write down on these three yellow strips of paper three positive qualities, traits, characteristics, or behaviors (like having a good sense of humor) of your person that you loved or admired. On the three purple strips of paper, I'd like you to write down up to three qualities of the person that you don't admire (these may be things that bothered or upset you, or bad habits that caused problems for them or people around them). Feel free to write down whatever comes to mind.

Then, think about both the positive and negative traits and behaviors that you have chosen to focus on. Do you yourself share any of the same qualities (traits, habits, or behaviors) that you <u>loved about your person</u>? On the other hand, are there any negative or unhealthy qualities (traits, habits, or behaviors) that you also share with them that could be creating problems for you, either now or in the future?

In this exercise, we will symbolically <u>keep</u> the parts of the person that are most helpful to us (which we will write on the yellow strips) and let go and leave behind our unhealthy connections to the person by throwing out what we have written on the strips of purple paper.

First, invite the client to write up to three positive traits, habits, or behaviors that they admire about their person on the yellow strips of paper, one trait per strip, and to write up to three negative traits, habits, or behaviors that they do not admire or that created problems for the person on the purple strips, one per strip. Emphasize that talking about the not-so-positive parts of a deceased person's life can sometimes make people uncomfortable, because it may feel like being disloyal to their memory. For example, you can tell them the following.

I know it may feel uncomfortable to talk about the not-so-helpful parts of your person. It's important to remember that no one is perfect, and we need to remember them as real people with flaws as well as strengths. This is about a choice you are making about which parts of their lives are most helpful for you to hold onto and which parts you may want to leave behind.

If the client cannot identify any positive attributes that the person exhibited during his/her life, then invite the client to either (1) select attributes that they <u>wish</u> the person had exhibited or (2) have them select positive attributes they themselves already possess that the deceased person admired or praised them for having while they were alive.

Second, invite the client to share out loud the things they admire about their loved one that they want to keep with them as they move forward with their lives. They can keep these strips with them or add them to the Good Grief Jar. Next, invite the client to also describe the person's traits, habits, or behaviors that could really create problems for them or others if they kept it, and to leave this behind by placing the purple strip in a container or waste basket.

Processing for Both Options 1 and 2

Summarize the activity by asking the client to reflect on the following:

- How it felt to identify both positive and negative qualities of the person who died
- How it can be helpful to acknowledge and accept negative qualities, but not make them the focus
- How choosing to focus on the positive qualities of the person who died can help them (1) to feel more connected to the deceased person, (2) to honor the deceased person, (3) to make their own lives better, and (4) to help the people they care about

Thank you for sharing. It can feel uncomfortable, even scary, to let go of negative qualities that we share in common with the person who died. It might feel a bit like we are losing them. But we can choose to replace those with positive qualities and share these in common with them instead. As we continue our work together, we'll be problem-solving how to use these positive qualities to help you feel more connected to your loved one, make good choices, and move forward with your life.

Note that this activity (either Option 1 or 2) can take an entire session to complete. It can also be helpful and often powerful to have the client share their sticks and stones or positive and negative traits with the caregiver at the end of the session for further processing.

Chapter 8: Making Meaning of the Death (focus on existential/identity distress and circumstance-related distress)

Although the death of a loved one can be extremely painful, sometimes we can find ways to grow from the experience or change our pain into something that can help other people, even if it takes a while to get to that point. What are some ways that _____ (client's name) may have grown from their loss experience?

Allow the client to generate their own responses. Then feel free to use the following prompts:

- How can they make meaning of the person's death? Is there a reason why the person died (in their mind)?
- How can they turn the circumstances of the death into something that can help other people not suffer in the same way they did or make the world a better place (e.g., do a walk/run for cancer, donate to a related charity; go into a profession that helps others so they can prevent the cause of their person's death)?

What has the client learned about himself or others since the death? For example:

- Life has new meaning (e.g., "Life is short," "Live life to the fullest")
- Recognizing the support of true friends or close loved ones
- Having more empathy for others who have gone through hard times
- Not taking things for granted

- Recognizing their own strength/resiliency
- Becoming more spiritual or religious, drawing closer to God
- Drawing closer to relatives or friends who have also suffered losses
- Living the kind of life that their person would want for them
- Wanting to do things that their person wanted to do (but never had a chance to do)
- Wanting to take life more seriously, to accomplish something important

Have the client add positive meaning making or life lesson items to the Good Grief Jar as appropriate.

Chapter 9: Looking toward the Future (focus on existential/identity distress)

Even though it's easy to feel lost after our loved one dies, it's important to remember that we can still live a good life even if our person is no longer with us physically. This last chapter is designed to help remember or discover our hopes and dreams for the future.

Allow the client to generate their own responses. Then feel free to use the following prompts:

- Do they have career goals?
- Family aspirations?
- Hopes of traveling?
- What do they think their person would want for them? Is this in line with what they want?
- Where do they see themselves in 10 years? 20 years?
- How can they prepare for future transitions/events and feel connected to their person as much as they would like?
- If they were counting on their person to be there for particular situations/life events, who can help to fill that role for them? In the next few weeks? Months? Years?
- What steps can they take right now to reach their goals?

4 Activity 2 Preparing Caregivers

Following the completion of the loss narrative, the clinician should meet with the caregiver(s) alone to prepare them for the session(s) in which the client will share the narrative with them. As with previous sessions (e.g., see Session 4), it will be important to understand the caregiver's own capacity to provide support to the client and offer positive reinforcement. The private session with the caregiver can involve helping them to generate phrases that reflect supportive praise, reminding them to try not to correct the client if they present information that may not be entirely accurate, and preparing them for potentially distressing material. (See Parent/Caregiver Guidance [Handout 4.3].)

5 Activity 3 Sharing the Loss Narrative with Caregivers

For many youth, sharing the loss narrative with their caregiver is one of the most powerful, yet anxiety-provoking exercises in MGT. This is due to the fact that children are often highly attuned to their caregiver's own grief and may be concerned about making the caregiver upset or sad. It can be helpful to remind the client that sharing openly about the death of their loved one can make these conversations with their caregiver feel less scary and can in fact make it easier and more comfortable to talk openly at home. It is also helpful to remind them that it is OK if they or their caregiver become sad or tearful during the sharing of the loss narrative. In fact, that is completely expected.

If the client continues to express discomfort about sharing the narrative with the surviving caregiver, they can (1) identify parts of the narrative that they do feel comfortable sharing with the caregiver and only read those components during the sharing session or (2) find another caring adult with whom they feel comfortable sharing their story and include them in the sharing session.

Once the sharing session has been discussed with both the client and the caregiver, and they both feel adequately prepared, you can begin the sharing session by explaining the rationale for the loss narrative. You can use your own words or the following wording.

The more we're able to talk openly about the person who died, through creating and sharing the loss narrative, the less overwhelmed or upset we feel when we're reminded of the person or the way that they died. Sharing a loss narrative also helps to develop more open communication at home, which can reduce feelings of loneliness and help family members to understand and support one another better.

It can also be helpful to set some ground rules with the caregiver and child prior to sharing the loss narrative. For example, you can say: *While _____ (name of client) is speaking, we will listen to their story with an open heart and an open mind. After they are done sharing, you will have an opportunity to offer words of support and encouragement.*

Next, have the client read the loss narrative (or whatever sections they're most comfortable with) to the caregiver. This activity can be an important opportunity to model effective caregiver grief facilitation (i.e., being fully present while the child is sharing, actively listening, making good eye contact). Once the client completes the loss narrative, allow the caregiver to provide praise and support. You can also facilitate a discussion between the caregiver and client by asking what it was like for the client to read their story and for the caregiver to hear the story. You can remind them that this is the first of many opportunities to revisit and talk about the loss narrative together.

In some situations, the client may want to share the narrative with the caregiver but may be too uncomfortable to read it out loud. This is a good opportunity to explore why they feel uncomfortable (e.g., Are they worried that they will start to cry?) and what their concerns might be. You can offer reassurance that it may feel uncomfortable at first but reading the story out loud can make it feel less threatening. You can also determine a plan if the client becomes distressed, like having you (as the therapist) read a portion of the narrative or taking a break to do deep breathing all together. If the client remains uncomfortable, it can still be helpful for you to read parts of the narrative aloud to introduce the material and begin a discussion between the caregiver and the client.

For younger children (ages 7 to 10), it can be helpful to involve the caregiver from the start and have the child share portions of the narrative at the end of each session (as opposed to waiting until the entire narrative is completed). This can allow for more open dialogue in an ongoing way and can be easier for both the child and the parent to process by discussing the story one piece at a time.

6 Assign Practice Exercise

To encourage further discussion, your assignment for the client and caregiver can involve asking the client to re-read one section of the loss narrative that felt more difficult to talk about with the caregiver, when they are at home together. You can remind them that the more they can talk openly about difficult aspects of the death or the person who died, the easier it will be to think about and talk about these things, and the less overwhelmed they will become when they encounter loss or trauma reminders.

7 Check Out

- *How are you feeling now?* (Use feelings thermometer rating)
- If caregiver sharing was done, ask the youth: *What was shared today that was either surprising or helpful?* You can ask the caregiver the same question.
- *What did you learn about yourself today?*

**End of Session **

MGT Session

10 Graduation and Launching into the Future

What Does It Mean to Have a "Good Goodbye"?

Session Objectives

Increase the client's ability:

1. To anticipate and cope with difficult days and future bereavement-related challenges
2. To recognize important treatment gains
3. To process reactions to ending treatment and experience a "good goodbye"

Section Number	Session Overview
1	Check In with Grief Thermometers
2	Activity 1: Planning for Difficult Days Ahead
3	Activity 2: Coping with Daily Occurrences
4	Activity 3: What I've Learned in Treatment
5	Activity 4: Having a Good Goodbye

Session Materials

- Rating My Grief Reactions (Handout 1.3)
- Good Grief Jar

Prior to this final session, we encourage you to readminister the assessment battery to your client to determine whether or not termination is indicated. At this point, the client's levels of posttraumatic stress, maladaptive grief, and/or depression should have significantly decreased and should not be interfering with daily functioning. If they still seem to be elevated on any or all measures, continued treatment (such as further skill building or processing work) may be indicated.

1 Check In with Grief Thermometers

Have the child complete the Rating My Grief Reactions worksheet (Handout 1.3) and explore the current snapshot of grief experience. Sample prompts include the following:

- *How are you feeling on your grief thermometers?*
- *How did your grief thermometers change from last week?*

Additional check-in prompts as appropriate:

- *Did anything happen since we saw each other last that you feel good about?*
- *Was there anything we talked about in our last session that you thought about this week or that stuck with you?*
- *Is anything going on that may make it hard for you to focus during our session?*

2 Activity 1 Planning for Difficult Days Ahead

Purpose:

- To anticipate and plan for difficult events that may include loss reminders or trauma reminders

Materials: White board or paper.

Directions: Draw six equally spaced vertical lines across a white board/paper, creating six columns that represent the next six months. Write the name of the current month at the top of the far-left column and continue writing the names of consecutive months at the top of each successive column to the right.

Invite the client to write, under the appropriate month, special dates or upcoming events that may serve as loss reminders or trauma reminders during the next six months. These days should include specific times or settings in which they may expect to be reminded, either of their person's continuing absence or the event(s) that resulted in their person's death. These difficult days may include

Graduation and Launching into the Future

- birthdays, anniversaries, holidays, parties, seasons of the year;
- special events such as religious ceremonies, marriages, athletic events, or performances;
- important developmental milestones, like cultural rites of passage such as graduating from school, going on a first date, getting their driver's license, moving away for college, etc.

Help the client to identify two to three days or events that they think will be the most difficult to handle, and to think of why. Next, you can explain the following in your own words.

Now that we have identified a couple of difficult events ahead and what parts of those days might be most difficult to handle, let's work on developing a plan that will help you to cope.

For holidays and special occasions, direct the discussion to aspects of the upcoming event that may be most painful or difficult to handle. Prompts for this discussion might include the following:

- The holiday I am most worried about is …
- What makes me most anxious is …
- I will miss (deceased person: "my brother," etc.) the most when we …
- I start getting upset when …
- It's hardest for me when …

One of the challenges we face when we're grieving is how to enjoy the present and look forward to the future when we know our person won't be with us. One way to cope with this challenge is to set aside a special time when you and other family members or friends remember your person. This can be during events or situations when you wish the person was there with you. For example, you can each share a special memory of your person, or have a moment of silence, or pray together, or include the memory of your person in some way such as serving their favorite meal. This can sometimes make it easier to get through special days and create happy new memories, while keeping your person close to your heart.

Lead a discussion using the following prompts:

- One way I would like to honor the memory of (deceased person) during (the holiday or event) is …
- I'm going to try something new by …
- One thing I've done in the past that has really helped is to …
- One thing I've done in the past that didn't help (and that I'd like to avoid doing again) was to …
- I'd like to figure out a better way to …
- Someone who might be able to step in when I wish my person could be there is …

It may be beneficial to share the child's responses, if they are comfortable, with the caregiver(s) to better ensure that the family is able to implement the child's wishes or needs. It is often the case that caregivers are unaware of what may be most helpful to the child; this discussion can shed light on how caregivers can help to facilitate healthy connections with the deceased during important transitions or situations.

3 Activity 2 Coping with Daily Occurrences

Purpose:

- To provide an opportunity for clients to share daily interactions at school or with friends/family that can be challenging because of their loss

Directions: Explain the following in your own words.

In addition to special days, certain everyday conversations and situations can be another source of stress for people who have lost a special person. Kids tell us that it's hard to know who to talk to about the death, and exactly what to tell them, or how to tell them. Sometimes other people who know about the death can treat you differently, like avoiding you, or acting nervous around you, or not wanting to say the name of your person. Some kids who have had a parent or caregiver die say they feel uncomfortable when they are in situations where their parent would have been or is supposed to be involved, like getting permission slips signed, or parent-teacher conferences, or making plans with friends.

So let's spend some time talking about whether this happens to you. You tell me: what kind of everyday situations feel awkward or uncomfortable to you, or are difficult to deal with?

- Not knowing whom to tell or how to talk about the death
- How to help friends and teachers provide the kind of support that you need at the time
- How to deal with situations that usually would have involved your person
- Dealing with rumors about the death
- Dealing with others' expectations that you should be over the death by now

The following are problem situations that many children and adolescents encounter after the death of a loved one. There are no easy answers to these problems. Your role is not to have all of the answers, but rather to act as an empathic listener who is ready to hear about the pain and isolation that these circumstances may cause. Using the problem situations the client has already listed earlier, and any other situations below that resonate with the client, invite the client to think through how they have experienced this problem, how they reacted, and, if appropriate, explore together possible ways to deal with each issue. This can also involve writing out a script together or even doing a role play in which the client practices what they will say in certain situations. The guided language below is not exhaustive and should be tailored to the unique experiences of each client.

Problem Situation: Not Knowing Who to Tell about the Death

The key thing to think about when you're deciding whether or not to tell someone about the death is whether telling them will make things easier for you in the long run. For example, even though you might prefer not to tell a school counselor or certain teachers, it may be helpful to do that rather than having it brought up in a classroom with everyone around. It can also help to tell a school counselor if you think it would help to have them talk to teachers for you or if they could support you on difficult days. Remember, you get to choose who you want to share with – no one else gets to decide that for you.

If applicable, you can help your client to write out a script to help with different scenarios (e.g., how to tell a school counselor about the death) and the wording that feels most comfortable to them.

Problem Situation: Not Knowing How to Speak about the Death

You might want different people to have different amounts of information about what happened. It may be a good idea to have in mind what you might say to people who ask about the death so that you can give them the amount and type of information that feels most helpful to you. If someone gets curious and presses you for details that you don't want to discuss, you can say something like, "I'd rather not go into details, but I can tell you that it was one of the hardest days of my life." Just remember that you are in full control of how much you say and who you say it to.

Problem Situation: How to Help Friends and Teachers Provide the Kind of Support That Feels Good to You

It is important to remember that different types of stressful situations may require different types of support. You may be confused over an important choice and not know what to do. In this situation, information and advice can be most helpful. At other times you may be bored or feeling lonely, so, in this situation, being with friends may really cheer you up. Sometimes, a hug and maybe a shoulder to cry on are exactly what you need.

Point out that often people may have the best of intentions but may not understand or know what type of support would be most helpful. If appropriate, help identify the type of support that has been most helpful and/or what they would like more of.

We can sometimes make things easier if we let our friends and family know what type of support they could offer that would be useful to us. Instead of becoming frustrated with them, we can coach people about what type of support would feel most helpful. How have people responded with support that you really liked? What kind of support do you feel you need most when you are feeling upset? Nervous? Confused? Really missing your person?

Problem Situation: How to Deal with Situations That Usually Involve Your Deceased Family Member

You can avoid some of these situations by letting key people know (like teachers or coaches or friends' parents) about the death beforehand. If this is not possible, then you might want to speak with people privately. For example, if a teacher asks that both parents sign a permission slip, speak privately with him or her after class.

Problem Situation: Dealing with Rumors about the Death

Consider taking the first step and being the first one to talk with key adults and people you want to know. Once they hear the news from you, the need for gossip may go down. Remember also that rumors are very common, especially among teenagers, but they usually fade over time. Although that doesn't make them any less hurtful, it can sometimes help to know that they won't last forever.

You may need to assess for instances of bullying related to rumors surrounding the death and identify the possible level of intervention needed. You can also help your client to identify support people to talk to and confide in if rumors are impacting them in negative ways.

Problem Situation: Dealing with Stigmatized Deaths

Stigmatized deaths such as murder, drug overdose, suicide, or gang violence are often hard to talk about. Sometimes after these types of deaths, we can feel angry, embarrassed, or ashamed. Family and friends often don't know quite what to say in these situations and can sometimes come across as unsupportive. Remember that it is your choice about how much you want to discuss with a given person at a given time and place. If it doesn't feel helpful, you don't need to go into details.

Problem Situation: Dealing with Other's Expectations That You Should Be Over the Death by Now

Dealing with other people's ideas about what grief is supposed to look like can be difficult, especially if they don't understand very much about grief. We might feel pressured by comments like "It's been a month now; you better start concentrating on your grades" or "It's been a year – don't you think you should be moving on?" Sometimes it can even feel like people are pressuring us in quieter ways, like when people stop mentioning our person altogether.

It's during times like this that knowing there is no right or wrong way to grieve can be helpful, both for you and for those around you. You can even think about handing out some of the materials we have worked on in therapy to family, teachers, or friends who may benefit from reading them. Remember that grief is different for each person and there is no set timeline for grief. In fact, grief can be thought of as a reflection of the love we had for our person, or the role they played in our lives, so the grief will never actually go away. In truth, we will grieve in some way or another for as long as we feel the absence of our person. This is not a bad thing. It shows how important our relationship with that person was and what they meant to us.

---

4 Activity 3 What I've Learned in Treatment

Purpose:

- To revisit the client's grief goals and what they have accomplished in treatment

Materials: Grief Goals worksheet (Handout 1.4); Good Grief Jar.

Directions: Return to the client's original Grief Goals worksheet and the Good Grief Jar. Review the client's Grief Goals worksheet and encourage them to think back on where they were at the start of treatment compared to where they are at now. Invite them to reflect on the goals that they have accomplished. Specifically, encourage them to think about how they were thinking and feeling at the start of treatment with regard to

Graduation and Launching into the Future

problems at school, at home, or with friends; reactions prompted by grief; and with regard to their hopes for their future. Have them reflect on ways these things have changed over the course of treatment. Summarize and praise their observations and the growth evidenced in their changes.

You can also revisit the Good Grief Jar and examine what it now contains. Encourage your client to talk about the ways in which they believe the Good Grief Jar can help them in the future – either to feel connected to their person in healthy ways or to carry on their person's legacy. You can also help them to think about how they might use their Good Grief Jar when they encounter difficult days or developmental milestones when they wish their person was there (i.e., to find strength or possible guidance on how to respond to a difficult situation).

As appropriate, you can make a brief personal statement about what working with the client has meant to you.

- Review your perceptions of the positive changes that you've seen in your client.
- Convey your respect and admiration for their courage and hard work.

5 Activity 4 Having a Good Goodbye

Purpose:
- To instill confidence that your client has the skills to accomplish their goals and meet future challenges
- To process thoughts and feelings regarding termination
- To increase tolerance for separations

Directions: Cover the general points below in your own words.

Today is the last day of our work together. But instead of thinking of this as an ending, I'd like us to view this as an important new beginning – the beginning of your journey where you will be using all of the skills you have learned to help you cope with many situations in the future.

Give your client a chance to share their feelings about treatment coming to an end. If appropriate, plan for a booster session when the client will be able to check in with you. Consider upcoming events (developmental transitions such as graduations, making important life decisions, etc.) in planning booster sessions – are there times when they may need extra support? You can facilitate a discussion using the points below, as appropriate.

Sometimes, goodbyes like the one we are saying today can remind us of past goodbyes, including times when we didn't get to say goodbye at all or we didn't want to say goodbye.

- *Does today's goodbye remind you of other goodbyes in your past?*
- *What is the same about today's goodbye compared to other goodbyes in your past?* (e.g., feeling sad that we won't see each other again; I'll miss the support). They may have had to say goodbye when they didn't want to (such as when their loved one died, or when a friend moved away).
- *What is different about today's goodbye?* (e.g., we've done our work and are now ready to move forward; we can see each other or get in touch in the future). Express confidence in the client's ability to continue on without regular meetings and to achieve their goals for the future. Help them to discriminate between traumatic or tragic goodbyes versus healthy goodbyes by pointing out the ways in which this goodbye is different.

Our goodbye is happening because you have grown and learned new things, and you're ready to move forward. And (especially if you are scheduling a booster session or plan to keep in touch) *it's not necessarily final. We can see one another again at some point, but just with more time in between, to practice all of the skills you've learned. Then when we can come back together, you'll have a chance to tell me about how things are going.*

Conduct a final activity that provides an opportunity for you and your client to express your appreciation for each other. This can be as simple as writing cards for each other or writing down three things you each appreciate or have learned from each other. You may wish to provide a certificate of completion or have cake and ice cream with the client and their family members to celebrate their accomplishment.

End of Treatment

Index

Active Inhibition Scale (AIS), 31
activity/activities
    engaging in, 100
    physical, 99
adolescents. *See* bereaved children and adolescents
    card sorting activity for, 98
    sketches for, 127–140
adult model of grief, Horowitz's, 11
ambiguous loss, distress over, 126
assessment
    prepare for the, 19–20
    primary measures for, *20–22*
    secondary measures for, *23*
Assessment Feedback Interview, 1
assessment interview procedure
    concluding the, 25
    conducting the assessment, 24–26
    explain the purpose of, 24
    feedback session, 25
    meeting with the client, 23
    overview of, 20
    preparing to meet the client, 23

behaviors, 116–117
bereaved children and adolescents, 2–4, 11
    therapeutic tasks with, 1
bereaved, definition of, 5
bereavement
    definition of, 5
    difficult days and future, 159
    in youths' lives, 2
bereavement and grief, 44
    assessing for, 24
body, 151
    breathing exercises and, 99
    color your, 72, 77
    language, 33, 72
    rhythms, 11

card sorting activity, 98
caregiver grief facilitation, 32
    assessment of, 35
    essential elements of, 35–36
    guiding principles for, 33
    principle 1, 33
    principle 2, 33–34
    principle 3, 34
    principle 4, 34
    principle 5, 35
caregivers, 32
    as key grief facilitators, 84
    grief vs child grief, 34
    guidelines for, 93–94
    loss of, 11
    positive caregiving and, 32–33
    preparing, 157
    sharing the loss narrative, 157–158
    sharing with, 81, 85, 100
    support from, 84
    what kind of support given, 83
check out, 49
Child Assessment Feedback Form, 25
Child's Parent Dies, A, 12
children
    bereaved, 12, 33, 34–35, 150 *See also bereaved children and adolescents*
    grieving and, 33–34
circumstance-related distress, 6–7, 12, 15, 30, 50, 126, 134–135
    alleviating, 34
    brother's death and, 138
    COVID and, 125–126
    exposure to traumatic deaths and life threats, 16
    friend's suicide and, 137–138
    loss narrative and, 152–153
    upsetting thoughts related to and, 124–125

Colombia-Suicide Severity Rating Scale (C-SSRS), 31
connections
    creating, 47
    staying connected, 153
coping toolkit, 100
    coping toolkit handout,
Cora, 47
COVID-related death, 125–126
daily occurrences, coping with, 160–161
death
    anger about, 48–49
    brother's, 138
    children's understanding of, 12
    circumstances of, 134–135
    conceptual lenses for understanding, 17
    coping with the, 151
    making discussion simple, 34–35
    making meaning of, 156–157
    other's expectations of, 161
    rumors about, 161
    sharing story of the, 151
    stigmatized, 30, 161
    talking about, 161
    who to tell, 160–161

deceased, the
    missing, 46–47, 127–129, 131–132
    situations involving, 161
    staying connected to, 35
depression and suicide risk, assessing for, 25
developmental and ecological theory, 7
differential relations, 7
Differential Validity Matrix, 8–9
difficult days, planning for, 159–160
domain scores, 29

Index

emotional pain
    brother's death and, 138
    circumstances-related distress (COVID), 125–126
    reminiscing, 124–125
    shame and, 134–135
    suicide and, 137–138
    the way they died, 126, 135
emotions, 70, 80
    bereaved children's, 33
    check in, 70
    memories and, 150, 151
    regulating, 96, 99
    separating caregivers from child, 32
exercises, breathing, 99
existential/identity distress, 6, 11–12, 14, 30, 121–122, 129–131, 132
    loss narrative and changes, 153–154
    loss narrative and legacy, 154
    missing the deceased and, 120–121
    parents' grief and, 122–123

Feeling Thermometer Ratings, 158
feelings, 70, 116–117
    feelings thermometer, 70, 71, 73, 74, 151
    guess my, 72
    measuring, 73
    measuring activities, 71–74
    monitoring mood or, 78
    selfie handout, 76
    what they are, 71
feelings charades, 72
Feelings Faces handout, 75, 80
Feelings Selfie, 72
    Feelings Selfie handout, 76
friends
    connecting with friends or family, 100
    distancing from friends or family, 126
    friends or family, 138
    helping out, 118, 140
    or family, 24
future plans, 132
future, looking toward the, 157

goals
    selecting, 31
    statement of, 31
Good,
good attributes, 155
good goodbye, 159
    having a, 162
Good Grief Game, 85
    handout, 85, 95
Good Grief Jar, 10, 80–81, 85, 98, 100, 152, 153, 154, 155, 156, 157, 161
grief
    caregivers' and children's, 32
    definition of, 5
    dimensions of, 10
    exploring waves of, 80
    Good Grief Jar, 80–81
    how it changed, 79
    how it changes, 80
    waves of, 81, 82
    what is, 44
grief characters, 80
grief domains, 9
grief facilitation inventory, 84
    administering, 84
    child version, 87
grief goals, 161–162
    Grief Goals Worksheet, 49, 161
grief reactions, 50
    circumstance-related distress, 50
    Grief Reactions cards, 46
    identifying, 46–49
    identity distress, 50
    rating, 68, 70
    rating my, 96
    separation distress, 18–19
grief thermometers, 70, 71, 79, 96, 115, 149, 159
    Grief Thermometer worksheet, 83
    handout, 49
    ratings, 100
grieving process, 24
    ways of, 46–49

handouts
    Color Your Body, 77
    Color Your Body Handout, 72
    Feelings Faces, 71, 75, 80
    Feelings Selfie, 72, 76
    Feelings Thermometer, 74
    Good Grief Game handout, 85, 95
    Grief Facilitation Inventory, 87
    Grief Goals Worksheet, 161
    Grief Thermometers, 49
    Monitoring Changes in my Mood and Feelings, 73
    Monitoring Mood or Feelings, 78
    My Coping Toolkit, 114
    Parent/Caregiver Guidance, 93–94
    Personal Goals Worksheet, 26, 28
    Rating My Grief Reactions, 68, 70, 79, 83, 96, 115, 149
    Rating My Grief Reactions worksheet, 159
    Reminders Assessment Tool, 98
    Reminders Card Sorting Game, 98
    Riding the Waves of Grief, 82
    Sizing Up a Situation Card Game, 117
    STFB handout, 117–118
    What Helps Me Grieve, 92
helping out a friend exercise, 118
Horowitz's adult model of grief, 11

identity distress, 50
intervention, 2, 3, 5, 7, 10, 12, 30–31
    caregiver-child relationships, 33
    manualized, 8
    stepped-care model of, 7–8
    tiers of, 1–2, 10
intervention manualized, 7
interventions, 4
    tiers of, 3

journal, writing in a, 100
joy, frustration over others, 120–121

Laurence, 47–48
legacy
    carrying on their, 154
    leaving a, 49
listening, 93, 94
    active, 81
    caregiver grief facilitation and, 33
    skills, 31, 150
lonely, feeling, 47–48
Lorraine, 49
loss narrative, 149
    carrying on their legacy, 154
    checking out, 158
    creating the, 151–152
    eliciting the, 149–150
    favorite memories focus, 152
    how things have changed, 153–154
    outline for, 152–154
    practice exercise, 158
    separation distress focus, 152
    sharing with caregivers, 157–158
    staying connected, 153
    structure of the, 151
    what it is, 149–150
loss reminders, 96
    avoiding, 127–129
    loss reminders worksheet, 98
    preparing for, 99
lost
    feeling, 47–48, 120–122, 129–131, 132
    parents feeling, 122–123
loved one, anger over replacing, 118–120

Marcus, 48
Mindy, 47
Mood and Feeling Questionnaire (MFQ), 30
mourning
    definition of, 5
Multidimensional Grief Assessment Feedback Form, 24
Multidimensional Grief Distress Assessment Feedback Form, 25
Multidimensional Grief Theory (MGT), 5
    as a manualized treatment, 43

Assessment Feedback Form, 29
conceptual domains of, 6–7
grief reactions and, 150
model, 6
scientific roots of, 7–10
theoretical roots of, 10–12
Multidimensional Grief Therapy (MGT)
benefits of, 26
goals for participating in, 26
phases of, 1–2
tasks associated with, 1–2
uniqueness of, 2–4
when not appropriate, 26

National Child Traumatic Stress Network's Core Curriculum on Childhood Trauma, 8
Native American youth, 8
negative attributes, normalizing, 155

parenting/parents
guidelines for, 93–94
positive, 32–33
parents grief, 122–123
participants, selecting appropriate, 18–19
Personal Goals Worksheet, 26, 28
positive attributes, 156
promoting, 155
posttraumatic/post-bereavement factors, naturalistic studies of, 7
Pretreatment Assessment Interview, 1, 18, 19
problem statement, 31
Prolonged Grief Disorder, 2, 5
checklist, 30
PTSD Criterion A diagnostic criteria, 15

Rating My Grief Reactions, 149
handout, 70, 79, 96, 115
handouts, 68
worksheet, 159

religious beliefs, 153
reminders, 96
avoiding loss, 127–129
caregivers and, 100
coping with, 98–99
introduction to, 97
loss, 96
my, 98
preparing for, 99
what are, 96–97
Reminders Card Sorting activity, 98
resilience, theories of, 7
reunification fantasies, 129–131
rumors, dealing with, 161

screening/diagnostic test summary, 29
self-talk, calming, 99
separation distress, 6, 11, 12–14, 30, 50, 118–120, 131–132
feeling lost, 120–121
loss narrative and, 153, 154
loss narrative focus, 152
loss narrative focus on memories, 152
loss narrative focus on staying connected, 153
missing the deceased, 127–129
reunification fantasies and, 129–131
session, concluding, 31
shame, 134–135
situation
card game, 117
sizing up a, 115–116, 117–118
social support, 100
social withdrawal, 131–132
spiritual beliefs, 153
stepped-care intervention model, 7–8
Sticks and Stones exercise, 11, 155
processing, 156–157
suicide
friend's, 137–138

Suicide Prevention Plan, 25
supplementary measures
administering, 25
scores on, 26
support, providing, 161

TGCTA training curriculum, 8
theories of resilience, 7
therapeutic change, theories of mechanisms of, 7
thoughts, 116–117
trauma and grief, evidence-based treatments for, 149
trauma and PTSD, assessing for, 24–25
trauma reminders, 98
preparing for, 99
worksheet, 98
traumatic deaths, 10, 33 *See also* deaths
children's grief reactions and, 12
distress over, 15
witnessing, 9
treatments
grief, 1–2
grief goals and, 161–162
planning for, 1
true-false grief game, 44–46

UCLA Posttraumatic Stress Disorder (PTSD) Reaction Index, 30
UCLA RI-5, 24–25

weird, feeling, 121–122
Wendy, 48–49
What Helps Me Grieve
activity, 86
handout, 92
worksheet, 84–85

yellow and purple paper exercise, 155–156

For EU product safety concerns, contact us at Calle de José Abascal, 56–1°,
28003 Madrid, Spain or eugpsr@cambridge.org.

www.ingramcontent.com/pod-product-compliance
Lightning Source LLC
LaVergne TN
LVHW080249260326
834688LV00042BA/1192